I0518872

*A Humorous Take on
Navigating Trauma*

"You Should
Write a Book"

*Laughing Through the
Tears of Trauma*

by Krista Hale Skapinski, M.Ed.

SKINNY BROWN DOG
MEDIA

Copyright © 2024 Krista Hale Skapinski M.Ed.

Published by Skinny Brown Dog Media
Atlanta, GA /Punta del Este, Uruguay

All rights reserved. No part of this book may be reproduced in any form or by any electronic or mechanical means, including information storage and retrieval systems, without permission in writing from the publisher, except by a reviewer who may quote brief passages in a review.

Skinny Brown Dog Media supports copyright. Copyright fuels creativity, encourages diverse voices, promotes free speech, and creates a vibrant culture. Thank you for buying an authorized edition of this book and for complying with copyright laws by not reproducing, scanning, or distributing any part of it in any form without permission. You are supporting writers and allowing Skinny Brown Dog Media to continue to publish books for readers like you. Scripture quotations are taken from the Holy Bible, New International Version (NIV). Copyright © 1973, 1978, 1984, 2011 by Biblica, Inc.® Used by permission. All rights reserved worldwide.

For Information, Contact:
Krista Hale Skapinski
kristahaleskapinskiauthor.com

Distributed by Skinny Brown Dog Media
SkinnyBrownDogMedia.com
Email: Info@SkinnyBrownDogMedia.com

"You Should Write a Book"
Laughing Through the Tears of Trauma.
by Krista Hale Skapinski, M.Ed

Library of Congress Cataloging-in-Publication Data
eBook ISBN 978-1-965235-03-4
PaperBack ISBN 978-1-965235-02-7
Hardback ISBN 978-1-965235-00-3
Case LaminateISBN 978-1-965235-01-0

DEDICATION

To every person (and there are A LOT of you)
who has ever truly listened to any portion of my story...
jaw dropped, eyes as big as hubcaps, frozen like a statue
with a look upon your face of utter terror
and disbelief from what you have heard,
and then said to me "you should write a book," ...
it is to you I dedicate this, my life's work.

TABLE OF CONTENTS

ACKNOWLEDGEMENTS

You will notice I have made every effort to keep the "cast" in this book anonymous, however, I would be remiss if I did not offer my sincerest gratitude to those who have made this book possible.

To all of those who are nearest and dearest to my mind, heart, and soul, who love me without reservation, as I do you. I cannot adequately express my gratitude to you for what you mean to me...

... for your patience with me as I struggled through this entire arduous process.

... for understanding and embracing my sarcastic, often dark, sense of humor.

... for your encouragement that helped me see my worth even when I felt worthless.

... for your inspiration to keep going even when I wanted to give up, on writing my book and on life itself.

... for reminding me that the ultimate reason I "should write a book" is to help others who are hurting see the light at the end of their very dark tunnel, just like what I needed when I was there in that numbingly dark place trying desperately to find any tiny glimmer of light. You... my friends, my family... my fra-mily... from the depths of my soul, thank you.

And, as much as I do not want to, I need to acknowledge those who are a part of my story in the complete opposite role. It really is true that hurt people, hurt people. To those who chose to inflict the physical, mental, and emotional anguish that are now in black and white on these pages, I can only hope and pray (if you are still living) that you will someday find your peace and reconcile your wrongdoings. Now that I am no longer influenced by you, I can finally say that I am stronger because of you. In my acknowledgement, while I'm not grateful for you, I'm grateful for the strong woman I became because of what I went through.

To God: thank You for keeping me in Your protective hand through every tragedy, trauma, and triumph I have experienced, for never giving up on me, for the humbling love that You so freely give because You ARE love, for leading me back to my walk with You and helping me realize that You aren't just some invisible entity out there in the cosmos.

You are merely a breath away and always have been.

And finally, to you, the reader. Thank you for investing your hard-earned money and your valuable time reading my book. If I can help or inspire you in any way, I will rest assured that everything I've endured and survived will not have been in vain.

INTRODUCTION

Why Should I Invest My Valuable Time Reading This Book?

"I wouldn't wish my life on my worst enemy, but I'm so very grateful for the journey."

Everyone has a story that needs to be told. Everywhere we go, we carry our story on our hearts. Some choose to keep it inside and contemplate; okay, they "stew" on it. Some stuff their story deep down inside so no one will ever see or hear it. They overanalyze and "shoulda, woulda, coulda" themselves to death.

That's me. I'm an over-analyzer. Call it genetics, call it a "teacher's mindset," call it being a woman (yes, men, I freely admit)—whatever the reason, I overanalyze EV-ER-Y-THING. Therefore, I tend to keep everything inside... that is, until someone asks. Then? Look out, because the floodgates will open.

A nice and caring person who seems truly interested in my story, typically someone who knows I have two children—yes, you read correctly, TWO children—who are cancer survivors (I'll get into that later), well, that nice and caring person has no clue the can of worms they've just opened and dumped. I almost feel sorry for them because they truly have no idea what they're about to discover. Usually, the conversation goes a little something like this:

Them: Wow, you have TWO children that fought cancer?

Me: Yep.

Them: Wow... do you have other children?

Me: I have four living children.

Them: You said you have four LIVING children...?

Me: Yes, I have two babies who have passed on. One through miscarriage and one through stillbirth.

Them: You've lost TWO babies? Wow. You've been through so much!

Me: Yep. *At this point, I show them my tattoos honoring all six of my babies, including the cancer ribbon heart.*

Them: Those tattoos are beautiful! *brief silence* You've just been through so much. You should write a book!

And so, here I am, putting my story in black and white so that maybe someone else can feel like they're not alone; like they're not the only ones going through some traumatic, life-altering, "stuff-it-down-so-no-one-sees" experiences—which is how I've felt far too often.

Something I've caught myself saying time and again is this: I wouldn't wish my life on my worst enemy, but I'm so very grateful for the journey. Seems like a contradiction and believe me when I say I've not always felt this way, especially when in the middle of what feels like the entire universe crashing down on your heart and mind in one fell swoop. I was anything but grateful. I was miserable—no, I was BEYOND miserable. What word describes beyond miserable? Well, whatever it is, if you look it up for its definition, a picture of my face would be right there.

Am I still in that miserable place? Honestly? I still have my rough days; doesn't everyone? I'm grateful to say that currently, my good days far outweigh the bad ones. As I type these words, I reflect on everything I've suffered, everything I've endured, everything I've survived. Yes, I'm still facing so many things that turn my stomach into knots, and I want to just go and hide and GIVE UP. However, I cannot give up. I refuse to give up!

Every day, everyone has a decision to make: how will I view this day, as beautiful or a bummer? Every day, I must ask myself, am I going to sit and mull over the extreme difficulties I face every day, forcing me into a deeper, darker depression? Or am I going to use my traumatic life experiences to help other people? Seems like an easy choice, doesn't it? And someone looking in from the outside can very easily say, "Of course you should use your experience to help other people." Sounds easy; however, when we're at the darkest place in our life, when we feel there will never be a "light at the end of the tunnel," the last thing on our mind is, "How can this life experience help someone else in the future?" If you're anything like me, you've lived through several week- or month- (okay, YEAR)-long stanzas of "Why me, God?" followed by a rousing chorus of "I CAN'T TAKE THIS ANYMORE!" I didn't care about how this living hell would end; I just wanted it to end, and end yesterday, please?

And I gotta tell you, if I hear one more person say to me, "God doesn't give you more than you can bear," with their uncomfortable and condescending inflection, I'm going to take their Mary-Poppins-spoon-full-of-sugar and shove it up their... well, you get the idea.

So, as you can see, despite the urge to stay in the muck, I'm choosing to use my story to help others. And, if nothing else, I hope to at least be entertaining enough to take someone away from their current reality and escape by reading about mine.

You are about to take a trip down what I like to call Whiskey Tango Foxtrot Avenue, so buckle up. You're in for a bit of a hair-curling (unless you're bald, then it's a blood-curdling) ride.

I decided to break up this PTSD-inducing story into five parts. Four of the five, individually, could send one to a looney bin. I found the glittery pink straight jacket to be the most bearable of the appropriate attire necessary for survival in each of these eras of my story. Most of what you will read is chronologically organized. Those of you who have OCD as I have (although, CDO is more appropriate of a label because the letters are in order—aren't coping mechanisms fun?), you will appreciate how I've chosen to organize this book.

I've started writing this book many, many times. Every time I'd have my outline complete and ready to write, yet another crisis would take my attention. And, every time another crisis came up, I would say, "Well, I guess it's just another chapter for the book." Many days, I have felt as if a proverbial bull's-eye is on my chest and life keeps on taking shots at me, which is why I've been told so often by so many that I need to write a book.

Thus, the reason for my philosophy that has developed over the course of about 49 years. I wouldn't wish my life on my worst enemy. No one should go through any ONE of the traumas I've endured, and boy, have I endured a LOT of traumas. HOWEVER, I am so incredibly grateful for the journey I have survived because it has made me who I am today.

This book is for those of you who have been through it, those who feel that proverbial bull's-eye on your chest as I have. This is for those of you who have loved ones who have endured more than you can imagine, and you have no idea how to help them through. This is for anyone who feels like things cannot get worse, only to find that, yes, they can.

You are not alone!

And now, my friend, get comfortable, wrap yourself in your favorite throw blanket (and if you happen to be menopausal like me, be ready to periodically throw that blanket to the side as you gasp for a breath of cool air), grab your coffee (or, for my non-coffee drinkers, your beverage of choice), prepare your sarcasm detector and sense of humor (and a flashlight, because at times there will be a bit of dark humor), and get ready for the roller-coaster ride of my life. Please keep all arms and legs inside the vehicle for the duration of the journey until we come to a complete stop and enjoy the ride.

I hope this book can give you a bit of hope, a few laughs, and perhaps a new perspective on life.

PART 1

Innocence

CHAPTER 1:

Nature vs Nurture?
A Prisoner of My Environment

Remember as kids how desperately we yearned to be grown-ups? What were we thinking? Countless times, I've preached to my own children, "Stay young as long as you possibly can because once you hit the age of 'adulting,' there is no going back." For most, life was much simpler before being launched into the world of adulting. Notice I said, "for most." No one had a completely perfect childhood. Even Cliff and Claire Huxtable made mistakes. Me? I envied Vanessa Huxtable. She and I were the same age when I first watched The Cosby Show, and I related to her on many levels, mostly her mistakes. What I couldn't relate to was how her parents handled those teachable moments in such a positive and loving way.

Whether we like it or not, we are all products of our environment. Even though, as adults, we need to take responsibility for our choices, we humans tend to lean on what we've been taught as children to steer us on our life's path. Thus, the great debate of Nature vs. Nurture. "Some philosophers suggested that certain things are inborn, or that they occur naturally regardless of environmental influences...Some characteristics are tied to environmental influences. How a person behaves can be linked to influences such as parenting styles and learned experiences. For example, [one] child might learn through observation and reinforcement to say 'please' and 'thank you.' Another child might learn to behave aggressively by observing older children engage in violent behavior on the playground...One example is Albert Bandura's social learning theory. According to the theory, people learn by observing the behavior of others. In his famous Bobo doll experiment, Bandura demonstrated that children could learn aggressive behaviors simply by observing another person acting aggressively."[1] But what about those who learn behaviors based on experience as opposed to observation? Does nature vs. nurture apply to victims of childhood trauma? I'm asking for a friend. Okay, you guessed it. I'm referring to my own experiences growing up.

The brain is an amazing instrument! Coping mechanisms, mnemonic devices, and self-protection are all beautiful means of survival. My brain's preferred means of surviving the plethora of childhood trauma that I endured is a healthy helping of coping mechanisms alongside a heap of self-protection, specifically repressed memories. "Some memories can be haunting or traumatic... perhaps the experience was so upsetting that it prompts the individual to subconsciously banish these memories from their conscious mind. Clinically, this phenomenon is referred to as repressed memory... Repressed memory is a condition where a specific memory has been unconsciously blocked by an individual due to the high level of stress or trauma contained in that memory. Therefore, repressed memory occurs when that person has pushed down a specific memory into their subconscious as a way to avoid facing the feelings associated with it."[2] The vast majority

---

1   https://www.verywellmind.com/what-is-nature-versus-nurture-2795392

2   https://psychcentral.com/health/repressed-memories#definition

of my childhood, I cannot recall. What I can recall, well, I'd really rather repress those memories as well. Although, truth be told, the memories I easily recall do explain a lot about me: my quirks, my idiosyncrasies, how I think, my neuroses, my perfectionism.

I was raised in an extremely strict religious home. Now, before anyone chases the religion rabbit down the hole, let me specify my opinion of the difference between religion and faith. In my opinion, religion is the legalistic rules and regulations of what one can or cannot do. Personally, I abhor religion. In my opinion, faith is complete trust or confidence in someone or something. I do have personal faith in God, but whether you agree or disagree with my opinion is not the focus of this particular narrative. What I would like to focus on is the issue of not practicing what you preach.

The funny thing—funny strange, not funny "ha-ha"—is that while I was taught every Sunday and Wednesday about the love and acceptance of Jesus in children's church by several truly kind people, in my home, I did not experience either: love or acceptance. Quite the contrary! I was taught that making mistakes is not an option. I learned that appearances are more important than anything. I realized I was to be seen and never heard. Everything that happened in the house where I was raised was never allowed to be discussed with anyone. The female parental figure tried so hard to make our family look like the perfect nuclear family. I was constantly given explicit instruction to never discuss what happens at home with anyone, lest the truth be exposed. Luckily, I was able to temporarily forget events so much more often than I could remember. As a result of the façade, no one truly knew the hell I was forced to survive. In those years of hell on earth, I discovered that, according to those in position of "parent," no matter how hard I tried to please them, I could never be good enough. I understood that it was my responsibility to earn their love and acceptance; however, earning their love and acceptance would never be possible.

Don't believe me? Try this on for size. I'm no more than 9 years old, and while I can't fully recall the circumstances, what I do remember went a little something like this:

Female parental figure: What did you do?

Me: *Looks at the floor*

Female parental figure: Why did you do that?

Me: *Continues looking at the floor*

Female parental figure: You go to your room and think about how much you've hurt Jesus.

Apparently, a 9-year-old has the ability to "hurt Jesus" by making a mistake. Seriously? See what I mean? If this is one of the memories I have not repressed, can you imagine the ones I have? Ready for one more example? Here you go...

Fast-forward about 4 years. I'm in the dressing room of K-Mart trying to find school clothes.

Female parental figure: Oh MY! Take that outfit OFF!

Me: *Looks at the floor*

Female parental figure: You should NEVER wear a dress like that (it was one of those sweater dresses that all the girls were wearing in 1987).

Me: *Continues looking at the floor*

Female parental figure: You know, you'd be so much prettier if you weren't so fat!

What the female parental figure failed to remember is that she made me a non-negotiable member of the clean your plate club. My dinner plate, which would often be filled for me, had to be completely empty before I was given permission to leave the table. Something else I inadvertently developed along with my memory repressing and coping mechanisms is my association of food with comfort, but that's a topic for a subsequent chapter.

I have a feeling you're wondering, "Why does this author keep referring to the mom as female parental figure?" I would be wondering that as well. Well, the woman who raised me from infancy was my grandmother. Her firstborn daughter was my birth mother. Nowadays, that sort of family dynamic seems much more common than it was when I was a child in the '80s. I grew up with a mom and a mommy. As a child, I rarely saw my mommy (that would be birth mom). From what I remember and what I've seen in old photographs, I usually saw her at Thanksgiving and Christmas, and maybe Easter and my birthday. Otherwise, I had no contact with her. What I didn't understand back then is that she was avoiding the female parental figure as much as she possibly could. While hindsight is 20/20 and I completely understand now why she stayed away, at the time, I resented—no, I hated her for abandoning me. I didn't understand why she didn't love me either. Something else you might be wondering: "Where is the birth father in this messed-up story?" According to the female parental figure, birth dad wanted nothing to do with me. And as for the male parental figure? Well, let's just say, thus begins the first of many difficult and uncomfortable chapters of my story.

CHAPTER 2

The "Funk" in Dysfunctional
Sorry, this subject is off limits!

I was an elementary music teacher for 25 years. Now, for anyone not involved in the education profession, I'll let you in on something that we were not taught in college. Every year, all teachers and support staff must go through something called "mandatory training." We are given a long list of topics of which we are to be trained. Everything from copyright laws to food allergies are covered, and those of us veteran teachers who sat through the same information for two-plus decades could probably give the training in their sleep. When I began my teaching career, mandatory training did not include something that is finally being presented. This is a topic that, until recently, and in many circles is still considered, a terribly uncomfortable and taboo subject matter. The subject I'm referring to is childhood sexual abuse. Just how taboo and off limits is this issue? As I was attempting to research the topic online, as I began typing in the search bar, it didn't even pop up as an autocomplete option. In fact, when typing "statistics childhood…" a long list of choices presented. Then, when I added "s—e—x," every bit of the autocomplete list disappeared. Coincidence? I think not!

As I opened the first link in my search, I was taken to this site: https://victimsofcrime.org/child-sexual-abuse-statistics/. On the bottom right of the home page, I found a button that said

"Safety exit." Upon clicking that button, it changed the site to weather.com with no ability to go back to the victim's site. Yeah, my Spidey-sense is saying, "Sorry, this subject is off limits!" And, for my entire life, I have adhered to that strong recommendation. NOT ANYMORE! It's time we give victims the voice they not only deserve; we need to give them the voice they so desperately need. No longer should the offender be protected simply because they're family or a close family friend. No longer should the victims feel like if they do expose the abuse, they will be shunned from their family because "How dare you embarrass OUR family!" Now, as I carefully step away from my soapbox, let's look at some statistics, shall we?

On the victimsofcrime.org site, this is what I found. Buckle your seatbelts, here we go.

"The prevalence of child sexual abuse is difficult to determine because it is often not reported; experts agree that the incidence is far greater than what is reported to authorities. Studies by David Finkelhor, Director of the Crimes Against Children Research Center, show that:

- 1 in 5 girls and 1 in 20 boys is a victim of child sexual abuse.

- Self-report studies show that 20% of adult females and 5-10% of adult males recall a childhood sexual assault or sexual abuse incident.

- During a one-year period in the U.S., 16% of youth ages 14 to 17 had been sexually victimized.

- Over the course of their lifetime, 28% of U.S. youth ages 14 to 17 had been sexually victimized.

- Children are most vulnerable to CSA between the ages of 7 and 13.

- According to a 2003 National Institute of Justice report, 3 out of 4 adolescents who have been sexually assaulted were victimized by someone they knew well.

- A Bureau of Justice Statistics report shows 1.6 % (sixteen out of one thousand) of children between the ages of 12-17 were victims of rape/sexual assault.

- A study conducted in 1986 found that 63% of women who had suffered sexual abuse by a family member also reported a rape or attempted rape after the age of 14. Recent studies in 2000, 2002, and 2005 have all concluded similar results.

- A child who is the victim of prolonged sexual abuse usually develops low self-esteem, a feeling of worthlessness and an abnormal or distorted view of sex. The child may become withdrawn and mistrustful of adults and can become suicidal."

I feel safe to suggest that, if you are reading this book, you either are a victim or know someone close to you who was a victim of childhood sexual abuse. And, if you didn't previously know someone, well, now you do. With great fear and trepidation, I am typing my confession. I am a victim of childhood sexual abuse. Who was my offender? The offender was my male parental figure. I don't want, nor do I need, accolades or sympathy of any kind. I struggle daily to make peace with my childhood. What I DO want is acknowledgment of my trauma. The acknowledgment I want needs to be from those who committed the crimes as well as anyone who knew it was happening and chose NOT to stop it or report it. For me, I doubt that will ever happen because everyone directly involved is either deceased or is someone from whom I have chosen to distance myself. Have I forgiven? I'm somewhat ashamed to admit that I have not yet fully forgiven, but I'm working on it (it is yet another reason I'm in weekly private therapy sessions). Although, isn't true forgiveness a daily choice we make? And, as I have in the past with this terribly delicate topic, I'm going to put that can of worms on the back burner for the time being. Yes, I will eventually address and hopefully conquer this extremely tall brick wall of unforgiveness because, as Neil Peart so eloquently wrote and Geddy Lee sang, "If you choose not to decide, you still have made a choice."

As an adult, I've come to the realization that "de-nial" ain't just a river in Africa! Denial does not make bad things go away, as much as we wish they would. Denial cannot change events, and just because we refute the truth does not mean the truth will change. What is denial? Of course, I looked up the definition. My favorite statement given is "failure to acknowledge an unacceptable truth or emotion or to admit it into consciousness." Yep! I like to describe denial as that smell in your house when you come home from a long trip away and you forgot to take out the trash after cleaning out the raw chicken from the refrigerator. It didn't start out that bad because few people knew about it, but if allowed to sit and fester without being removed, it will become that thing that no one can get rid of without A LOT of work from anyone in the general vicinity of its offensiveness. I'm also on the fence as to which is worse: pedophilia or denial? Now, before you say, "DUH, Krista... of course it's pedophilia," hear me out. Yes, the offender in my abuse was a pedophile. I was only one of his victims. No, I am not letting him off the hook by any means. Yes, I started my anger (more like rage) towards the offender first. But, as time continues, my perspective has shifted. I wholeheartedly believe that anyone who knows of abuse that is happening and does nothing to protect that child by any means necessary deserves the same, if not harsher, treatment as a pedophile. A pedophile is an extremely sick individual that obviously experienced some sort of sordid trauma of their own. Those who protect, deny, or otherwise encourage through the act of complacency or apathy, in my opinion, are just a hair worse.

Who else knew what was happening? That, I do not know. As I said, my severely repressed memory bank contains sketchy details at best. And, as much as the female parental figure tried to live in an altered universe of non-reality called denial, hoping I would either join her on insanity island or forget everything that I had survived (she was almost successful with that one), the memory of those events, much like spray foam, is finding its way through the cracks and has been oozing into a place it cannot be denied any longer.

Your next question might possibly be, "How did this woman end up in that household, and why would anyone leave her in such a volatile situation?" As I mentioned before, "Mommy" was rarely in the picture, and birth dad, at the time, was not in the picture at all. "Mommy" left me with her parents because she had nowhere else to go. And she, as I learned in my early adult years, was dealing with her own severe issues regarding the parental figures and her life choices. I do not fault "Mommy" with any of this. In fact, I found a way to fully forgive her. While her story is fully relevant to mine, from what I understand, she was the first victim of the male parental figure. How about we put a pin in her story for now?

As a child, I exhibited so many warning signs that nowadays would cause a mandatory reporter to hotline my home. When researching the warning signs, I found this information from a document published by Michigan State University.

"PHYSICAL SIGNS

- Pain, bleeding, or discharge in the genitals (check)

- Persistent or recurring pain with urination or bowel movements (I had chronic bladder infections as a child so, check)

- Toileting accidents unrelated to toilet training (check)

- Physical symptoms such as headaches or stomachaches that cannot be explained (check)

BEHAVIORAL SIGNS

- Knowledge about sexual topics that goes beyond the child's developmental stage or what is expected for them to know about at their age (check)

- Withdrawal from previously regular interactions and conversations with peers and parents or activities they previously enjoyed (check)

- Desire to spend an unusual amount of time alone (check)

- Reluctance to leave school or other activities; not wanting to go home (check)

- Trying to avoid certain places or people, especially if they used to be excited to be around those people (check)

- Regressing to behaviors they had grown out of such as wetting the bed or sucking their thumb (check)

- Sexual language, knowledge, or behavior that does not match a child's age such as acting out a sexual act with toys or inappropriate sexual contact with other children (check)

- Removing clothing at inappropriate times (check)

- Running away from home (I wish)

- Fear of closeness with others (check)

EMOTIONAL SIGNS

- Self-harm behaviors (check) or suicidal behavior (check)

- Nightmares, trouble sleeping, or fear of being alone at night (check)

- New or increased depression, aggression, worry, or fearfulness (check)

- Changes in eating habits (check)

- Thinking of their body as bad or dirty (check)

- Decrease in confidence or the way they feel about themselves"[1](check-ity, check, check, CHECK!)

Yep... that was me.

The problem was the female parental figure volunteered at my school, and everyone thought she was a model parent. According to her, my problems weren't because of her or my prison, ummm... I mean, my home environment. She obviously had an uncanny ability to sweep everything under the rug. Either that, or the obvious signs were just ignored. You think this subject is off limits now? Back then, in the early 1980s, this sort of thing, childhood sexual abuse, never EVER happened! Right? RIGHT??? Please forgive my deafeningly loud eye roll.

In the public education world, during our yearly mandatory training, we must sit through one specific training video that is the same every year. It demonstrates the warning signs for which we educators need to always be on the lookout. Every year I sat through that training, I had an overwhelming feeling of jealousy and frustration. I nodded my head like a bobblehead toy through the training as those warning signs were listed and detailed through anonymous examples from Jane Doe and John Q Public, and I thought to myself, "Why couldn't this have been mandatory when I was a kid?" Yet another rousing chorus of "shoulda, woulda, coulda," I suppose.

My repressed memories, as you can imagine, are a blessing as well as a curse. I have to rely on what I've been told, the few family photos I have seen, and piecing that together with what I

---

1   https://www.canr.msu.edu/creating-safe-environments/uploads/files/
Warning%20Signs%20of%20Child%20Sexual%20Abuse%20Final.pdf

can vaguely remember. Oftentimes, my attempts at remembering anything from my early years result in nausea, terror, and my limbic system going mach-3 with its hair on fire. It's like my body wants to simultaneously fight, flight, and freeze. I have decided that I need to come with a disclaimer. You know, like what is shown just before a TV show or story that isn't safe for a child to view. Something along the lines of "This program contains violent material, strong language, and adult themes which may be unsuitable for children. Viewer discretion is advised." Maybe that should be my next tattoo?

So, you've been warned...gird your heart, my friends.

Right now, I can picture in my mind being on the school playground one afternoon at my elementary school. I had to be in 1st, 2nd, or 3rd grade because that particular school was only for kindergarten through 3rd grade, and I only attended AM kindergarten. I can see myself on that playground sneaking to the back of the school with boys and initiating acts with them that no 6–8-year-old should know anything about. I learned early that the only way to gain acceptance and attention is through physical acts, specifically acts that involve oral stimulation and being naked in front of them. I can see myself at my neighbor's house in their basement. I was 12 years old. How do I know? They had just bought Bon Jovi's new album Slippery When Wet. I see myself in their bedroom, it's dark, and we're playing a much-advanced and very inappropriate-for-children version of "house." During those years, I do remember the need to eat... to eat A LOT. I desperately hated being alone in a room without the ability to lock the door. And more than my hatred of an unlocked door, I loathed bathing or doing anything at all in a bathroom. Coincidence? Hardly!

Again, if these are the memories I have not repressed, imagine what my brain is keeping under lock and key!

My clearer memories start at around age 13. Remember the K-Mart incident with the female parental figure? Yeah, it was right around then. I can remember, vividly, how uncomfortable I felt being alone in a room with the male parental figure. There were times he would tell me to sit on his lap and say something to me like, "If I were your age, I'd be following you around like a lost puppy." Creepy? Absolutely! My response to this scenario was always trying to hide my hysterical panic and crying. I didn't understand why that was always my response until many years later. How many years later, you might ask? Well, I was a mom of four living children and was in the midst of my first divorce.

I'm living proof that trauma begets trauma. While in the throes of dealing with yet another personal blow as an adult, specifically divorce and facing life as a single mom, I started having severe nightmares. Well, that's what I thought they were. What I was experiencing were vivid memories. I was telling my then-therapist about the dreams, and as she continued asking very pointed questions, the realization of what she was uncovering came to light. These were not contrived scenarios created by a brain processing during REM sleep. No, I was experiencing flashbacks of childhood. The scenes were always in my childhood bedroom at night. In some, I would be holding my doorknob trying desperately to keep it from turning. I would awaken from that nightmare, well, that flashback, to physical pain in my hands. In another flashback, I was silently crying and trying to get a hand and a blanket off of my face.

Excuse me while I take a breath and try to regain my composure.

I used to think a trigger is the mechanism that fires a bullet in a gun. While that might be true, a trigger in the psychological world is much more complex. "A trigger can be anything that sparks a memory of a trauma, or a part of a trauma. When you encounter a trigger, memories and thoughts associated with the trauma come back without warning. You cannot stop the intrusive thoughts, and in response, you feel a turn in your emotions and begin to react. A trigger might make you feel helpless, panicked, unsafe, and overwhelmed with emotion. You might feel the same things that you felt at the time of the trauma, as though you were reliving the event. The mind perceives triggers as a threat and causes a reaction like fear, panic, or agitation. Think of the reaction to triggers as a defense mechanism: the memory of the traumatic event places you right back into the experience, which causes your walls to go up against the perceived threat in an attempt to protect yourself."[2]

Ah, yes, that good ol' limbic system working overtime to protect us. It's downright frustrating, as an adult, to still be dealing with triggers. There are times I'm able to avoid triggers; however, often I'm unprepared and thrown into a place of utter panic: fight, flight, and/or freeze.

So, despite the fact that it's rare for a flashback to be caused by a trigger, I was experiencing nights alone, and it was the first time I had ever been alone in a room at night after childhood. I went from graduating high school straight to a college dorm with a roommate, then married my first husband after my sophomore year of college. Based on the flashbacks I was having, the oc-

---

2   https://www.choosingtherapy.com/triggers/

currences of the trauma imposed on me happened usually in the middle of the night in my bedroom.

Now, being a true Missourian (Missouri is the Show Me state), when reading or hearing about someone having flashbacks triggered by being alone and going through a divorce, my first thought would be, "Prove it! If you say you can't call to mind this so-called abuse, then how do we know it truly happened to you?" I was thinking the same about myself. How could I know for sure all of this truly happened to me? How could I prove this is just bad dreams and not truly flashbacks? How could I prove my therapist isn't just filling my mind with psychobabble? For the sake of anonymity, I will not specify the source of my proof. What I will tell you is, I have had extensive conversations with another of the male parental figure's victims. We have discussed at length what happened to them and how it follows my story in parallel. As for this victim, I'm leaving their story for them to tell, as it is not my place.

I guess the positive side to being taught from such an early age to put on that mask and show the outside world all is peachy keen is that I'm quite an actress, at least that's what I'd like to think. The reality, however, is the development of yet another defense mechanism: dissociation. Psychology Today tells us, "Dissociating is the experience of detaching from reality. Dissociation encompasses the feeling of daydreaming or being intensely focused, as well as the distressing experience of being disconnected from reality. In this state, consciousness, identity, memory, and perception are no longer naturally integrated. Dissociation often occurs as a result of stress or trauma."[3] To this day, there are

---

3   https://www.psychologytoday.com/us/basics/dissociation

times I sense myself in, what I've called, an out-of-body experience when I've had to deal with confrontation or when I feel a
trigger rear its ugly head. The thing about dissociation is that it
can lead to dissociative amnesia. "Dissociative amnesia usually
follows a stressful event and cannot be attributable to explicit
brain damage. It is thought to reflect a reversible deficit in memory retrieval probably due to memory repression."[1]

Forgive my reiteration; however, if what I've described to you
are the memories that I am able to recall, I shudder at the thought
of what my brain has buried.

---

1   *https://www.ncbi.nlm.nih.gov/pmc/articles/PMC5573566/*

CHAPTER 3

Fighting the Demon: *Life Circumstances – 100, Self-Worth – 0*

So, how does one cope with so much trauma? How much of an effect does a life of constant turmoil, stress, and trauma have on a person? I've had people tell me they recognize symptoms of PTSD, Post-Traumatic Stress Disorder, in me. Huh? What in the world is PTSD? I decided to do some digging online.

There's a lot out there on this subject. I first went to Wikipedia because (tongue firmly planted in cheek) that's the most valuable resource, right? I hope you sense my sarcasm. Wikipedia says, "Posttraumatic stress disorder (PTSD) may develop after a person is exposed to one or more traumatic events, such as major stress, sexual assault, terrorism, or other threats on a person's life."[2] Well, I would say I fit in the major stress category for sure. Wiki also suggests C-PTSD: "Those who experience prolonged trauma, such as slavery, concentration camps, or chronic domestic abuse, may develop complex post-traumatic stress disorder (C-PTSD). C-PTSD is similar to PTSD but has a distinct effect on a person's emotional regulation and core identity."[3]

On the Mayo Clinic website, it states, "Post-traumatic stress disorder (PTSD) is a mental health condition that's triggered by a

---

2   https://en.wikipedia.org/wiki/Posttraumatic_stress_disorder
3   https://en.wikipedia.org/wiki/Posttraumatic_stress_disorder

terrifying event."[4] I do believe I have had enough terrifying events to put me in the PTSD category. On one of the websites, I found one of those "answer-these-questions-to-see-if-you-qualify" surveys. So, out of twenty questions, I answered "yes" to sixteen of them. They suggested I seek psychological help. Lovely!

Although, I've decided to label it as it should be for my situation. I don't think I'm dealing with PTSD, and C-PTSD doesn't seem adequate either. Nope. I believe I'm dealing with OTSD. That's right, ongoing traumatic stress disorder. I don't think that's a real psychological term, but if it is, I'm sure I'm the "poster child." The bigwigs in the psychological world might want to use me for current studies. Although maybe not. It would probably be somewhat like opening a Pandora's Box.

The problem with dealing with any traumatic stress disorder, whether it be post, complex, or ongoing, is the repercussions it has on the way you think about and see the world as well as how you see yourself. I've always struggled with self-image. I've never felt good enough for anyone or anything. I know I've always been melancholic—the personality test we took at a teachers' professional development workshop told me so as well. Although I didn't need a test to tell me my personality is analytical and that I'm susceptible to depression and moodiness. However, take an already melancholic personality, add to it a series of traumatic events, multiply that by an ingrained sense of feeling worthless, and voila, you have a recipe for a life of fighting one of the most difficult "demons" there is or ever will be. This demon is another reality that makes everyone uncomfortable, and yet many

---

4   https://www.mayoclinic.org/diseases-conditions/post-traumatic-stress-disorder/symptoms-causes/syc-20355967

have been touched by someone they love losing their battle to it. I know of many people who have condemned someone struggling with this demon because "even the thought of this is so very selfish and is the coward's way out." And until you've gotten in the wrestling ring with this demon, you'll never know just how difficult it is to defeat it instead of just giving up and letting the three-count happen. What reality, what demon am I referring to? Suicide! And I have fought this demon for an awfully long time.

I remember the very first time I had the overwhelming desire to find sweet relief from the emotional prison I endured day in and day out. I was 13 years old. I was talking to a friend about how worthless I feel, how I'll never be good enough for anyone or anything, and how I desperately wanted to end my life. Bad move! My friend was terrified and feared for me, which is why they immediately contacted the female parental figure to tell her what I had said. They were only trying to do what they thought was best for me; I understand that now. However, at the time, they didn't know the trouble I would get in at home. I walked into the kitchen where I heard a phone conversation ending with the female parental figure thanking someone for letting her know about what I had said. I was then immediately sent to my room, where I would then be told how selfish I am for thinking such a stupid thing, how stupid it is to even consider doing something so very stupid, how I would go straight to the pit of hell if I did something so stupid... do you notice a theme here? So, rather than try to help me, rather than try to love me and talk me down off of my suicidal ledge, rather than try to find out what I need to get past such a "stupid" thing, I was met with anger, criticism, and judgment. Seems logical—again, I hope you sense my sarcasm.

Yep, at 13, I was already fighting my suicidal demon. Would my life be different today if the female parental figure had shown empathy rather than contempt? I don't know. Of course, those events that are out of my control would have been the same; however, the way I've handled those situations, and the self-made issues could have definitely had a more positive spin. Am I blaming the female parental figure for any of this? Well, now that my four children are older, I completely understand how difficult parenting is. However, the way she handled this, along with every other difficult situation, is inexcusable, so yes, I do have bitterness and unforgiveness there that I'm still working on.

Now, where was I? Oh, yes...

As I was researching the subject of suicide, one page had this statement in big red letters: "Suicide is not chosen; it happens when pain exceeds resources for coping with pain."[5] Absolutely! It goes on to say, "When pain exceeds pain-coping resources, suicidal feelings are the result. Suicide is neither wrong nor right; it is not a defect of character; it is morally neutral. It is simply an imbalance of pain versus coping resources."[6] If this is true, which I believe it is, then why is the subject so terribly taboo? According to Counselling-Directory.org, "Suicide is a public health problem but is not treated as such. People tend to avoid the subject of suicide – death is scary enough, but suicide is even more so – as is the link to potential mental illness that people imagine goes with it. A common reaction today is 'you can talk about mental health, but not about suicide.'"[7]

---

5   http://www.metanoia.org/suicide/
6   http://www.metanoia.org/suicide/
7   https://www.counselling-directory.org.uk/blog/2017/05/25/why-is-suicide-so-hard-to-talk-about

Attemptsurvivors.com blog writer, psychologist, and attempt survivor Bart Andrews says, "It is crucial that more providers speak up to reduce the tremendous prejudice and discrimination that WE have created around mental illness and suicide."[8]

I'm not sure why, but it seems we, as a society, feel the need to exude an air of perfection. I don't know about anyone else, but I've always felt I had to put on a "mask" when in public. Have you ever noticed, when meeting someone in passing, whether that is at work, school, walking through the grocery store or wherever, we nod and smile and say something like, "How are you doing?" But do we genuinely care how that person is doing? Exchanging pleasantries is the polite thing to do; however, are we genuinely concerned about that person's well-being? I'm just as guilty of this as anyone. There have been many times I've seen someone I know that has said, "Hey, how are you?" and I hold back how I truly feel. Yes, there are situations when there isn't enough time to be open and honest and the greeting is in passing; however, when I'm approached and someone asks, "How are you?" now, I always hold back. Why? There was a time the conversation would go something like this:

Friend: Hey, Krista, how are you?

Me: Honestly? I'm not doing well at all.

Friend: *Uncomfortable expression on their face* Really?

Me: I'm just going through so much in my life. Sometimes it's just too much to bear. Between my two cancer kids, issues with fi-

---

8   https://attemptsurvivors.com/2017/10/17/the-future-of-suicide-preven-tion-according-to-dr-bart-andrews/

nances, trying to continue with life and work while being thrown every possible curveball, dealing with…

Friend: Interrupts I know how you feel. Well, just remember, God doesn't give you more than you can handle. What doesn't kill us makes us stronger.

Me: *Puzzled expression on my face* If that's true, I should be able to bench-press an 18-wheeler with my pinky finger.

Friend: *Uncomfortable sympathy laugh*

Awkward pause

Me: Ever feel like life just…

Friend: *Interrupts* Well, it was nice talking to you… *Friend walks away*

I understand when someone tells you something and you have no idea what to say or do, it can be difficult. Although, I've learned through my plethora of life challenges, there are some things you just DON'T do. Empty clichés like "God doesn't give you more…" or "What doesn't kill you…" are not the best choice. If you are uncomfortable hearing what someone else is going through, don't ever, EVER tell them, "I know how you feel." Even if I've experienced something similar to another person, I still cannot know how they feel… I'm not them.

Now, I've never broached the subject of suicide with anyone other than a select few. I haven't been open about it because I just don't want to hear the clichés or the "I-know-how-you-feels." I certainly don't want anyone to call the police to come and protect the crazy lady who can't cope with life anymore. When I was a public-school teacher, it was kind of important that I seem as lucid as I possibly could. If I ended up in a mental hospital, that pretty much negated me being sane. But do my suicidal thoughts truly make me crazy? If it's true that suicide happens when our amount of pain outweighs our ability to cope, is that insanity? Maybe these are rhetorical questions, but they shouldn't be.

So, then I thought to myself, "Okay, self, what is the true definition of insanity?" And no, the dictionary did not say that insanity is doing the same thing over and over, expecting different results. It shows the definition of insanity as "the condition of being insane; a derangement of the mind... psychosis."[9] All righty then! Their example is psychosis, which is any severe form of mental disorder, such as schizophrenia. So, what exactly is schizophrenia? According to Webster's, it's a "psychotic disorder characterized by... noticeable deterioration in the level of functioning in everyday life... expressed as disorder of feelings, delusions, hallucinations, and behavior."[10] Wow, that's a lot! So, I'll break it down. In my suicidal battle, I still function in everyday life. I've been known to go through each day in a complete fog, feeling like I'm just going through the motions, so to speak, but still function as a mom, wife, teacher, friend. I don't think my behaviors have disintegrated... still the same Krista, just an incredibly sad version. I don't have delusions (except maybe in my singing career), I don't hallucinate (despite my vivid imagination), and my behavior, albeit sometimes not conducive to being a 49-year-old, isn't out of the ordinary. So, I think it's safe to say I'm sane.

---

9   https://www.merriam-webster.com/dictionary/insanity
10   https://www.merriam-webster.com/dictionary/schizophrenia

Do I agree that I need psychiatric help? Absolutely! Not just for the suicidal issue; as you are beginning to realize, there are so many reasons why I should see a shrink... DAILY. Has my pain exceeded my ability to cope? More often than not, yes. And, while life circumstances have far outweighed my feelings of self-worth, my story isn't over. Nope, my story has just begun.

CHAPTER 4

Where Did I Come From?
Why didn't the stork use a map?

I've never liked puzzles. I don't mean those free puzzle games we play on our phones. Now, those I could play until my fingers fall off; such a great mind escape when I'm feeling overwhelmed. What I'm referring to are the jigsaw puzzles you find in the toy section of a store, the kind that have a pretty picture on the front and so many pieces on the inside just waiting to be reunited into the essence of what it once was. As symbolic and inspiring as that depiction sounds, I've never had the patience nor the desire to find the pieces that fit together to create a pretty picture. Perhaps there's an underlying subconscious reason for my dislike of jigsaw puzzles. Or it might be that I dread the possibility of getting to the end of a puzzle only to discover not all the pieces are there and there's no way I can complete the picture. That, my friends, would turn my CDO (remember, OCD but the letters are in order as they should be) into an obsessive tailspin that, frankly, I do not have time to fumble through. And maybe these two scenarios are linked? For 35 years, I had a missing puzzle piece in my life that I could not have peace about until that puzzle piece was found. What was missing from my life? My birth father.

When I was a child, there were two things I knew of my birth father: 1) His first and last name and 2) He was career Air Force. I can remember being told by the female parental figure that she kept an open-door policy with him, that he was allowed to visit whenever he wanted. She also told me that he wanted nothing to do with me; otherwise, he would have attempted to contact me. Furthermore, she told me she just knew deep down that I was meant to be her child anyway, and that I didn't need anyone else, especially not someone who would abandon their child. So, apparently, the "stork" didn't use a map. My young mind couldn't understand. Maybe the stork got me mixed up with someone else's baby? Either way, the female parental figure tried to convince me to completely forget about my birth father. I remember being told he had moved on with his life and had other children and he had forgotten about me. I would ask, can parents forget they have children? The answer from her? Yes.

As I grew older, I stopped asking questions about my birth father. I have a feeling the female parental figure thought she was successful in her attempt to erase him from my mind and my heart. In reality, she fueled a drive in me to find him and ask him why. Why am I not good enough? Why didn't you want to visit me? Why didn't you want me to be a part of your life? Why did you let me stay in such a prison... ummm, I mean house, with such horrible parental figures? WHY?

At one point, I had almost completely given up on ever seeing or talking to my birth father. I believe it was the summer of 1988, or was it 1989? I was either 14 or 15, and I know I wasn't in school when this particular event occurred, and it had to have been during the day because the male parental figure was not at home. The phone rang, and the female parental figure answered the phone in her bedroom. I was told to join her, there's someone on the phone who wanted to talk to me. I said, "Hello?"

and I heard a voice I didn't recognize say, "Hello, Krista. This is your dad." I remember starting to tear up and forcing myself to stop getting emotional. Why? Because under the regime of the female parental figure, we were not allowed to show our feelings. Feelings were not allowed; good or bad. So, as I choked back tears, I heard him say he was on leave for two weeks and he was going to visit me. He told me to keep watch out the front window because I'd be seeing him very soon. I was so nervous and excited all at the same time. Finally, I'd have my answers. And maybe, just maybe, I would have an adult in my life that would, dare I suggest, love me?

So, for the next two weeks, I stayed at that window and watched every car pass my driveway, trying to catch a glimpse of the driver. Was that HIM? Did he change his mind and drive away? Maybe this car coming down the road is him? Nope, not him either. After those two weeks of watching at the window, I tried to distract myself from even acknowledging that blasted window, but just couldn't help myself. I would just about jump out of my skin every time the phone rang. Nope, not him on the phone either. Two weeks I waited for him, and he never showed. The following weeks, I would continue to look out that window periodically to no avail.

"See, I told you he didn't want anything to do with you," is what I heard from her yet again. What she refused to accept is that I had a gaping hole in my heart, a huge puzzle piece, so to speak, that just wouldn't be filled with anything but answers from the source of that hole. So, I continued going through the motions of living, and everywhere I went, I would wonder if I had maybe passed my birth father on the street, at the mall, or

ANYWHERE. I would try to picture him, what he looked like, if he liked music, was he fun to hang around with, did he like going on adventures, what job did he have in the Air Force? I tried desperately to remember the sound of his voice. I just couldn't accept that "the stork" made a mistake. And, despite wanting to give up on him, I just couldn't do that either. And I'm so glad I didn't.

CHAPTER 5

Adoption: *Adding to the House of Cards, or Is That Jenga?*

One of my favorite movies of all time is My Cousin Vinny. Released in 1992—ah, yes, 1992. That was a good year. It was the year I graduated from high school, but I digress. There's a scene in My Cousin Vinny where Vinny Gambini, an attorney, is talking with his nephew, Billy, who was arrested and on trial for murdering a convenient store clerk. The circumstantial evidence is rather stacked against Billy. Vinny is making a point that the prosecution is trying to build their case, much like building a house, and is going to make it look like each piece of evidence is a solid brick, building a strong, airtight case against Billy. The problem for the prosecution is that Billy is innocent, and their solid bricks are actually as thin and delicate as playing cards.

Every attempt I've made at building a house of cards has resulted in a jumbled mess, a pile of cards, if you will. There's no substance, there's no strength, and sooner or later, at the slightest hint of wind or shaking of the foundation, that structure will collapse and fall.

Much like a house of cards, but on a whole other engineering level, we have Jenga. If you've never had the pleasure of a game of Jenga, it starts out as a seemingly solid structure of fifty-four rectangular wooden blocks stacked three blocks per level, arranged in opposite directions, creating a tower. Each player removes a block from the tower and places it on top. This, obviously, leaves holes within the tower, and, ultimately, the tower will collapse.

I haven't decided if the female parental figure was building a house of cards or was in advanced stages of Jenga fever. Whichever way the analogy swings, for a time, all seems to be on the up and up. The problem for her was, eventually, collapse was inevitable.

Yet another attempt at protecting the façade was to create a means that would give her definitive control over my situation. To ensure that I could not be ordered to live with anyone else, when I was in the third grade, FPF (female parental figure) and MPF (male parental figure, who I now refer to as "the pedophile") legally adopted me. I don't remember much of the process nor many of the details surrounding my adoption. What I do remember is walking out of that courthouse, FPF said to me, "Now that you're legally my daughter, no one can ever take you away from me." I don't remember how I felt at that moment because all I remember feeling is numb. I also remember how grown up I felt going into my elementary school's office to tell the secretary about my legal name change. Little did I know the difficulties that name change would pose for me as an adult.

As much as I'd like to continue with that train of thought, for now, let's switch tracks back to the game of choice: cards or Jenga? In my mind's eye, I can see how perfectionism, the disease that it is, was built into every facet of my personality. I learned at an incredibly early age that perfection is the only option. Case in point, I remember a time as a child being told to hang up my laundry, so, as expected, I hopped to and promptly hung my clothes in my closet. As I was hanging those clothes, the FPF walked into my room, and you would've thought I had intentionally tried to make her entire life miserable. I heard from FPF, "How could you even consider hanging up clothes like THAT? Can't you do anything right?" And, just like that, every article of clothing in my closet that was on a hanger was removed and piled on my bed. I was then directed to correctly hang everything in my closet, and do not leave this room until it's perfect. Now, did FPF teach me how to hang those clothes as expected? Of course not! I was expected to just KNOW. I mean, doesn't everyone just KNOW the perfectly correct way to hang shirts, pants, skirts, and dresses? And this scenario was the case for pretty much everything I did. From incorrectly washing dishes (we didn't have a dishwashing machine at this point) to dusting to laundry to, well, basically anything that was "women's work." I cannot remember ever being taught HOW to do anything that was expected of me. It was my responsibility to just know how to do, well, everything! Did I ever ask FPF to teach me anything? Not in so many words. I can remember standing in front of that closet door sobbing as I wondered exactly what it was that I did wrong. FPF must have heard my crying because she stormed back into my room and was told to quit that crying or I'd be given something to cry about. So, did I ever ask to be taught how to do anything? No, thank you! I guess I figured it was better to try and possibly do it "wrong" and just hope for the best. Trial and error seem to be how I learn best? Sounds about right considering the choices I made in adulthood.

Something I find funny—funny strange, not funny ha-ha—is that if I ever DID do something correctly, there was no direct positive reinforcement. My positive reinforcement was that nothing was said at all. So, for me, positive reinforcement was that I didn't cry and feel like I was completely worthless. Did that stop me from trying to please FPF? No, it made me try even harder to be perfect.

As I try to pull one positive scenario from the catacombs of my mind, I remember an occurrence that happened more than once involving my ability to sing. I was told, at church, that I would get on that platform and sing for Jesus. Apparently, this was an ability that was accepted by FPF. So, the congregation knew I was able to carry a tune. I remember being... somewhere out in public... and we ran into a couple from church. I was told to "sing for _____," whoever it was for whom I was expected to sing. Let's call them Joe-Schmoe and Sally-Schmoe. I was TERRIFIED that I would make a mistake and proceeded to freeze like a block of ice. FPF would tell the Schmoes that I was just shy and would turn to me with a look that shook me to my core, and through clenched teeth said, "I told you to sing for the Schmoes!" to which I would squeak out whatever the selection was for that encounter. The Schmoes would proceed to ooh and ahh over my "pretty little voice." FPF would respond with something to the effect of it being so aggravating that I wouldn't listen the first time. In the world I knew, I was to be seen and not heard unless I was told to perform like a trained circus monkey. In every circumstance, I was to present perfection no matter what, and under no circumstance was I to speak of anything that happened in our family because it's no one else's business. And, as I'm thinking about all of this, it occurs to me that we rarely had anyone who wasn't family over for anything social. We didn't entertain any of their adult friends, never had anyone over for dinner. I think, maybe, the only real friend outside of church FPF had was the Avon lady, who would stop by for a minute or two to deliver Avon products and then left rather quickly. Although, I'm not so sure that qualifies as a friend. Even more odd, when the mail carrier would deliver our mail (our mailbox was attached beside our front door), FPF would literally hide so they didn't see her, and she'd peek out the window to see if they were gone and only then would she open the door to retrieve the mail. It was as if she was scared of the mailman. What's even sadder is that I thought that all of this was completely normal.

It seems logical that when one, namely the FPF, strives to project a family of perfection to the outside world, they would fully believe they have effectively offered the world a veneer of perfection. And when looking from a great distance, from the outside looking in, I can see how her house of cards could look like a solidly engineered, strong structure. Keeping everyone well beyond arm's length should keep that façade protected, and that's exactly what happened for far too long.

As I sit here reflecting on how I'm pulling FPF's Jenga tower apart block by block, it seems apropos to include a Scooby-Doo ending. The villain has been caught, and their mask is pulled off, to which the villain, in this case, the FPF, exclaims, "And I would've gotten away with it, if it weren't for those meddling kids!" If only it could be that simple. Instead of being like an episode of Scooby-Doo ending in a pretty little tied-up bow, I feel like I'm clawing myself through some very thick mud, trying to keep my head up so I can keep breathing.

And so, my friends, if you're still with me in this narrative, let's take a deep breath, wiggle ourselves out of that sparkly sequined straitjacket I mentioned in the Introduction, and stand up from the fetal position that we've folded ourselves into. Let's stretch those legs, shake out those arms, maybe find a stiff drink, and buckle up for the next section, where we head into adulthood territory.

PART 2

Adulthood

CHAPTER 6

Settling, But Not Like the Pioneers: *So Few Tools, So Many Poor Choices*

I've never understood the draw of so-called reality TV. I'm a skeptic as well as a Missourian, so I see those avenues of time investment to be more of a time suck. However, there was one show I felt myself being drawn into its gravitational pull. While I cannot remember the name of this specific show, the premise was something like this: a few participants are dropped into Canadian wilderness with very few tools to aid in their survival. Their task was to survive with those tools as well as the resources available to them in that wilderness for a set number of days. The one who lasted the longest won the prize money, which I'm thinking whoever won should've used all of that money towards much-needed psychological therapy, but I digress. As I watched that first episode, I couldn't understand why I was being captivated by this genre of entertainment. As I pondered my why, I found myself likening their reality show task to my adulthood.

Before I tackle that subject matter, let's establish a few universal ideals. What is the ultimate purpose of parenting? Is it to prove to those youngsters in our care just how cool, fun, and awesome we are? Contrary to current American societal standards, that is NOT the purpose of parenting! No, I'd like to think we can all agree that the ultimate purpose of parenting is to train our younglings in how to be strong, viable, positive contributors to society. That purpose develops their personalities to be strong and independent adults who can take those tools they've been given and, in turn, do the same for their own younglings. Thus, the perpetuation of the human race. And now I have a mental picture of Rafiki holding Simba at the top of a rock as the song "Circle of Life" plays with a crescendo in sound and ends with the title The Lion King in big letters, but again, I digress.

Parents have the responsibility to equip their children with the necessary tools to survive life as an adult. If one has not been given adequate adulting tools, it's much like trying to survive in the Canadian wilderness. Mistakes will be made, some potentially fatal. If this is true, then why in the world would anyone set up their children for failure? Are people truly that selfish? Excuse me while I attempt to get the lid back on that large and very messy can of worms. Now, as Snoop Dogg says, "Back to the lecture at hand."

Navigating life as an emerging adult with very few tools for adulting survival is difficult at best. Top that with feeling worthless as a human being, and there's a twice-baked disaster on the verge of exploding. My poor choices started quite early. There I was, a freshman in high school. I was on the color guard team with our marching band. Fourteen years old and about as naïve as one can be. There was a junior that talked to me a lot before and after marching band practice. We were also in symphonic band together. I was strongly warned by various people to stay away from that particular boy. Did I listen? Of course not! And why not, one might ask? Because someone, a BOY mind you, was giving me attention. It didn't matter to me if it was good or bad. He said he liked me and asked if I'd go to Homecoming with him. A date? A real live date with a boy that seemed to like me? Yes, please! So, as tradition holds, I found a dress suitable for a Homecoming dance. I felt like a princess in a fairy tale. I was given a corsage and everything! I had a boyfriend! Just the thought that a boy wanted to spend time with someone as worthless as I was a dream to me. And just like that, my dream turned into a nightmare. I soon found out why I was being warned about him.

Remember in Chapter 2 where I listed the symptoms and side effects of childhood sexual abuse? Do you remember the statistic: 63% of women who had suffered sexual abuse by a family member also reported a rape or attempted rape after the age of 14? Yep, I'm one of those 63%. Out of the frying pan into the fire? I seem to be the source for the meaning of that cliché. What happens to a girl's brain after enduring years of childhood sexual abuse and then the very first relationship outside of the "funk in dysfunctional family" is one that ends up in date rape? That's right! The affirmation that the only way to gain a man's love is through physical acts. Remember, I was not shown love in my childhood, so a terribly warped definition of love developed as well as the reliance on co-dependency. Without the tools of self-respect, self-worth, confidence, and healthy coping skills, the result will be one poor choice after another. This is exactly what set the stage for my adulthood. I didn't realize that I was settling for subpar rather than reaching my potential. In my defense, I didn't believe I had any potential in which to reach.

Now, despite the overwhelming feeling of worthlessness, I sought activities and pursued interests in which I wanted so desperately to excel. Music, theatre, speech, and any other performance-based extra-curriculars I could find filled my spare time. I tried gaining my family's approval for my efforts, and those activities kept me from being at home any longer than necessary. Win-win! So, I was involved in the fall and spring theatrical productions, I was on the speech team, and one year I was in both symphonic band and concert choir. And, yes, the parental figures did attend those events (remember, the façade of being the perfect parents was the goal, however, their attendance only gave ammunition for their nit-picking my every mistake).

Let's do a short fast-forward. It's my junior year in high school. The pedophile had been diagnosed with colon cancer and was in the final stages of life on this earth, and when he died, I had an overwhelming feeling of relief wash over me. I felt guilty about that feeling. Why? At the time, I didn't understand it was because the prison I had survived had finally opened a window of respite. While emotions were not allowed to be demonstrated, the expected sense of sadness (rather than the subdued joy I felt in my gut) was something I could not hide, so I sought refuge in a boy who was currently giving me attention. However, this boy was unlike all the others. Due to the fact that my perception of what was expected of me was so warped, when it came to boyfriend-girlfriend relationships, I basically scared him away. I did what I thought I was supposed to do and often gave him opportunity to use me as he wished, but instead, he broke up with me. I was dumbfounded and bewildered. Rather than understand the respect he had for me, rather than accept his desire to retain his integrity and purity, rather than step back and see the situation from the outside and recognize that physical acts do not equate to mental and emotional connection, I chose to push the issue, and as a result, I was rejected. An abused 16-year-old does not have the tools, nor the ability to distinguish like vs. love, much less love vs. lust, and yet another poor decision was made. Looking back on that relationship, as an adult, I can see how that boy was trying to show me he liked me as a person, not as an object with which to play. He wasn't directly rejecting me as a person; he was making the choice to create a boundary for himself. And, as much as I respect that NOW, at the time I was utterly devastated. I didn't have any other boyfriends in high school, and adult-me is rather grateful for that. However, for high school me, it only reinforced my self-deprecation and loathing.

If only I'd had those necessary adulting tools! Would my ultimate dreams have come to fruition? Of course, there's no way to know. At the time, I felt my dreams were so far beyond my reach there was no point in even trying to take that path. The first time I allowed myself to dream was when I went with my drama group to Chicago. It was the summer of 1991, mere days before the pedophile passed away. During this trip, we saw a live musical. It was my first time attending a musical in a theatre. We saw Les Misérables. It changed me in ways I didn't understand at the time. I walked out of that theatre dreaming of going to New York City and landing my dream role as Fantine in Les Misérables. I became obsessed with that musical. I bought the original cast double cassette tapes and wore them out. I had every word of the entire score memorized. I figured, since there's no way I'd ever be able to land any role on Broadway, Fantine included, I'd enjoy singing every word to myself. It never occurred to me that the voice lessons I was taking, the exemplary ratings I had received at both district and state contests for my solo singing, and the encouragement of my teachers were an indication that maybe I should pursue that career path. No, I had experienced enough rejection, so I decided to play it safe. I chose to go into music education. I developed a love and passion for music early in life, so I thought this would be a safe and stable career. Another bad choice? That's still up for debate.

I graduated high school in June of 1992 and started my music education program that year in August. I chose Hannibal-La-Grange University in Hannibal, Missouri, for my undergraduate degree. I originally wanted to dual major in music as well as elementary education, however, it would've taken twice as long, so I chose earning a BSE in secondary education with an emphasis in vocal music. I would be certified Kindergarten through 12th grade, so I could be hired just about anywhere. I chose H-LG University because I thought going to a private school would be safer than a state school. I had just enough sense to realize that I would need boundaries to keep me on the "straight and narrow." Having specific rules for dorm life, I hoped, would keep me from going completely crazy with this newfound freedom. I didn't take into consideration that the tuition would be considerably higher than a state school and that having student debt carried into adulthood is a horrible choice. Again, no adulting tools as well as zero guidance from anyone except for the financial aid officer who offered to help me apply for the maximum amount of available funds to be borrowed. Excuse me while I go bang my head against a wall.

CHAPTER 7

Age Does Not Equate Maturity:
There Ought to Be a Law!

There I was, a freshman in college. I was thrilled and terrified at the same time. My grades were excellent, and I felt like I was really in control of my life. I found a fabulous group of friends within the music department, my roommate and I got along swimmingly, and I was thriving! I genuinely wanted to make better choices and be successful. I decided to date a boy who showed interest in me and was a really nice guy. And, while we weren't truly compatible (we're still friends to this day), our break-up wasn't the end of the world for me. My first semester of college was under my belt, and everything was going well. And then came second semester. It was January of 1993, and a new crop of students arrived on campus. I was walking to one of the boys' dorms to see a friend and felt eyes on me, watching my every move. I turned to see a guy smiling at me. That made me terribly uncomfortable, so I kept walking a little faster. Later in the cafeteria, smiley-guy approached and asked my name. I found out he was twenty-three. Oooo! An older man? And he wanted to date... ME? I told myself: SELF?!? Don't blow this!!!

He and I were inseparable! Although, I found it rather odd that I'd have to wait in his car while he'd go call his mom. Ummm... red flag? Yeah... it should've been, but I was so excited about my "grown-up relationship," I chose to ignore all of the warning signs, and there were a LOT of them. Yep, ignoring warning signs is a skill I was honing much like an artiste hones their skill of sculpting. I was shaping my future with tools of my own making. I hadn't been given adequate tools, so I eventually had to create my own, which were inadequate at best.

I can't decide which of the red flags was my favorite. Was it waiting in his car while he "called his mom," which I found out later was actually his probation officer? Or maybe it was the fact that he was spending a ridiculous amount of money on me and didn't have a job? It could be how freaked out he got when I started to open one of his desk drawers in his dorm room. Or possibly the fact that he was twenty-three and living in a college dorm? So many red flags! But, but... he was nice to me! And, regardless of the plethora of warning signs to get away from this guy, still I reveled in my oblivion and continued the relationship. We met in January 1993, and he proposed marriage to me, with quite the expensive diamond ring mind you, in June of 1993. With as much excitement as a newly engaged 19-year-old can muster, I called FPF to tell her the news. I was met with anger and frustration. I don't know why I thought I'd have a response that was anything besides a doom-and-gloom-what-are-you-thinking attitude. Still, I was planning a winter wedding. I thought just before Christmas would be the perfect time. That summer was, at that point, the best summer of my life. I was engaged to who I thought was my knight in shining armor (armor can be made of aluminum, right?), I was working full time at a daycare while still living on campus, and had my entire life figured out. At least, that's what I thought.

As my sophomore year of college began, I was living with three roommates in an on-campus apartment. As I was getting ready to go to my first class of the day on a brisk September morning in 1993, the phone rang, and it was him. The conversation went like this:

Me: Hello?

Him: They're coming to get me.

Me: Who is coming to get you?

Him: They are... I'm so sorry.

Me: What's wrong? What's going on? Who is coming to get you?

Him: Marion County police. I don't know what's going to happen, just know that I love you.

Me: But WHY are they coming to get you?

Him: They have a warrant for my arrest. I have to go.

Click—dial tone

That's right, the man I was supposed to marry was wanted in seven... SEVEN counties between Illinois, Iowa, and Missouri. Very quickly, puzzle pieces were turning into a clearer and rather disturbing picture. This genius had opened a checking account upon arriving in Hannibal that January, had it long enough to have a box of checks for the account delivered to him, and then promptly closed that account, which he continued writing checks on. The really sad part is that he had come from a different private college in Missouri to H-LG for a "fresh start" after having done the same illegalities there, and when the law caught up with him, rather than serve time since it was his first offense, he was given three years' probation. Well, this time he took it to the next level and had written one check to purchase an entire computer system, which pushed him into class A felony territory. And, just like that, my entire world came crashing down around me.

I decided the best way to get over what was, in my opinion at that time, the most devastating blow a 19-year-old could ever experience was to push it out of my mind as if it had never happened. Yeah, THAT'S healthy! So, I made it abundantly clear to the male population on campus, those in and around my circle of friends, that I was more than available to date and have fun. I decided I was young and shouldn't be tied down to one man. And that's exactly what I did. The remainder of my first semester sophomore year was spent having fun and pretending I hadn't been virtually destroyed by my own poor choices.

As second semester started in January 1994, one of my roommates and I decided to go to McDonald's to share 6-piece chicken nuggets. We had just finished one of our evening classes, and she was dealing with a personal crisis. As I sat in that booth with her, I noticed one of the workers mopping near us. He smiled a lot at me, and I promptly wrote my name and number on a napkin and gave it to him. He picked me up that night after he closed the restaurant, I broke curfew to sneak out with him, and we went to his apartment that was in town and talked all night. And, just like that, co-dependency reared its ugly head again. I spent every waking minute with him. My grades were starting to slip, but I didn't care. I had all but moved into his apartment, and by the summer of 1994, we were living together. The level of guilt I was feeling was overwhelming because of my current relationship. I knew deep in my spirit that living with him outside of marriage was not the best choice for me. I was still working at the day-care that summer, and in June of 1994, during a lunch break, he picked me up from work, and while driving, he asked, "So, are we getting married or what?" That was my proposal. No ring, no kneeling, no happy tears. I know what you're thinking... how romantic! Right? That noise you just heard was the rumbling of my eyes rolling. What's even more eye-roll inducing is that we were married six weeks later. Six weeks? I have a carton of milk in my refrigerator I've had a longer relationship with! At least, that's the logic we've heard from Chandler Bing on Friends.

I've since decided there ought to be a law! That's right, there ought to be a law against anyone getting married before the age of thirty. Okay, maybe twenty-five if the correct fiery hoops have been successfully jumped through and enough psychological evaluations have been administered. This may seem like over-the-top extreme thinking to you, and I know there are many couples who married young and had a successful marriage and family. However, a 20-year-old and a 25-year-old are usually two completely different species of adult. Nevertheless, I was 20 years old, my husband was 19 years old, and we'd live happily ever after, right? RIGHT?!?

Wow, those are some loud crickets chirping!

CHAPTER 8

Ummm... No, I'm Not!
You'll Never Graduate...
Watch Me!

I'm sure it goes without saying that my marriage was strained and difficult at best. And, while there was severe abuse that I endured, I will save that story for a subsequent book.

Since Broadway was absolutely out of the question, I decided to focus my attention on a new plan. I would finish my BSE in music education, find a job teaching music at a public school, and once I had achieved tenure, would think about maybe starting our family. At that point, I could stay home and focus on just being a mom until the baby started kindergarten, then return to the classroom. Seemed logical and reasonable... until...

It was my junior year of college. In terms of academics, first semester was rather uneventful, barring the horror that was my Music Theory III class. I'm convinced that anyone who can not only survive but can pass Music Theory III deserves some sort of gold medal or badge or... something. I was finishing my second semester. It's the end of May 1995. I had the privilege of participating in the music for my brother and sister-in-law's wedding, and I was much weepier than the norm for a wedding. I wasn't feeling well at all and had zero energy. This went on for a couple of weeks until I decided to visit the free women's clinic just across the street from campus to find out what's going on with me.

I was sitting in that small, cold room on the protective, crinkly papered patient's bed with the stirrups. Ah, yes, a woman's FAVORITE exam. After peeing in a cup, wearing that lovely gown that covers virtually nothing on a big girl like me, and their completion of the full-on exam, I was asked to get dressed and wait for someone to talk to me. Soon, I was walked into a small office with lots of pamphlets hanging from racks on the wall. I'm sitting in a folding chair, and there's a nurse with her back to me, rustling some papers and getting a folder together. The conversation we had went like this:

Her: Now, you're going to want to find a doctor, so I'm putting together some information for you to look over and make some decisions.

Me: *awkward silence*

Her: I'm assuming you're going to want to see a doctor in town. Do you already have an OB/GYN that you see?

Me: No, why? Is something wrong?

Her: *turns around to look at me* Well, you're pregnant.

Me: *deer in headlights stare, pregnant pause (see what I did there?)*

I'm WHAT, now??????

Her: You're pregnant.

Me: Ummm... no, I'm not!

Her: Ummm, yes... you are!

Me: But I can't be, I'm still in college.

Her: You CAN be, and you ARE!

Me: But... but I CAN'T be!

Her: WELL, I DIDN'T DO IT!!!

I didn't believe it. So, I promptly went to Wal-Mart and purchased a pregnancy test. I bought the 2-pack just to be sure. And, yes, every indicating line appeared. I still didn't believe it.

When my husband arrived home from work that day, he found me staring into space in an almost catatonic state. I showed him the two pregnancy tests. He was elated! We were pregnant. And I still didn't believe it. As I said before, "de-nial" ain't just a river in Africa.

I applied and was accepted for Missouri Medicaid for Pregnant Women as well as WIC. I chose an OB/GYN in town and found out my due date was January 25, 1996.

My first phone call was to FPF. Surely, SURELY this would cause a positive interaction. You're going to be a grandma again. Isn't that exciting? You probably already have an idea of the terribly hurtful and disappointing result of that conversation; however, I'll be specific.

The response was not only less than happy but also one of condemnation. It was silence, followed by the spewing of angry questions. "What were you thinking? How do you expect to support this child? How are you going to afford a baby?" But my favorite part of the response was this: "You'll never graduate college. You'll drop out and not finish. You'll never graduate!" My response was silence and choking back tears. My brain and my soul screamed, WATCH ME!!! And that's exactly what I did.

I spent that summer working at a local bank, I enrolled and successfully completed my first semester of my senior year in college, and was preparing for my senior voice recital, which was set for December 1995. I successfully performed my senior voice recital that I had literally been preparing for the last four years of voice lessons. Yes, I was my own planet, waddling on and off that stage singing songs that before I was pregnant was no problem, but as the pregnancy continued, my voice continued to change and made those soprano arias terribly difficult to squeak out and, if I were lucky, would sound okay. Aren't hormones lovely?

I blinked, and the second semester of my senior year began. I wasn't due for about two more weeks, so I had enough time to go to each class, obtain the syllabus, and discuss with my professors the impending arrival of baby #1. Most of those professors were kind and understanding and only asked I turn in every assignment on time. No problem! And then, my baby girl decided to make her arrival 8 days before she was due. On January 17, 1996, I became a mom to the sweetest little girl.

Two weeks—that's correct, folks—only two weeks after her arrival, I went back to my classes. The best thing about living in married-student housing on campus is the number of available babysitters within walking distance who were more than excited to watch my baby girl while I attended classes. Surviving on little to no sleep, I finished that semester with a 3.06 GPA. Not too shabby for a zombie, ummm... I mean a new momma who was also a full-time music education major. Those summer months were spent at home with my baby girl, and it was such a precious time. I wish I would've had enough maturity then to fully appreciate that gift I was given as a new mom. I look back at those days and, as financially lean as they were, I wouldn't trade them for anything.

My final semester of college was the fall of 1996. My last "class" of my undergraduate degree was a professional semester, also known as Student Teaching. I could write an entire series of books on my 25 years of experience in the trenches of public education, starting with student teaching, but again, that's for another time. And, while I won't speak directly about the specifics of student teaching, I will say that the most difficult aspect of that semester was the realization of my heart's desire flying from my grasp. As I dropped off my 7-month-old baby girl at the daycare where I had once worked, a piece of my heart withered and died. The dream of staying home to raise my child the best way I could for her died that day, and in its place was conceived a new-and-improved monster of guilt and self-loathing. This is where those self-made tools I developed up to this point came in rather handy. Knowing how to stuff down every feeling and emotion had become second nature to me, so I pushed into full-on adulting survival mode.

As I feel the overwhelming need to step away from the current subject matter (grabbing for the tissues), I'd like to use this opportunity to explain why my tools of adulting survival mode are so damaging and destructive. When I started seeing a therapist, she chose to utilize a therapy method called CPT: Cognitive Processing Therapy. "Cognitive processing therapy (CPT) is a specific type of cognitive behavioral therapy that has been effective in reducing symptoms of PTSD that have developed after experiencing a variety of traumatic events including child abuse, combat, rape, and natural disasters."[1] So, in that season of therapy, I learned that my tools of choice are avoidance, detachment, and at times dissociation.

You probably remember in Chapter 2 where I touched on dissociation. And, while my adulting survival tools are undesirable at best, being validated by my therapist identifying them was at least a little reassuring.

Oh yeah, self-doubt is huge in all of this mess as well... but I'm not completely sure about that.

Let's first look at avoidance as it's the most obvious and conscious of the three. According to Michael Patanella, "...avoidance is usually a pre-planned action, which we put together in order to avoid certain scenarios, situations, and people. It is something that comes knowingly and consciously. A behavior that is counterproductive."[2] For me, this is intentionally making myself late to an event and then reasoning it's just too late to attend and choose to stay home. Or I "lose track of time" doing something like, perhaps, writing an autobiographical book (excuse me while I check the clock), knowing full well I have other unpleasant obligations to fulfill. Mr. Patanella also indicates, "Experts often call our avoidance behavior a 'maladaptive coping mechanism'. Avoidance itself, is not a mental illness. It is however one of the key symptoms and behaviors of multiple mental illnesses."[3] All this time, I deemed myself a professional procrastinator when,

---

1   https://www.apa.org/ptsd-guideline/treatments/cognitive-processing-therapy

2   https://medium.com/@michaelpatanella/the-psychology-of-avoidance-f140a05b18f2

3   https://medium.com/@michaelpatanella/the-psychology-of-avoidance-f140a05b18f2

in fact, I'm a professional avoidance artist. I could further my proof of avoidance and go on with the analogies, but that would be avoiding the other two coping mechanisms, wouldn't it? See? There's some progress!

In regard to dissociation, allow me to elaborate. If we're getting abused, insulted, or attacked verbally, or mentally, dissociation is one of the brain's strongest ways to react as a subconscious defense mechanism. In my opinion, dissociation is a result of tenacity through a traumatic experience. Now, before you disagree, hear me out on this. Our amazing and powerful brains have the ability to not only convince us to keep going through trauma but also develop ways to help us keep going through trauma. This is my attempt at throwing a positive spin on a really horrible situation. Yeah, I know, I'm avoiding again.

Detachment, another of these subconscious means of coping, is similar to dissociation; however, there are distinct differences. In my research, I found a blog-type article that gave thoughts on the difference. It says, "Dissociation is really an involuntary process of the mind to protect us, whereas, on some level, emotional detachment can be intentional. Dissociation is being emotionally disconnected and not present, where detachment is more like being distracted and not fully present but still somewhat present. Emotional detachment can be likened to 'numbing' one's feelings by avoiding being with an emotion because it feels too overwhelming or painful. Both of these coping skills are often associated with having experienced trauma in the past. Emotional detachment can also be related to other anxiety and stress disorders. Sometimes, when we are emotionally detaching, we may appear present to others in the cognitive sense (speaking logically) but our emotional affect may be lacking."[4]

Okay. If I'm going to practice what I preach, it's definitely time to stop all of this avoiding and get back to our regularly scheduled outline already in progress. Where was I? Oh, yes... student teaching.

I managed to finish that last semester of college, successfully earning a 4.0 GPA, my very first 4.0 semester in my college career. Yes, I only took one class, and I earned an "A" in that one class; however, I'm still going to enjoy the success of having a 4.0 semester. More importantly, I'm enjoying the success of a well-earned I TOLD YOU SO! Did I say "I told you so" to the FPF? Of course not! Did I scream it in my head along with a rousing chorus of "neener-neener-neener" while walking across that stage when I participated in my graduation ceremony? You bet your boots I did! Did I want to hear "I was wrong" from the FPF, you know, the one who is NEVER wrong? Yep! You want to hear a shock? She did not say "I was wrong." That's not the shocking part. She said... wait for it... "I'm proud of you." It was the one positive reinforcement from FPF I can remember. Wait, WHAT? Now, before you faint from such a ginormous shock, it was said in true FPF style: quietly and away from any other ears. I guess that was her way of saying "I was wrong"? I don't know, but the point of the matter is, I proved her wrong. I DID graduate! And I'm allowing myself to feel proud of that accomplishment.

---

4   https://www.counsellingconnection.com/index.php/2015/01/26/dissoci-ation-and-emotional-detachment/

CHAPTER 9

Back to Life, Back to Reality: *A Crash Course in the Politics of Public Schools*

Are there any 1980s and 1990s peeps out there? I have to know; did you sing the first part of the title of this chapter like I always do? Anyone? Bueller? Moving on...

Because I finished my undergraduate degree in December of 1996, I had six months until my graduation ceremony and a few hoops to jump through in order to finish obtaining my teaching certificate. I heard there was a part-time job open in Hannibal at the Catholic school for a music teacher. It was for grades pre-K through eighth on Tuesdays and Thursdays. Before taxes, I made a whopping $75 a week; however, the experience was what I was most interested in. I taught at that school from December 1996 until the end of their school year in May of 1997. It was decided the best choice for our family was for me to apply to every possible music teaching job in the state of Missouri, and we'd move to wherever I found employment. After graduation, amidst the dozens of resumes I had mailed, I was contacted by a district I had not heard of, nor had I sent a resume to. The principal of the school was going to be in the St. Louis area that week; would I like to meet somewhere for an informal interview? The beauty of that situation, at least what I thought was a "God thing," was that the school was in way south Missouri, just north of the Arkansas border. I reasoned it couldn't just be a coincidence with the timing and her being so close to the St. Louis area for other reasons. That week, I met with that principal and was immediately offered a job. I was on cloud nine! Surely this is the path I'm supposed to be on! I had visions of establishing our family literally on the other side of the state and having a long and full career in that small town. There was one slight problem I was overlooking: my naivety. I had no clue that something was rather suspicious from the beginning. I was basking in my oblivion that, in hindsight, should have been screaming RED FLAGS!

We secured housing, a cute little two-bedroom duplex, that we thought we would be able to afford because my husband would SURELY have plenty of job offers at one of the nearby factories. Well, there were not plenty of job offers... and don't call me "Shirley" (as per the movie Airplane!). He could not find a job anywhere. Here is the problem that we had no idea was a problem. We were not from there. Why is it a problem, you ask? Well, because in that particular small town (I'm choosing to leave it unnamed out of respect for the one person who was truly kind to me), if you haven't lived there a minimum of 25 years, you are an outsider! We were REALLY out of luck considering in August of 1997, I was the ripe old age of twenty-three, and he was twenty-two. And there I was, getting lost amid the myriads of red flags! There was no going back at this point. My contract had been signed, and I was committed to a minimum of one year. I still had hope that happily ever after would happen there. My classrooms were ready, and there was no stopping that tardy bell.

In case you are wondering, I did not misspell classrooms. That is not a typo at all. My very first year of teaching music full time involved grades kindergarten through eighth. I was responsible for general music K-5 as well as sixth through eighth grade music appreciation, "honors" choir, beginning AND intermediate band. I had a total of 3 classrooms. Why? Well, I was originally in charge of just K-5 as well as music appreciation and choir. At the beginning of the year, there was a separate band teacher. That guy up and quit before the first quarter was over, leaving me to take on everything. And the red flags just keep coming. But wait! There's more! As if that weren't enough to throw a first-year music teacher over the edge, my mentor was a kindergarten teacher who had no clue about anything outside of teaching kindergarten. Now, you might wonder, why not assign my state-required teaching mentor from a different school within that school district? Ready for this? It was the only school in that district. Read that sentence again! That's right! The entire district was housed within that facility, including the school board full of "good ol' boys," as well as the district's superintendent. So, there was literally no one else in that district teaching music besides me. Lovely!

While anyone else in public education would have seen the overabundance of red flags covering every aspect of my work life as it was, I continued in my determination to make a good name for myself in that community. I wanted a stable upbringing for my daughter and, as a terribly naïve individual, I was convinced small-town USA far from any of my family was the perfect place for it.

I had completed almost two months of teaching when I was asked to see the principal after school. I was then told that the school board had been receiving complaints about me. The crime? I dared to assign homework to my sixth through eighth grade music appreciation students. I mean, how DARE I?!? Homework? In a MUSIC class? For shame! I was then told the teacher who had just retired, the one whose place I was taking, the one who had been the only music teacher in that "district" for the last 25 years, followed her own curriculum of showing any movie her students wanted to watch. Thus, the explanation for the boxes full of VHS tapes I found when going through the choir classroom. I had the audacity to attempt teaching those students basic music theory. What a horrible thing to do! Pardon my need to find a towel to wipe all of this sarcasm off of my laptop. I chose to apologize for any inconvenience, and in the next breath explained to my boss that I felt I would be doing a disservice not only to those students, but to their parents and the entire school as a whole if I didn't do what I was hired to do: teach music. I then made a vow to no longer assign homework; whatever wasn't finished that day would continue into the next class time. My question to my 23-year-old self is, how in the world did you not see the setup happening? Setup of what? Patience, grasshopper, you will soon understand.

In that meeting with my principal, I was reminded that I was in charge of the school Christmas concert. Back in 1997, in small-town Missouri, it was still called a "Christmas" concert. I was surprised as well. I asked, for clarification's sake, I need to conduct a Christmas concert. Which grade levels should be involved? I was told to make it my own, to create a concert centered on Christmas to be performed in the evening for the community as well as for the Christmas assembly. No problem! And so, I prepared my students for a Christmas concert. Now, I've been involved in all thing's music for as long as I can remember. Any time I participated in a concert, it was a choir standing on risers singing selected songs, a symphonic band playing selected songs, and maybe a cute appearance by Santa Claus in a big finale combining those ensembles. The actual definition of a concert is a performance given by one or more singers or instrumentalists or both. That is a concert. Keep that in mind and hold on to your hat...

Two weeks... TWO WEEKS before the concert in December that I had been preparing my students for since September, my principal approached me after school.

Principal: So, how's the play coming?

Me: I'm sorry, the WHAT?

Principal: The play!

Me: The play???

Principal: YES! The play!

Me: In our meeting, you said a concert was the expectation.

Principal: Yeah! Concert... play. Same thing, isn't it?

Me: Ummmmm...... begging your pardon, ma'am, but no, a concert and a play are not the same thing.

Principal: Well, our community expects a Christmas play. We've had one every year for the last 25 years!

Me: *blank stare*

Principal: Your concert is a play, right?

Me: *pregnant pause while my brain is going Mach 3 with its hair on fire* ....Yes, ma'am. Our community will have a Christmas play.

Principal: Great! Good to hear!

You know that analogy about the duck? You know, the duck above water looks like he's calm without a care in the world, but underwater his legs are frantic? Yep! I went straight home and after a full-on sobbing, panicky cry fest, I went to work. Before that evening was over, I had written a script tying all of my concert songs together. The next day during choir, I assigned speaking parts. The beauty of it? I made it to where those students had props with their speaking parts written on them. I went to the art teacher, the only person who was genuinely nice to me, and asked if she might have time to have her students create backdrops for the stage. Thankfully, she volunteered to help in any way she could. Within those 2 weeks, I had written, assigned, rehearsed, made costumes, rehearsed, made props, dress rehearsed, and directed a "Christmas Concert" (it was actually a musical, but... meh...) for that community. Not only was I successful in fulfilling their expectations, I had nothing but positive feedback from everyone I encountered. I was told it was the best Christmas Concert that community had ever seen... and it wasn't so long and boring as in years past. I was certain I had planted those positive seeds and had, hopefully, earned their respect. I still had no clue about the world of public education politics. I didn't know they had an endgame, and I was only a pawn for them to achieve their ultimate goal.

We survived through Christmas break and plowed into the second semester of that overwhelming school year. I directed pep band for the eighth-grade basketball games, I took the "honors" choir to a district choir festival, I was getting along beautifully with all of my students. All was right in the world, until...

Around the end of February, I was feeling pretty rough. I figured I was dealing with a stomach bug that was going around the school. The strange thing was that it only affected me in the mornings. Uh oh! Yep, you guessed it! I was expecting baby #2. I was not ready to hear that news; however, I was much less surprised than I was with baby #1. Mornings were ROUGH! It was not at all like with my first pregnancy. I was convinced this precious little bundle of joy was determined to kill me slowly through the means of vomiting everything I had ever ingested since 1982! I was exhausted, I couldn't find much of anything that I could tolerate smelling, much less eat. That's okay, I would tell myself, we're finally getting somewhere with this school and the community, so all will be well. I had finished preparing and directing the "Easter Concert" (again, it was a musical, but whatever... I chose a patriotic theme which was a smash hit with the community), and the following week, the end of April 1998, I was again called into the principal's office.

Me: You wanted to see me?

Principal: Yes, have a seat. First of all, I want to congratulate you on the success of the Easter Concert. I've heard nothing but good from everyone.

Me: Thank you!

Principal: Unfortunately, I have to have this difficult conversation with you. The school board has decided not to offer you another year here. Rather than choose to let you go, we wanted to give you the opportunity to offer a letter of resignation. You'll want to get your resume together and start your search for other employment.

Me: WHAT??? But I thought I was doing so much better. My classes are all going so well, I've developed such positive relationships with all of my students. Why? What could I do better? I can do better!

Principal: I'm sorry. The board has made its decision. I, as well as the Superintendent, will be more than happy to offer a letter of recommendation for you as you find another teaching job elsewhere.

Me: *blank stare*

Principal: Also, we'd appreciate it if you'd keep this between us for now. No use in upsetting the kids this far from the end of the school year. I'm sure you understand, don't you?

Me: *blank stare*

Principal: If there's anything I can do to help you, please let me know.

I could not believe it! How could I lose that job? I had done everything they asked of me and then some! I was pregnant, had a 2-year-old, and had just lost my job. Not only that, I had to finish that school year knowing I wouldn't be back the following year. This couldn't be happening! What would we do? No one would want to hire someone whose due date was Oct 2! Like always, I continued on in a fog, trying to pretend all was well. I had become quite a good actress at this point. I was completely miserable in my marriage, I had just lost my job, I was raising a potty-training 2-year-old and was expecting the fourth member of our family in a mere 5 months, and yet I had learned how to "forget" all of the bad and keep going as if everything was sunshine and rainbows. Detachment is real, y'all!

I had already told everyone about my pregnancy, and when May arrived, my sweet eighth-grade band students threw me a baby shower. I was overwhelmed with gratitude and cried a lot. The kids didn't know I wouldn't be returning the next school year, and I was asked not to say anything. I felt like I was stealing from these amazing students. I used those tears to mask the fear, hurt, and anger I was seething and brushed it off as surprised happy tears. Thankfully, they bought it. As I was leaving school that day, it was two weeks before the last day of school, I was stopped by my principal and some lady that was with her. The strange lady was introduced to me as the newly hired music teacher. Now, I don't know about you guys, but there are times when I have the proverbial angel on one shoulder and devil on the other. The angel reminded me that we should always give everyone the benefit of the doubt. Maybe they got lucky and found a new candidate quickly because they were already offered so many fine applicants... in May... before the current school year was finished. The devil promptly jumped in and said, REALLY??? There's something fishy going on here, and we need to get to the bottom of all this insert expletive here.

The principal told me she'd like for me to show the new girl around the building to get her acquainted with the layout of the classrooms and the building. That's right, folks, I was expected to be the tour guide for the person they deemed better than me at the music, choir, band teaching gig. Humiliating? Well, let's just say I went from 5 foot 11 inches tall to about the size of a micro-machine toy within the matter of the five seconds it took for the principal to make the request. And so, like the puppet I was indoctrinated to be from childhood, I nodded, smiled, and proceeded to be the most pleasant tour guide in the history of tour guides. As we finished our time that day, this woman, who was obviously extremely uncomfortable with the entire situation, apologized to me and said she couldn't imagine how humiliating it must have been for me to be in that position. To that, I shrugged and said, "Is there anything else you need from me?" She quietly said no and thanked me for my time.

During the last week of the "this-is-how-NOT-to-treat-people" education I earned that school year, the art teacher, my only friend in an over 200-mile radius, asked to talk with me after school. She then painted me a clear picture titled "It's Not Your Fault." She had been talking with another of our colleagues. Now, you've probably already realized that in a small town like this, news travels fast. What's really sad is that these people in this tiny town considered themselves to be a metropolis because they had not only a Wal-Mart but also a McDonald's AND a movie theatre that had three screens. Of course, every movie started at the exact same time, so when the movie Titanic was released, that was the only movie offered at their theatre. Allow me to wait for all of you who live in a REAL big city to finish laughing at such a ridiculous concept.

So, as the art teacher painted the scenario, I began to realize that it truly wasn't my fault and that the people involved in this scam ought to be ashamed of themselves for the way I was treated. Here's the scathing reality. When the former music teacher announced her retirement, one of the school board members made it clear that their son was engaged to a girl who was finishing the requirements for her music education degree and that she needed a job. This school district needed someone to fill the position of music teacher for only one year in order for this girl, who was soon to be the board member's daughter-in-law, to finish getting all of her ducks in a row before she could take on the position of music teacher. Yes, that's right, rather than submit the job as a one-year contract, these people chose to find an unknowing victim to accept the open music teacher job, sabotage said person to the point that they'd fail so they'd have reason to not rehire that victim, and the intended could swoop in and take over the position. The problem for these schlubs is that they had no idea who they were dealing with when they met me. The principal felt so bad, she gave me her washer and dryer, and I later found out she wanted to keep me as her music teacher. When she offered me her washer and dryer set, she said she wanted to get rid of them when, in fact, she wanted to somehow apologize in a way that didn't truly apologize for being the snake in the grass that she ended up being. And so, my crash course in public education politics at the time was devastating and burned me in a way I cannot even explain. The disadvantage of being a detail rather than big-picture person is not being able to see the positive outcomes on the horizon. Also, the disadvantage of being in the eye of the storm is not being able to adequately prepare for what lies ahead. Although, I don't think anyone could be truly prepared for what was on my "horizon."

CHAPTER 10

Return to Civilization: *There Has Got to Be More to Life Than This!*

In homage to Sophia in that classic 1980s sitcom The Golden Girls: picture it, St. Louis, Missouri, 1998. It's Memorial Day weekend, and I'm moving with my husband and 2-year-old daughter, back to an area where movies are scheduled at various times, on more than just three screens in one building, and no one cares where you were born or how long you've lived in "town." Ah, yes... back to civilization. I was 22 weeks along with baby number two, husband had secured a decent job at a factory, and I was actively seeking employment. Now, there is a law that states an employer's reason for not hiring someone cannot involve medical reasons, such as, you know, pregnancy. However, we all know that a medical reason, pregnancy, will not be stated nor implied as to why a candidate is not chosen for a job... especially for a teaching job. That being said, over the course of the next two months, I went on a myriad of music teaching interviews. Being the honest person that I am, I would always end the interview with the mention of my due date and how it would not hinder me from being an excellent choice for their position, hoping maybe they'd want to overlook my motherly condition and focus on my honesty. Yes, the naivety is strong in this one! Of course, no one would hire someone who, within the first quarter of school, would require maternity leave. Duh! And so, the job search continued. Thank goodness husband had a decent job. And then, before I could secure employment, husband was injured on the job, and was hurt badly enough that he couldn't work. Surviving on worker's compensation alone was not going to pay our bills, much less feed our babies, so I had no choice but to hope someone in a field that is somehow related to education would hire me. I interviewed at a daycare/preschool. Lo and behold, I was hired as an assistant to the 3-year-old class teacher. I was given full-time hours, and because I had a teaching certification, I was offered just over minimum wage. At least it was a job working with kids, and it would be a decent resume entry. As my pregnancy progressed, I noticed my amount of swelling increased more than with my first pregnancy. Yes, it was the summer months, and my due date was October 2nd; however, it wasn't just a symptom from the heat and humidity of summer. I was diagnosed with preeclampsia and was ordered to reduce my hours from 40 to 20 per week. So, not only was my pay cut in half, but my baby was also at risk if I didn't behave myself. I was just grateful I wasn't ordered to bed rest. Some pay is better than none.

I stated earlier that I wouldn't get into the whole religion/God thing, and I have no intention of proselytizing, but I will give you my experience and opinion, which you can take or leave. Anyone who knows me personally will tell you how my faith has gotten me through a lot of my experiences and traumas. That staunch devotion gained its foundation at this point in my journey. As you know, I was raised in a church where there were good people who genuinely loved others and did not fit the stereotypical hellfire-and-brimstone kind of Pentecostal/Assemblies of God church. And, while I vowed never to go back to attending that particular church, I had decided that raising my own children in a loving church family was a priority. My little family had visited several churches in the area close to our apartment. None of the places we visited felt right to me. I felt a pulling in my soul to give my former church, yes, the one to which I vowed never to return, a chance. The funny thing about my plan, funny "ha-ha" AND funny strange, is that it was completely contrary to what I originally felt led to do. I started attending that church consistently and developed friendships that, at the time, were strong and more like family than I'd ever experienced up to that point. Now, some people deem "Christians" to use the church and religion as a crutch because they're weak-minded. If that is you, please know that I completely respect your opinion. In my opinion, and to be fair, opinions are like armpits... everyone has two, and they sometimes stink. As I've previously stated, there is an enormous difference between following a religion and having a relationship with the One whom I believe is the creator of everything. I don't use the church as a crutch, and I'm far from weak-minded. In actuality, it takes a strong person to follow the teachings found in what I believe to be Holy Scripture. Being a Christ-follower (I prefer this term to "Christian") is not for the faint of heart, that's for sure. Why do it? Trust me, it's worth it!

I decided during this incredibly stressful time of my life, there has to be more to this life than just existing and scraping to survive. I had been playing church, so to speak, for quite some time, and my epiphanic moment came on a Sunday evening service at my church. I was about 36 weeks along in my pregnancy, sitting with our youth pastor's wife, deep in thought, when I heard our head pastor say from the pulpit that if anyone needs prayer, now is the time. The youth pastor's wife turned to me and asked if there's anything I need that she'd like to pray for me. I started sobbing pretty hardcore and said I didn't even know where to start. Suddenly, I was surrounded by every lady in the church, and at that moment, I prayed something like this: "Okay, God, I've played church long enough. There has to be more than what this world has served to me. At this moment, I'm devoting my life to you. Take my life and show me how I can best serve you. No more halfway for me... I'm all in. Forgive my sins and help me to be used in your service." I had no idea the gravity of that prayer, but I meant it with every fiber of my being. What I couldn't fully grasp at that time was, it completely changed the trajectory of my existence.

For those of you who do not know, when one gets to the 36th week of pregnancy, OB visits are weekly. It was week 38 for me. My swelling was so bad, I could no longer fit into regular shoes. I did find some extra-large men's slippers that I was able to shove my sausage-looking appendages into. Seriously, people, my feet were so swollen, I could no longer see most of my toenails. As I waddled into the doctor's office and went through the same routine: pee in a cup, weight, blood pressure, I was kind of seeing stars and felt rather woozy. After the nurse took my blood pressure, she gave me a funny look and told me she'd be right back. My doctor was summoned to my room, and I was promptly directed to go to the hospital that was adjacent to his office. Do not pass GO, and do not collect $200. I was to check in on the maternity floor for an overnight test. What was wrong? My blood pressure was about 210/125. I was ordered to stay in bed unless I had to pee, and I was told to be sure that all of that pee was collected every time. Can I get a witness from all the mommas out there? During the last month of pregnancy, the extent of your day consists of standing up, going to the bathroom, returning to your easiest sitting chair, sitting down, standing up, going to the bathroom, returning to your easiest sitting chair, sitting down, and loop that on repeat ALL DAY AND ALL NIGHT. I'm convinced this is to prepare new mommas for the same continual sequence of events with their newborn baby. Mother Nature is a sneaky and conniving prankster, isn't she? And so, I spent the next 18 hours in and out of that bed to empty my bladder. Around 6 am, my nurse walked in:

Nurse: Good news! Doctor said he thinks it's best that we go ahead and induce labor. Isn't that wonderful?

Me: Absolutely! Can I please go ahead and take a shower now? I didn't get to do that before my appointment yesterday, and I'm feeling pretty yucky!

Nurse: No, ma'am! You are now on strict bed rest until the doctor gets here.

Me: So, I can't even get up to pee?

Nurse: That's the only reason you're allowed to be out of bed.

Me: Okay, so I'm going to need to pee for about 10 minutes, please???

Nurse: Nice try, missy! No shower!

Fabulous! So, class, what have we learned? Always …ALWAYS shower before going to the doctor. YUCK!

Around 8 am, the nurse wheeled me into one of the labor/delivery rooms to start the induction. There with me was husband

and FPF. Doctor says to be prepared for a long labor. How long? He had no idea but assured us that husband had time to go to work and come back. Fabulous! Husband had just started at a temp job delivering mail for a company in downtown St. Louis. Where was I? In a hospital approximately 40 miles due west of downtown St. Louis. When the doctor said it could take more than 24 hours to deliver this baby, my BP skyrocketed beyond the stratosphere and lingered there for the duration. Unfortunately, that caused quite a bit of alarm, so after the initial start of Pitocin, the doctor upped the dose to the maximum allowable. If you aren't familiar with Pitocin, allow me to paint a clear picture for you. Pitocin is an evil substance that was contrived in the deepest depths of hell. Pitocin is a foul and nefarious substance whose sole purpose is to initiate labor and then make a woman's labor contractions more intense and effective in order to speed up the labor process and help that baby make its entrance into our world much sooner than normal. Boy, does it work! How intense, you ask? The epidural I was given did not alleviate ANY of the pain. And the contractions? The monitor should have shown beautiful bell curves as each pang of labor slowly increases, hits its high point, then slowly decreases, and then momma can catch her breath for about a minute or so. My contractions did not show those bell curves. Nope! My contractions looked like the path of a bullet. To be more accurate, it was not contractions with an "S," it was really one continuous contraction that, as it would start to decrease, would immediately jump up to above the normal high point. This went on for almost three hours... that's right, almost THREE solid hours of one contraction!!! The only good thing about this situation is my first real labor pain hit around 3:15 pm, and my second beautiful baby, a boy, was born at 6:14 pm. He really was a bullet baby! And, at two weeks early, he weighed eight pounds, three ounces.

The next six weeks I spent learning how to be a mom to a newborn while attempting to finish potty training my two-and-a-half-year-old. And as my dream of being a stay-at-home mom flew further from my grasp, we couldn't afford for me to stay home, I returned to that daycare job. It was a difficult job, not because of the children in my care, but because the administrators of that daycare were terribly difficult individuals who must have had the same problem as the Tin Man in The Wizard of Oz; they seemed to be missing their hearts. I stayed as long as I could but was so miserable. I was praying for a way out that would provide for my family.

It was the first Sunday in April of 1999. I was serving in the music department of our church and was on the platform for that Sunday evening service. A gentleman in the congregation publicly asked for prayer for their granddaughter because the day before, her music teacher had committed suicide, and he was a beloved member of that community. It was a great loss for the school and that small town as a whole. Now, normally, my prayers would be immediately directed for that family. Instead, I thought, "Music teacher? There's a music teaching job open?" After service, I asked the man what school his granddaughter attends. The next morning, bright and early, I called that school to offer my condolences as well as to be their sub and cover those music classes for them. I was asked to interview two days later and was offered the position of permanent substitute for the remainder of the school year. I successfully finished that last quarter of school for them and subsequently interviewed for the permanent position of music teacher, to which I was offered that job. An answer to prayers, indeed! I started my long-standing career with that school district in July of 1999 as a music teacher for kindergarten through fifth grade as well as beginning band.

The school where I taught was on a year-round cycle schedule, which is why I started the school year in July. Our schedule was 9 weeks on, 3 weeks off for four quarters, and then off 6 weeks in the summer. I had completed the required new teacher informational meetings and all of the in-service hours necessary to fulfill my contractual expectations and had finished one full week of that school year. Things were on an upswing, and then, well, it wouldn't be a complete year in my life without another trouble, tragedy, or trauma. I was in the middle of teaching a fifth-grade class when our building administrative assistant walked into my classroom and said I needed to take a phone call. This was before each classroom had its own phone as well as before we were all issued our own computers of any kind, and laptops were way out of the realm of realization in my school. I asked if she could take a message, and she told me I needed to take the call in the library. I picked up the phone, and it was husband. He told me that my birth mother had passed away unexpectedly. Why was this a troubling, traumatic tragedy? My faith is the root cause. You see, when I chose to go all in with my relationship with God, I meant it. That means doing my best to live to a biblical standard. In other words, I needed to forgive in order to continue the process of cleansing my soul and spirit. I continue to struggle with the debilitating disease of Irish Alzheimer's. That means I forget everything except the grudges.

I have the uncanny ability to hang on to a filthy, unforgiving grudge with both hands and feet... it ain't going anywhere! I felt deep in my spirit that I needed to completely forgive my birth mother for everything I ever held against her. I learned through sound teaching that forgiveness is not a one-and-done deal. Forgiveness is a choice that must be made daily, and with each passing day, it gets easier. So, I decided to start with her. Just after my son was born, I wrote her a letter spelling out my feelings. I wrote to her how I was doing my best to forgive her and that I genuinely wanted to have a healthy relationship with her. It took a lot of attempts because, at first, I didn't WANT to forgive her. I wanted to hate her and blame her for everything. That's something else I've learned in therapy, all about displaced anger. She wasn't to blame because she was just as much a victim of that toxic environment as I was, but it was much easier to cast blame on her because she wasn't around to defend herself. And so, that letter was the catalyst to finding true forgiveness for her. It was beautifully freeing! I finally felt like I could find a way to a healthy mother-daughter relationship, and I was so grateful and excited about that. March of 1999 was when our conversations were more frequent, and I truly looked forward to talking with her. I started inviting her to my home and offered to let her babysit my kids. We were getting close, and I was the happiest I had ever been in my life up to that point. When my son was seven months old, birth mother was diagnosed with gangrene. As a result of her poor choices and her mismanaged type 2 diabetes, she had to have a below-the-knee amputation. She had that devastating surgery and still lived in an apartment that wasn't wheelchair accessible with no means to improve her situation. She was in and out of the hospital starting in April

1999. I visited her with the kids as much as I could. She was so proud of me and the career I was starting, and she was so good to my babies.

So, that day, that horrible July day, I received that horrible phone call that she was gone. Just like that... gone! She was preparing to go home from the hospital the very next day. How could she just be gone? I was so angry! I was finally feeling loved. I only had four good months with her before she was taken from me. It seemed just so... so... WRONG! As arrangements were made for her memorial, I was informed that in her will was a specific detail that she wanted for her funeral; she wanted me to sing a specific song for the service. And that, my friends, was my first time down the road of needing to grieve as an adult. Up to that time, I had never been allowed to grieve anything. Remember, no emotions allowed. Even if I did feel like I was allowed the privilege to show any emotion, especially grief, I didn't know where to start. Little did I know the extent of grief I was going to encounter in the months ahead.

The end of the decade, the millennium, was upon us. Would "Y2K" be a thing? Would Prince be on New Year's Rockin' Eve with Dick Clark singing "1999"? I sat in my living room and watched on our TV as time turned over much like the speedometer on a car clicking over another 100,000 miles. The year 2000 started uneventfully. The world did not end as projected, life continued as we knew it, and my little family was renting the house owned by our church. It was formerly the parsonage, and we were able to live there for a rent amount that didn't break us. I was deeply involved in both the music ministry and the women's ministry at our church and was helping prepare for a traveling evangelist to speak at our multiple evening revival that was scheduled that summer. It was the third night of our revival. I arrived early to make sure everything was ready for that evening's service. The evangelist, with whom I had some really fascinating conversations, asked to speak with me before people started to arrive. Now, usually when someone approaches me and says, "God told me to tell you...," I am quite skeptical. I also have the gift of discernment, so I'm normally able to sense whether I should really listen to this God-given message or take it with a grain of salt. With this guy, my Spidey-sense was telling me I should pay close attention to everything he tells me. The message he gave me was rather general at first and then became much more specific to my situation. His message was this:

Evangelist: God told me to tell you to get ready and hang on.

Me: Hang on to what?

Evangelist: He's got really big things in store for you. He's preparing you for a ministry that will be more than you could ever imagine; however, you will have to go through some really tough times to get where He wants to take you. He will not reveal to you any specifics as to what's going to happen because if you knew the big picture from his perspective, you would not be able to handle what you will face in the years to come. Just know that you need to hang on because better days are coming.

Me: Ummmm... O...K???

Evangelist: You've been through some pretty tough times already, haven't you?

Me: I couldn't even begin to tell you the difficulties I've survived in my life.

Evangelist: Yes, I know. You've been hurt deeply and terribly by those who should have been loving you and protecting you.

Me: *wide-eyed stare*

Evangelist: God's got you, my friend. Just get ready and hang on. It will be worth it all, and there will be a time you'll look back on the past years and remember this conversation and how God brought you through everything. And he will use all of your experiences to help other people. Just get ready and hang on.

Me: Uhhh... thank you?

The summer of 2000 was, for me, the calm before the storm. I was about to go through everything that had been told to me that day; all of that and then some. I was about to develop more reason to never wish my life on my worst enemy. I just hadn't yet encountered the part about being grateful for the journey. That wouldn't manifest for quite some time.

PART 3

Tenacity

CHAPTER 11

No, I Need to Finish This!
When Delusions Nearly Turn Fatal!

The end of the year 2000, which, I guess, is technically the end of the decade/century/millennium, was rather uneventful. Status quo had crept into life as we knew it. At this point, husband was working at a better job in a factory, I was teaching elementary music, I was consistently serving at the church in both the music and women's ministries, and my children were growing way too fast. Things seemed a little too ordinary for my norm. And then, I noticed my sense of smell had heightened to a bloodhound level of accuracy. I had an inkling another entity had developed, and sure enough, another positive pregnancy test. Boy, those lines on that little stick aren't very shy, are they? At least not when I'm involved. So, in late February, my doctor confirmed that baby number three would be due to arrive on November 4th. I felt so much more exhausted during this first trimester. I shrugged it off as, of COURSE I'm exhausted! I'm the mother of two who works full-time as an elementary music teacher. Regardless, I was excited to have another beautiful addition to my little family, and both of my other babies were excited as well.

On April 13, 2001, I was on spring cycle break, and it was Good Friday. Husband decided to take our girl and boy with him fishing, which gave me a good amount of time to rest that morning. Around 9:30 am, I decided to get up and make some decaf. I'm usually a fully-leaded-caffeinated kind of gal; however, I was trying to limit my caffeine for baby's health. When I went to the bathroom, I noticed I had started spotting blood. That hadn't happened in my other pregnancies. I tried to remain calm and called my OB. The nurse said it's probably nothing to worry about; however, if I had concerns, to have someone drive me to the ER and get checked, if nothing else, for my peace of mind. Remember, this is early 2001. We had prepaid flip phones that had a horrible connection in most areas. Husband was unreachable out on the other side of east Egypt at a lake fishing with the kids. I called FPF to ask if she'd please keep trying to get ahold of husband, and I drove myself to the ER. Due to the fact that the pregnancy was so early, I was only 12 weeks along, I was not seen on the maternity floor. I was taken to triage for their battery of questions and vital signs check, and then I was taken into a room rather quickly. I was told to undress and put on that lovely won't-cover-my-backside hospital gown, and a doctor would be in soon. Meanwhile, the spotting continued. Husband still hadn't been located, so yes, I was in there all by myself. I was wheeled into an ultrasound room where an ultrasound technician administered an internal look around in there to see what was going on with my baby. On a side note, I don't know why, to this day, I giggle so much when they're preparing that internal ultrasound probe and cover it with a condom and that special ultrasound gel. Forgive my inadequate attempt to, yet again, use humor as a defense mechanism, as what follows isn't pleasant to recall.

As the technician poked, prodded, and typed whatever indicators necessary for a doctor to read, I tried desperately to read her face, and I gotta tell ya, that tech would be well-advised to take a turn in a professional poker circuit; no tells whatsoever. When I asked what's going on, the response was a generic "I am not able to give any results, only the doctor can do that." Lovely! And so, I was wheeled back to that ER room, still alone and waiting... and waiting... and waiting. As my mind was racing through every possible scenario and even impossible ones, husband finally arrived. FPF had gone to our house and written a note on the counter telling him I was at the hospital and to take the kids to her place so he could be with me. The timing was impeccable because almost immediately after he arrived, the doctor made an appearance. The details are rather sketchy in my recollection. Usually, when I hear something I would rather not hear, it seems like what I hear most is the sound of static along with Charlie Brown's teacher.

Doctor: We cannot find your baby.

Me: Ummm... I didn't think babies could be missing from the womb???

Doctor: We believe this is an ectopic pregnancy, which is extremely dangerous. We would like to keep you overnight for observation.

Me: *blank stare*

Doctor: You are on strict bed rest, which means no getting out of bed for any reason.

Me: *blank stare*

Doctor: I've contacted your OB. He will be in later to speak with you.

Me: *blank stare*

Doctor: Do you have any questions?

Me: *blank stare*

Husband: Thanks, doc.

Me: *blank stare*

And so, I stayed in bed the rest of that night. I asked husband to go home and get a few things to bring back and then pick up the kids from FPF. I tried to sleep, but that wasn't happening. Me alone with my thoughts is never a good thing.

That terribly long night turned into daylight. Bright and early, my doctor came in to see me. He said it looks like baby was not ectopic, it just didn't develop as normal, and the heart was no longer beating. He was genuinely saddened and held my hand as we talked.

Me: What did I do wrong?

Doc: You did nothing wrong. Unfortunately, sometimes the baby doesn't develop as it should, and it's no one's fault.

Me: You're sure about that?

Doc: Yes, I'm sure.

Me: So, my being extremely overweight didn't kill my baby? *choking back tears (I weighed over 300 pounds at this point)*

Doc: Oh, no! Your weight had no impact on the situation. In fact, I find women who are UNDERWEIGHT to have more complications in pregnancy. You did NOTHING wrong! I have no explanation as to why this happened right now. He paused.

Now, I'm going to release you to go home. We need to wait for this miscarriage to finish what it needs to do.

Me: Wait... WHAT???

Doc: Baby is still in the womb at this point, so you need to go home and wait for it to finish terminating.

Me: But tomorrow is EASTER! I'm supposed to be singing for the service at church!

Doc: I know. I'm so sorry! You need to try to stay off of your feet for as long as you can. No strenuous activity.

Me: How will I know when it... is finished... terminating? *again, choking back tears*

Doc: You'll know. As soon as it passes, please call me. I'll want to see you ASAP. I don't want you to be in a dangerous situation.

Me: Dangerous situation?

Doc: There's a potential you could bleed a lot, and I want to be sure you're watched carefully.

Me: Ok??? How long do you think this will take?

Doc: Maybe a day, maybe two days, maybe 6 weeks. There's no way to know for sure.

Me: SIX WEEKS???

Doc: That very well could be. We won't know until your body decides it's time.

Me: Ok???

Doc: Go home and rest. Stay off your feet as much as possible and call when you need anything.

And so, once husband was able to pick me up, I got in the car to leave the hospital. We did not go straight home. Nope, we had to go to FPF's house. Why in the world, you might ask, would you subject yourself to that torture knowing full well how things would go with FPF? Obligation. My babies were there, so was other family from out of town because, you know, Easter.

When we arrived, I was met on the front porch by my sweet sister-in-law, who had no real idea of how horrific life is with FPF. She ran to me, hugged me tight, and said, "I'm so very sorry for your loss!" Of course, I started to cry again. We walked in the front door, and she said, "I can't even imagine what you're going through right now." As I started to open up to her, FPF walked in the room, and I watched the most disturbing phenomenon happen before my eyes. Along with my sister-in-law and me, there were a few other family members who expressed deep sympathy and compassion. The moment FPF walked in the room, every one of us stopped any emotional expression and stood stoic-faced and silent. Remember, no emotion allowed! At that point, the fact that I had a dead child residing in my womb was no longer allowed as a topic of conversation.

Later that day, as I was preparing to take my babies home for the evening, I was on FPF's front porch trying to wrap my brain around what was happening to me and my baby, and FPF decided to join me. Apparently, she felt the need to "comfort" me in my situation. As I stood there looking out at the adjacent street, I heard this person who was supposed to be a mother to me utter the most cold-hearted statement. She said, and I quote, "At least it wasn't a REAL baby. You couldn't afford another mouth to feed anyway." To this day, when I recall that horrific memory, I feel like I've been given a right hook to the chest. Unfathomable!

Yes, that weekend was beyond horrendous. And yes, I plastered on my "I'm just fine" face for my family as well as for everyone at church. I still went to church. I still sang the songs I was scheduled to sing for the service. I still did everything I was expected to do for everyone else, all the while I felt like I was dying from the inside out. My babies got their baskets from the "Easter bunny," they had their Easter egg hunt, we had our ham for dinner and our lemon-coconut cake for dessert just like we did every year, my family recalled the same stories they did every single year, we ate way too much, we helped clean up after dinner, and we all went our separate ways. That day couldn't end fast enough for me. Once home, I set up everything I needed to go to work the next day and decided to prepare my plans and classroom in the event I needed to be gone for the next six weeks. Luckily, the day after Easter, we were scheduled to be off school anyway.

I wasn't supposed to be driving, so husband drove me to the school where I walked to my classroom on the other side of the building and began preparing my plans for my potential six-week absence. I had a plan of attack... I'd plan by grade level. Remember, I teach kindergarten through fifth grade music and see all six grade levels daily. I was about halfway through having all of my plans finished when I decided to take a break. I walked to the teacher's lounge, although I don't understand why it's called a "lounge" because teachers do not have time to lounge at all during the school day. The "lounge" was on the opposite side of the building from my classroom, and I had to walk two awfully long hallways. When I was about to walk into the restroom, I felt the strangest sensation. The only way to describe what I felt is, if you can imagine, a muffled pop like when you pop your toes, but then your middle toe releases itself from your body. So, I felt a muffled pop in my pelvis and then a WHOOOSH like floodgates had opened. I froze in my tracks. I turned to go to the phone room adjacent to the restrooms and immediately called my doctor. Luckily, everyone there knew me and my situation, so I didn't have to go through the entire story to the nurse who always answered.

Nurse: How can I help you?

Me: I think my baby just... I think I just passed my baby?

Nurse: Where are you now?

Me: I'm at work trying to finish my plans for my impending absence.

Nurse: You're at WORK???

Me: Well... I had to be sure plans are ready for whomever teaches my classes...

Nurse: Are you in any pain? Are you bleeding a lot?

Me: No, and I don't think so. It literally just happened.

Nurse: I need you to collect the specimen, put it in something, and bring it into the office.

Me: *blank stare*

Nurse: Krista?

Me: You want me to put my baby in a container and bring it to you??? For real???

Nurse: Yes, the doctor will want to have the lab conduct tests.

Me: But I'm not finished with my plans yet! I'm only half-way finished...

Nurse: Ok, well, as long as you're not bleeding a lot and you're not in pain, put the specimen in a box and put it in the refrigerator until you leave and come straight to the office from work. If anything changes, please promise me you'll leave immediately and come to the office?

Me: I promise... I just need to finish my plans.

Nurse: Ok, we'll see you today. Sooner rather than later, please?

Me: Ok

And so, I went to the nurse's office. She had a baby wipes container that she emptied and handed it to me. I went to the bathroom and, as best as I could, tried not to look at my baby that I was about to put in a baby wipes container (oh, the irony!). I cleaned up as best I could because, yes, I was bleeding, put baby in the nurse's mini-fridge, and proceeded to walk back to my classroom to finish my lesson plans. As I sat at my desk frantically trying to finish the last 3 grade levels, I kept feeling wave after wave of that WHOOOSH-flood-gates-opening feeling and was becoming more and more weak by the minute. I remember thinking the entire time, "I just need to finish this."

I don't know how much time had passed; however, I had only two grade levels left to finish when a colleague of mine walked into my classroom.

Colleague: WHAT ARE YOU DOING HERE???

Me: I have to finish my plans. I'm almost finished, just have K and first grade to go.

Her: Aren't you supposed to be in bed resting?

Me: Sure, but I have to finish this.

Her: No, you HAVE to go home and rest.

Me: No, I have to finish this.

Her: *walks beside my chair* Ummmm, NO! You need to get to the hospital.

Me: No, I need to finish this first.

Her: There is a lake of blood behind you, my dear... YOU NEED TO GO TO THE HOSPITAL!

Me: What???

I look at the floor and, sure enough, it wasn't just a little trickle.

Me: But I'm almost finished with my plans!

Her: I'm going to get the wheelchair. You're GOING TO THE HOSPITAL!

She quickly walked out of the room, and I frantically wrote as fast as I could. I still had two grade levels to finish. She returned with the nurse, who had the baby wipes box in hand. The two of them helped me into the wheelchair, plan books and pen in hand. I was under the delusion that I'd be able to go home and finish those last plans before going to the doctor's office. Yeah, I know... I know... The sound of your rolling eyes is deafening. So was theirs.

Another colleague had her minivan waiting for me, passenger seat covered in large plastic trash bags. And yes, the entire time, I continued wave after wave of blood rushing out of my body. I didn't realize just how bad it was. As we drove from the school, my colleague asked which hospital I wanted. My response? Are you ready for THIS?!? I said, "I just want to go home." After a bit of discussion, she relented and took me home. I tried calling husband to let him know I was almost home, but that sad flip phone wasn't connecting. Besides, I was too weak to hold the phone to my ear. I felt myself drifting off to sleep, so I didn't hear her finally get Husband on the phone. We pulled into the driveway with Husband and my two children on the front porch waiting for me. I opened the passenger door, and as I tried to lift myself out of the van, I felt the strongest WHOOOSH of all, and down I went. At that point, all I remember is hearing sirens, feeling the back of my head hurting and then something soft under it; I was going into shock and convulsing on the driveway. I felt myself being lifted and opened my eyes long enough to see a river of blood flowing down that driveway. I can remember thinking to myself, "Who is this guy, and why does he keep asking me stupid questions?" Yeah, that was the ambulance driver trying to keep me conscious as he was starting an IV.

I closed my eyes, and when I opened them again, I was on a gurney hooked up to a whole lot of wires and tubes and in a horrific amount of pelvic pain. They had given me a strong med to get my uterus to, basically, clamp down and stop bleeding. Husband was to my right, and when I looked up at him, I tried asking where I was. I heard him say, "She's waking up," and as I started to talk, I was told, "Don't talk, don't move." I looked at the monitor and saw very scary numbers (BP 90/60? YIKES!). I asked if that was my stats monitor to which he nodded and told me not to talk, just be still.

Long story short, I was near death. When the doctor came in to examine me, it was determined that I needed an emergency D & C. I was required to stay overnight for observation. I had lost so much blood and was so very weak I slept most of the time I was there. The next morning, I was released to go home under orders to stay home and rest for the next two weeks.

At the time, what amazed me most was not the fact that I survived the miscarriage, or the fast-acting colleagues who took care of me, and it wasn't even the genuine tears my doctor shed with me. Nope, at that time, what amazed me the most was that the nurses took the pants I was wearing, the ones I thought I'd have to throw in the trash, and they removed any remnants of blood from those pants! How did they do that??? Ah, the secret magic of cold water! And yes, looking back on this experience, I would say Gloria Gaynor wrote that song about me; I will survive... hey, hey! (You just sang that in your head, didn't you?)

CHAPTER 12

Work, Work, Work: *"But wait... there's more! If you act now, you too can become a Stepford wife!"*

If I remember correctly, it was Charles Darwin who came up with the whole survival-of-the-fittest theory. It figures that a man would be the one to develop a theory based on whomever is the strongest in a given situation. And, since I'm on the subject of whomever is strongest in a given situation, if you ask a man (not a boy, mind you) which is the strongest, a man or woman, an honest man will tell you it's the woman that is stronger, every day and twice on Sunday. No offense intended, gentlemen, so please allow me to elaborate. The strength I'm referring to is not only pertaining to physical strength; I'm looking at the big picture here. Please understand, I'm not saying men are weak by any means. Many times, a man's physical strength does tend to be more on the "stronger" side than a woman's. What I'm talking about is mental, emotional, psychological strength; the ability to confront, tackle, and overcome whatever obstacles arise and subsequently to conquer and thrive on the other side of that which tried to defeat.

Case in point, one of my favorite chick-flicks ever: Steel Magnolias. Before I continue, I must say SPOILER ALERT! If you've never seen this movie, I'm about to tell you one of the most pivotal scenes within the story. Don't say I didn't warn you! The story involves characters, women, who prove just how strong a woman must be and still retain a sense of delicate grace and beauty; hence the term "Steel Magnolias." Towards the end, the youngest of the main characters, Shelby, fell into a coma due to complications of type one diabetes. When it was decided to take Shelby off of the life support, the men couldn't handle it and walked out of that ICU room, but M'Lynn (Shelby's momma) stayed and held her daughter's hand until the very end. After Shelby finally let go and passed away, M'Lynn took a deep breath, walked into the waiting room where every male character stood, and immediately started organizing the arrangements for the funeral. This is what women do. We keep everything on the rails, oftentimes to our detriment. It is ingrained and deep-rooted in women to take care of everyone else first. This was the self-imposed situation for me after such a traumatic loss that I had survived. I continued serving in the music and women's ministries, I continued working as an elementary music teacher, I continued being wife and momma.

I decided to give my baby a name. I wasn't able to have a funeral, but I still wanted to give that little person the dignity of having a name. I am convinced to my core that my baby who is waiting for me in Heaven is a boy, and I named him Jonah. As a mom of two other little ones and a household to run along with teaching full-time, I decided that I didn't have time for grief. Although, to be fair, I didn't know HOW to grieve. I had lived, up to that point, without the permission to experience grief, or any other emotion for that matter. So, rather than allow myself that grieving process, I stuffed all emotions down, just like I always did. If I ignore it, it'll just go away, right? Pfft! Boy, was THAT dumb!

Here's what I eventually learned: you WILL grieve, regardless of any attempt made to avoid it, but I'm getting ahead of myself.

And so, as I did my best to avoid my grief, status quo reared its ugly head and set up shop in my existence. Deep down, I felt as though my insides were withering away, so I desperately tried to replace that with being busy. That's not a difficult task for a working mother of two who was the music minister at church. Summer came and went; another school year began, and then came November. If you recall, my due date was November 4th of that year. I did my best to keep it together on that particular day and tried to keep status quo in the forefront of everything. Subsequently, I decided to be the absolute best wife and momma ever. I immersed myself in Bible reading and decided I would do everything possible to be a "Proverbs 31" woman. If you are not familiar with what I'm referring to, here's a sample of what my intentions were:

"A good woman is hard to find, and worth far more than diamonds. Her husband trusts her without reserve, and never has reason to regret it. Never spiteful, she treats him generously all her life long...She's up before dawn, preparing breakfast for her family and organizing her day...First thing in the morning, she dresses for work, rolls up her sleeves, eager to get started. She senses the worth of her work, is in no hurry to call it quits for the day. She's skilled in the crafts of home and hearth, diligent in homemaking. She's quick to assist anyone in need, reaches out to help the poor...she always faces tomorrow with a smile. When she speaks, she has something worthwhile to say, and she always says it kindly. She keeps an eye on everyone in her household and keeps them all busy and productive...Charm can mislead, and beauty soon fades. The woman to be admired and praised is the woman who lives in the Fear-of-God."[1]

Some might say I "drank the Kool-Aid" of religious teachings and relented to the propaganda of those determined to keep women subservient. Some might say I was in the throes of a Stepford Wife syndrome of sorts. To that, I will remind you that I loathe religion because of the legalism and stigmata it creates. Furthermore, keep in mind that I wanted to be the polar opposite of what I witnessed growing up in a home where there was no love from the FPF, only intimidation and dictatorship. Along with all of these points of possible contention, I was merely surviving in a marriage that was terribly difficult at best. I wanted my children to see a healthy marriage example, and if that meant I needed to lose myself in the process, then so be it. Yes, of course, looking back at that time in my life, I realize my line of thinking, my intentions, created the opposite effect. What I wanted so desperately to be healthy was, in fact, the epitome of dysfunction. How was I supposed to know the difference? Yes, I knew what I did NOT want my home to be for my children, I just didn't know how to manifest a truly healthy environment for them to thrive in rather than merely survive as I was doing.

As the year 2001 quickly became 2002, the hole in my heart left by my Jonah and the events causing him to no longer be with us was the silent scream I faced every single day, and I longed to fill that void. In the middle of March 2002, that familiar heightened sense of smell returned and, sure enough, I was expecting again. I hoped and prayed this little one would survive and thrive. At my first appointment with my OB, the same who had been

---

1   Proverbs 31:10-31 (The Message)

there for my son's birth as well as the recent loss, I asked him what measures I could take to ensure that this baby would be full-term and healthy. In addition to the normal bloodwork that is done in the initial visit, he ordered a test of my progesterone level. As he suspected that particular hormone level was dangerously low and said this was probably why Jonah didn't continue to develop as my other two children had. He prescribed, along with my prenatal vitamins and calcium, a medication, progesterone supplement, to keep that bun in the oven baking. He then gave me the due date of this new little one: November 12. That's right, this baby had a similar due date as my Jonah. I tend to overthink every little thing, so of course, I stewed on this information a little too much. Was this redemptive by design? Is this baby a means of restoring me and my broken heart? I mean, no one could replace my sweet Jonah, but is this a means of helping me find closure with my loss? What if... what if... what if...?

I found, as the pregnancy progressed, I was becoming more and more preoccupied with the possibility of another loss. I was becoming afraid to sneeze, cough, or do anything requiring me to breathe. As I sought a distraction, I was made aware of an opportunity to pursue my master's degree strictly online. In 2002, this was quite a new venture and, to be honest, seemed rather daunting to take on the task of full-time student along with everything else filling my already overwhelming schedule. Did that stop me? Goodness, no! I jumped in with both feet, just knowing my pursuit of a master's in education with an emphasis in curriculum and instruction would not only advance me in my career and aid in what I then considered my dream job—district-level fine arts coordinator—it would be the perfect distraction to help me get over all those yucky feelings that kept creeping up despite my efforts to force them back down into the depths of my being.

There I was, in my second trimester of my pregnancy, pursuing a master's degree. Let's see… full-time wife, full-time mom, full-time teacher, head of the music department at church. Hey, how about we tack on full-time student to that life description? No problem! Excuse me as I return to that brick wall against which I need to bang my head. Now, if anyone knows how I can get ahold of a DeLorean along with the whereabouts of Doc Brown, I'd really like to go back to the June 2002 me, take her by the shoulders, and shake the ever-loving snot right out of her. And you'll be so happy to know that other than the fact that I never allowed myself to grieve the loss of my baby and the traumatic event causing me to face my mortality, my goal of keeping my mind completely occupied with anything else was a complete success. Most days, I felt like I was meeting myself coming and going all at the same time.

The beauty of online learning is the flexibility. I didn't have to worry about a babysitter for my two little ones, I was able to complete assignments and "attend" classes through question-and-answer threads on my own time, which was usually between the hours of 10 pm and 2 am, give or take. So what if I was only running on about 4 hours of sleep a night? I was earning my master's degree; I would justify to myself. This is going to help my family in the long run.

Looks like I had it all figured out, doesn't it? I thought I was being the epitome of a "Proverbs 31" woman. The saddest thing about all of this is how much of a Stepford Wife I became. I mentioned that phrase before. If you're unfamiliar, the Urban Dictionary defines a Stepford Wife as "a servile, compliant, submissive, spineless wife who happily does her husband's bidding and serves his every whim dutifully."[2] In an effort to be the best wife and mother I could be, I completely lost myself in the process. Although, is it possible to lose something that had never really been attained? I didn't truly know who I was because, well... you know. And, as I sit and ponder all of this, I'm thinking to myself, perhaps, that was the time I realized I didn't know who I truly was underneath the plethora of hats I chose to don each and every day. To which I answer, self, I believe you are correct!

Now, you may be asking, what about the grief? How could anyone continue with that much weighing on the heart, mind, and soul? The grief? Yeah, it was definitely still there, fermenting in a dreadfully dark place underneath all of those chosen "hats" and stomped-on, pushed-down painful feelings and memories I thought I had completely eliminated. What I was avoiding, that I didn't even realize I was avoiding, was what I like to call the Sorcerer's Apprentice Effect. In the original Disney's Fantasia, Mickey Mouse was depicted as an apprentice to a great sorcerer who, after what seemed to be a long day of labored sorcery, was retiring for the evening, leaving his sorcerer's hat behind. Mickey Mouse, who had been doing some chores, decided to try on that hat and maybe use it to make his job easier. He directed a broom to grow arms and fetch water with two buckets to fill the reservoir for the next day, and Mickey promptly fell asleep. He was awakened to a flood in that room because the broom continued doing the job it was given. Mickey took a hatchet and chopped the broom into many pieces. Each piece came to life and

---

2   https://www.urbandictionary.com/define.php?term=Stepford%20Wife

became its own broom with two buckets, and all continued filling the reservoir with water. Poor Mickey was helpless in getting the madness to cease because he had no idea how to stop it. He was drowning in the flood of his own making because rather than risk embarrassment by asking for help and finding means to stop his error, he chose a way that he thought would avoid causing the sorcerer to know what he had done and would be the easiest and least difficult for him. Unfortunately, it only made matters worse… A LOT worse. And much like Mickey Mouse's calm before the storm, at this point in my experience, I was in full-on sleeping mode, at least figuratively.

I continued meeting every obligation I had lain on myself; work, mom, wife, church, and full-time student, along with the baby I was growing. I decided to start my maternity leave a full workweek before my due date to get things in order between home and HR paperwork and getting everything ready for the arrival of our newest family member. That Monday morning, November 4, I started my day at the administration building finishing necessary paperwork for my leave, then went to my OB appointment to make sure all was well (and thankfully, that beautiful heartbeat was loud and strong), then to my chiropractor because the misery of late third trimester pregnancy causes any and every attempt at relief. I went home, did the typical mom/wife stuff, finished my homework for the day for my classes, and finally crawled into bed around 1 am. At approximately 5:15 am, I felt a pop and a WOOSH. Baby's water breaking woke me out of a dead sleep. Wait… WAIT! But I wasn't due until November 12! I still had so much I needed to do that week before baby's arrival! It's almost as if I heard that little one saying, "Sorry, mom, it's time!" And so, to the hospital we raced. That baby was so eager to escape from the confines of my uterus, the water had exited so quickly, baby was starting to go into distress. Again, that lovely labor-aid Pitocin entered the scene. She needed to be born, and FAST. Fast, indeed! A mere 4 hours later, there she was. A healthy, beautiful little girl. As I stared at her, I realized it was November 5, 2002; exactly one year and one day after her big brother was due. I didn't know if my sobbing was happiness or grief.

Nope, couldn't be grief. I wouldn't allow it! How in the world could I be grieving when I was holding my brand-new baby girl? I asked myself, why am I being so ridiculously selfish?!? Grief? Grief...schmeef! I had much more important things on which to focus my time and energy. Besides, I should be OVER my grief by now, right? Those are the ridiculous justifications I came up with to continue avoiding what I didn't realize was destroying me from the inside out.

CHAPTER 13

Ignorance Is "Bliss"?
It's Groundhog Day!
But Where's Punxsutawney Phil?
Oh, THERE He Is!

If you've ever seen the 1993 movie Groundhog Day starring Bill Murray, that will give you an indication of what my life was like at this point. My weekdays looked something like this:

6:00 am—up, shower, dressed

6:15 am—get older 2 kids up, dressed, eating breakfast...prepare my breakfast

6:30 am—get baby up, changed, and nursing while I'm eating my breakfast

6:50 am—load all kids in car, take baby to sitter, son to daycare, daughter with me to work

8:00 am—4:00 pm—teach K-5 music

4:30 pm—pick up all kids and go home

5:30 pm—prepare dinner, prepare everything for the next day, help oldest with homework, clean up dinner, do my work/schoolwork (grading papers, lesson planning, etc.), give kids bath, get older kids in bed, change and nurse baby, get baby to sleep.

10:00 pm—start master's classes assignments

Somewhere between 1 am-2 am—go to bed for sleep

6:00 am—up, shower, dressed

This schedule repeated Monday through Friday. And then there's the weekend.

Saturday 7:00 am through around midnight—up with baby and the kids, grocery shop, pay bills, laundry, clean, cook, master's homework, bathe kids, nurse baby, collapse in bed to sleep.

Sunday 7:00 am—up, shower, dressed

7:30 am—get kids up, dressed, fed for church

8:30 am—Praise Team practice, church service

1:00 pm—Feed family, prepare kids' lunches for the week, set out kids' clothes for the week, set out my clothes for the week

5:00 pm—Return to church for PM service, dinner with friends

10:00 pm-1:00 am (sometimes sooner)—Master's homework that needs finished for the week

6:00 am—up, shower, dress

Imagine, if you will, a life lived in that never-ending repeat for almost 2 years straight. Some call my state of existence at that time a hypnotic state[1], some call it autopilot, others might go so far and label me as being in a dissociative fugue state[2]. I lean to-

---

1   https://www.merriam-webster.com/dictionary/hypnotic
2   https://www.ncbi.nlm.nih.gov/books/NBK541012/

wards calling it the Groundhog Day syndrome; all that was missing was Punxsutawney Phil and that guy Ned who tried chasing Phil Connors across the street. Regardless of the label, I was in what seemed like a never-ending time loop. The Groundhog Day syndrome in which I was existing could have been tolerable, maybe even bearable, or acceptable rather than merely survivable. The problem was the relationship I was in with my husband was only a marriage in the legal and technical terms.

At this point, if this were a Marvel movie, I'd be breaking the fourth wall with a disclaimer. Please allow me to preface the following description of my marital situation at that time by saying this: the fact that we married so incredibly young and neither of us had a clue as to how the whole adulting thing needed to be... and given the fact that he was dealing with his own trauma issues, keeping that marriage together was virtually impossible for us. And while this fact is legit, it does not excuse any abuse within the marriage. It does not excuse the abuse I endured at the mind and hands of my husband. And, for anyone to whom he chose to speak character-defaming lies about me and chose to believe those atrocities, it breaks my heart to think that those who I considered to be my friends would blindly believe such horrible lies without asking me my side of the story. Yes, I know that, despite my efforts, how I handled everything was far from perfect, and I own that. I just wish those people would have come to me in private and asked me about what they had been told by my husband. I guess it's true that you know who your true friends are when you're at your lowest.

As time went on, my husband and I were even less than roommates. Without going into detail regarding the condition of that marriage and the ongoing problems that evolved, allow me to say something that many staunch legalistic religious people will disagree with... staying in a marriage only for the children is never a good idea. Period! The toxic environment only permeates into their little hearts, and there's virtually no recovery from that except for ongoing and intense psychological therapy. And the harder I tried to be the Proverbs 31 wife and mother, the more that relationship crumbled. The more I tried to make our family something positive, the more I was met with negativity and discouragement. And it seemed like the more weight I packed on, the better for him. Not because he likes large women, per se. No, it was mostly because the worse I felt about myself, the more security it provided so that I'd stay in that marriage. I know that sounds twisted, and husband can try to refute that all he wants. However, this is not an inference; this is fact. There is a lot more that I had to endure as a result of that marriage; however, like many other issues I've already addressed, that is for another time and another book. And despite all of these facets, including the adultery he committed that he was terrible at hiding, I continued to accommodate husband's "needs" through my wifely obligations. Why would I willingly accept this obligation? There was still a gaping hole in my heart that I thought could be filled with another baby; I thought that eventually, at some point, I'd have another baby. Well, "at some point" was much sooner than I would have ever expected. About 2 weeks before my youngest's first birthday, I had yet another positive pregnancy test. Apparently, another good wind hit me, or there was something in the water, and BOOM! Pregnant again. I was almost as blindsided as I was with my first pregnancy. Then I did the calculations. My youngest little ones would be 18 months apart. I was due July 8, 2004. I was scheduled to graduate with my master's degree in early June. So what if I would be my own planet waddling across that graduation stage for my diploma, much like when I performed in my Senior recital in college? At least I wouldn't still be pregnant and going to school. One less thing! And as it seems that I perpetually need that brick wall on which to bang my head, so much so that the wall has developed a "my-head-sized-dent" in it, I will probably need to find a new one soon.

I continued living in blissful ignorance, for the most part, throughout those years with the focus of trying to raise my babies and be the best momma I could be despite the gaping hole that was still there without allowing myself to admit my need for therapy as well as my need to find other means to address what the root problem was. And despite bearing almost all of the household responsibilities, I was grateful husband worked second shift at his factory job. At least that cut back on the terribly loud arguments that were constantly plaguing our home. The worst element of this part of my story was that suicidal ideation had crept back into my daily thoughts. The only thing keeping me from following through at that time was my children, especially the little bun that was relying on me to be their life source. I also did not want any of my children to survive with the stigma of suicide and all the pain that goes with it and, most of all, I did not want any of my babies to be the one to find me. Oh, I had lots of thoughts on how I could follow through and make it look like an accident; however, none were feasible enough to consider, especially not as a pregnant momma.

And so, Groundhog Day continued. I was able to participate in a graduation ceremony, and on June 5, 2004, I waddled across that stage and accepted the diploma for my Master of Arts in

Education with an emphasis in curriculum and instruction. Then, the newest addition to our ever-growing family was born June 24, 2004, two weeks before my due date: another beautiful, healthy baby girl. And, as Tracy Lawrence sings, time marches on.

Over the next 3 years, Punxsutawney Phil continued to elude my existence. Although, I did have my one "shining" moment that will forever be emblazoned in my mind. Every once in a while, the FPF would watch my four little darlings at her place, and on this particular day, she volunteered to drive them back home to me. I was in the throes of scaling Mount Laundry and was folding the umpteenth basketful when she arrived with the kids. She decided to stay for a bit to chat. As I was folding a basket full of towels, my moment went like this:

Me: How were the kids for you?

FPF: *blank angry stare at me*

Me: Were they not okay for you?

FPF: What are you doing?

Me: Ummm... folding my towels?

FPF: YOU'RE DOING IT WRONG!

Me: I'm doing it wrong???

FPF: YES! You are folding those towels the wrong way!

Now, at this point in my life, I'm a 33-year-old mother of four, I had earned my Bachelor of Science degree, my Master's in Education, and I'm in my own home... MY HOME... the home that I paid the mortgage, paid all of the utilities, put groceries in my pantry, and clean clothes on MY children. I had enough of this tyrant, this 75-year-old woman, who had the gall, the audacity to sit on MY couch and tell me that I'm folding MY towels, that I paid for, wrong? Yep. She tried. And for a brief moment, I watched myself address that statement that I was folding my towels wrong. Dissociation and detachment to the rescue!

Me: Did you just tell me I'm folding my towels the wrong way?

FPF: Yes, I did. Because you're folding them wrong.

Me: Ummm... these are MY towels, and this is MY house.

FPF: That doesn't make any...

Me: MY house... and that means I am ALLOWED to fold these towels however I choose. I can fold them into a triangle, I can make swans, OR I can roll them up into a ball and throw them in a DRAWER if I want. And, furthermore, if I choose to leave them unfolded in this basket until they're used again, that is completely MY CHOICE! This is not YOUR house; this is MY house!

FPF: *silently stares at the floor* Well, fine then... fold your towels wrong.

And, at that, she picked up her purse, walked out my front door, and never stepped foot on my property again for the rest of her life.

From that day on, things were even more tense in the exchange of the children when they would stay with her in her little one-bedroom apartment. And during family gatherings, we all did what we were taught: strap on the neutral-faced mask and pretend all is well. Either way, very few words were exchanged between FPF and me from then on. Surprisingly enough, I really didn't feel any guilt for taking a stand. I can't decide if that's a symptom of insanity or indifference.

Besides this small glimmer of attempted self-preservation, Groundhog Day continued... at least for a short time. And then, Punxsutawney Phil showed up and FINALLY changed everything.

At this point in her life, FPF had several health problems from a heart condition to Parkinson's disease, her kidneys were shutting down, a severe thyroid condition, and that's just a few of the issues. From January of 2007 until January of 2008, she was in and out of the hospital a lot. Throughout that period of time, the family was called to her ICU room in the hospital several times because "she probably won't make it through the night." She would always pull through and recover enough to be sent home. The last time we were called to see her for "the last time," she decided she'd had enough of this world. The decision was made to put her on hospice at her home.

The day hospice was decided, with all of the family at the hospital, I experienced the second miracle that year involving FPF. Once the doctors left the hospital room to begin preparing everything for FPF to spend her last days in her apartment, FPF asked to see me in private. O...K???? At the time, I was completely clueless as to what was going on in that woman's mind. The miracle conversation went like this...

FPF: I want to talk to just you.

Me: O...K???

FPF: I just wanted to tell you I'm sorry.

Me: You're sorry???

FPF: Yes... *starts to get choked up* ...I'm so sorry.

Me: Why are you so sorry?

FPF: I'm just so sorry.

Me: Okay?

FPF: That's it, that's all I wanted to tell you.

AWKWARD SILENCE FOR ABOUT 2 MINUTES

Me: Okay

And that was it. At that time, I had no idea specifically why she was "so sorry." To this day, I still have no assurance of why she was sorry. I do have an idea why, but that will be addressed in another chapter.

And at that, we prepared for her to go home to her apartment for the last time. If you've never had a close experience with someone who is on hospice, it is a terribly unpredictable situation. There have been people who have been in hospice for up to and beyond several months, but there was no way to know what would happen with FPF. The day she was transported to her apartment, hospice also sent every bit of necessary equipment for her as if she were in a hospital room: the hospital bed, oxygen tank, bedside commode, and the like. We knew she needed 24-hour care at that point, so between my family and me, we decided on a schedule of which one of us would be with her at what time each day, and we decided we'd pay for a nurse to be in her apartment with a family member overnight. Everything and everyone arrived early the afternoon of that chilly January day, 2008. For a short time, she was awake and somewhat coherent. That didn't last long. She, rather quickly, started drifting into incoherence and by that evening was no longer responsive.

I volunteered to be with her that first night of hospice care. I would stay with her and the nurse from about 10 pm until about 6 am when the next family member would take over. Everyone left for my first shift to begin. Was I sad? Not really. Did I want those overnight hours to hurry up and be over with? Absolutely.

I've heard it said that the last sense to go when someone is near death is their hearing, so I decided the best choice at that moment was to read scripture to her. I chose to read from the book of Psalms, specifically Psalm 121.

A Song of Ascents.

Psalm 121

I will lift up my eyes to the hills—

From whence comes my help?

My help comes from the LORD,

Who made heaven and earth.

He will not allow your foot to be moved;

He who keeps you will not slumber.

Behold, He who keeps Israel

Shall neither slumber nor sleep.

The LORD is your keeper;

The LORD is your shade at your right hand.

The sun shall not strike you by day,

Nor the moon by night.

The LORD shall preserve you from all evil;

He shall preserve your soul.

The LORD shall preserve your going out and your coming in

From this time forth, and even forevermore.[3]

To be honest, I chose to read those scriptures out loud for me, not for her. I needed to feel... something. All I felt in those hours, alone with the woman who turned her eye from the depravity and evil I endured for so many years... SO many years, all I felt was numb. Oh, the irony! I spent the first 18 years, and most of the subsequent 16 years of my life, stuffing every feeling I ever encountered. I was not allowed to feel sadness, disappointment, pain—physical or emotional, anger, confusion, happiness, pride, anxiety, joy, excitement, or to demonstrate even a hint of being human. This person who was supposed to be my female parental figure or, dare I suggest, my mother, who seemed to take pride in finding new ways to destroy any semblance of my self-worth. This so-called Female Parental Figure was lying in a hospital bed in her one-bedroom apartment on her literal deathbed, and I felt nothing. Nothing! There was no sadness, disappointment, pain, anger, confusion, happiness, pride, anxiety, joy, excitement... NOTHING!

Nothing.

And less than 6 hours after we set her up for Hospice in that apartment, she was gone. Even now, as I remember that experience, I feel so empty and numb. And, as much as I dislike the

---

3   Psalm 121 (New King James Version)

empty numbness of that situation, I would have gladly experienced that emptiness a thousand more times rather than the trauma that awaited me.

CHAPTER 14

The Depths of Stillbirth:
When It Rains, It Hurricanes,
It Monsoons, It Tsunamis,
It Mudslides

Okay... deep, cleansing breath... WHEW!!!

Let's recap where we are. FPF passed on in January of 2008. The family had to make the final arrangements for the memorial, clean out her apartment, and divvy up her earthly possessions. Those few weeks were a bit of a blur. What I do remember is cleaning out her cabinets and finding lots of things that she had kept for reasons unbeknownst to all of us. Why would anyone keep an antibiotic ointment that expired in 1993? Or keep clipped coupons that were good until December of 1989? Regardless, we finally finished those looming tasks, and we all went back to status quo, at least for a bit.

As for me? I started a new chapter in my life. This chapter was full of possibilities. Yes, I was a 34-year-old woman and had been on my own, with my own family, for quite some time. The thing is, even though I was adult aged, I had still been under the iron fist of FPF until she was finally gone. This new chapter, this era, began with my realization that it was time... time for me to figure out just who I was and what I wanted for my life. I started making decisions for ME for the first time in my life. What was my first big decision for myself? I decided that I wanted a tattoo.

I wanted something that was in direct opposition to the legalism and tyranny that I had survived. Yep, a tattoo was definitely the way to go. So, the last week of June 2008, I did just that. Husband and I took our four little darlings on a camping trip at the end of every June for my youngest's birthday. As we were turning onto the road where we would be camping for the next week, I noticed a tattoo shop in a little plaza on the corner. "That's the one," I thought... that's where I wanted to get my first ink. And that is exactly what I did.

My newfound freedom didn't end there, no sir! I realized that I wanted to make some serious changes in myself, specifically for my health. At this point, I was the biggest and heaviest version of myself. I hated what I saw in the mirror. I hated the fact that I couldn't fit in regular clothes. I couldn't just go to Wal-Mart and buy pants because I was too big for their biggest women's size. I hated seeing the number 328 on the scale. I hated having to wear men's clothes all the time. I hated being such a bad example for my kids. I wanted to be a healthy mom that they could be proud of. I didn't want to be an embarrassment to my children because I was so morbidly obese. It was time to make a change. I decided I wanted to start making healthier food choices and wanted to lose weight and get healthy so I could go swimming with my kids, go on roller coaster rides with my kids, play soccer in the back-yard... with my kids! So, I joined a gym. I decided I would stop at the gym on my way home from work every day. There was a Club Fitness close to my work, so that was perfect. And so, that's exactly what I did. So, why is that so bad? Why would I take the time to add this particular story to this book? Because that was the beginning of the end of my marriage.

I've heard it said that we are either going forward or going backward. I don't completely agree with that. I believe we are either going forward, going backward, or hanging out in our happy little rut. That rut is comfy and cozy. That rut doesn't expect anything of us. In fact, it keeps us in a place of stagnancy. What happens when stagnancy happens? Stuff starts to stink! Okay, enough analogy and avoidance. I think I've made it pretty clear that my marriage was less than stellar. Remember, as long as I was morbidly obese, husband felt secure in his situation. When my self-worth was in the toilet, he was completely confident that I wasn't going anywhere. What he chose to NOT understand is that my striving to be a "Proverbs 31" wife and mother meant I wasn't going anywhere regardless of how I looked. I took my marriage vows very seriously! That's why I stayed in that so-called marriage as long as I did. The problem was my newfound freedom to find my true identity completely shook my husband to his core. His stability centered on that stinky, stagnant rut. I had the audacity to strive for growth in my personal life and wanted that growth to translate into my marriage and parenting. Husband could not have disagreed more. He found a NEW rut with how he dealt with me, and it became like a broken record. For those of you younger than Generation X, feel free to Google that idiom "like a broken record."

Anywho... the new back-and-forth between us went something like this... I'll set the scene for you. At this point, he was working weekend night shifts. Three 12-hour shifts on Friday, Saturday, and Sunday nights. This meant he was home during the week. Did he make sure dinner was ready when I got home? Uhhh... NO! Of course not! And, in a subsequent book, I'll go deeper into the psyche as to why he refused to help around the house. Suffice it to say, it was my responsibility to make sure that he and the children were fed. Now, the end of my day at school was 4:20, then I'd go straight to the gym for cardio and strength training. By the time I got home, it would be around 6 pm.

Him: Where have you been?

Me: What do you mean, where have I been? You know I go to the gym every day after work.

Him: The kids are hungry!

Me: So, make dinner for them.

Him: Why should I? That's YOUR job!

Me: Look, I get off work at 4:20 at the earliest, and I go to the gym. Either you can make dinner, or you're going to have to wait until I get home.

Him: Why is it so important for you to go to that gym? Are you trying to impress other men???

Me: *blank stare* ... WHAT? What are you talking about? I'm trying to get healthy for my children, so I can go outside and play with them, so I can fit in regular clothes, so my children won't be embarrassed by me. Don't you want me to be healthy?

Him: Not if it means you're trying to impress other men!

Me: Seriously???

After the first time I was asked if I'm trying to impress other men, my response became more and more dark and confrontational.

Him: So, you're still going to the gym and trying to impress other men?

Me: YEP! That's my goal in life. First, I'm going to impress other men, then come home and make you dinner.

But it wasn't just problems with me going to the gym. Anytime we'd be out in public anywhere, if a man I didn't know talked to me, I would be interrogated as to why he talked to me, and then... and this is my FAVORITE part... he would ask, "Are you f****ng him?" Absolutely ridiculous! I've been told one of the signs that your significant other is cheating on you is that they begin accusing you of cheating. The more weight I lost, the worse the interrogations. It was obnoxious, to say the least. I tried everything to convince him that I was faithful only to him and had no intentions of stepping out of the marriage. The most challenging aspect of this was how often I would throw myself at him physically only to be pushed away. He wasn't interested in me whatsoever. This was more heartbreaking than any accusations he ever made.

This back-and-forth continued into the year 2009. There were a few times that he didn't push me away. The proof of that was at the end of July when I found out I was pregnant for the sixth time. I was 35 years old and really didn't want to start over in parenting. My youngest was in kindergarten, and I was exhausted just thinking about having another baby. And much like most women, even though I was shocked and pretty freaked out when I found out I was pregnant, when I knew I had another baby on the way, that I had the privilege to be their momma, I was in love with him or her. So, again, I experienced morning sickness, cravings, and my favorite was hearing that strong baby heartbeat at the OB visits. I was due in early April and was so excited at the thought, the possibility, of sharing my birthday with my baby. I was still in a miserable marriage but was keeping my focus on my baby and what he or she needed.

All was going well. I had made it past the first trimester and sailed into my second trimester. It was Halloween of 2009. I was in week 20 of the pregnancy and had just got home from taking the kids trick-or-treating around the neighborhood. I sat down to rest and felt baby moving like crazy. It felt like baby was tapdancing and breakdancing at the same time... and then it stopped. It was still early in feeling those kicks and turns, so I didn't think much of it. Two days later was THE ultrasound. We would see if we were having a boy or girl. I had decided I wanted to find out so the kids and I could start preparing baby stuff. My three daughters were team girl, and of course, my only son was praying for a boy.

My OB was the same doctor that I had for my son, my miscarriage, and my two youngest daughters. The visit started like all of the other ones. I peed in a cup, checked my weight, and waited to be measured and check heart rate before going to the ultrasound room. Doctor put that cold goo on the doppler and started looking for baby. He tried left, he tried right, he tried high, and he tried low. The only heartbeat we were hearing was mine. That's weird! He didn't seem concerned at all... he said baby is just being stubborn. Let's go on into the ultrasound room and take a look. Oh, yay... more cold goo. Again, he looked left, he looked right, he looked high, and he looked low. I asked what's going on? What's wrong? Doctor said it's probably just a problem with the ultrasound equipment. He told me to go to the ultrasound specialist first thing the next morning. He said not to worry, he was sure everything was just fine. I tried to slap on a smile the best I could and said, "Okay, thank you, doc." Of course, I didn't sleep that night... how could I? I was reliving my horrific near-death miscarriage that happened only 8 and ½ years before. I counted the hours and minutes until we went to the specialist. Every minute felt like a week.

I remember sitting in the waiting room praying and praying and praying all was okay. Finally, I heard my name called. The zombie version of myself nodded and quickly walked into that room. More cold goo, more searching, left, right, high, low... with a solid poker face (I'm convinced ultrasound techs are required to take a poker-face class), that ultrasound tech said, "Excuse me just a minute... I'll be right back." I stared at the ceiling, begging God to calm me and strengthen me... and that when we finally see our baby, I'd be completely okay with not seeing if we'd be buying blue or pink when we left that appointment.

FINALLY, the tech opened the door, but... hang on. That's someone different.

Me: Um, where did the lady tech go?

Tech: I'm the head of this department. She asked me to help you today.

Me: Okay. Nice to meet you...

More goo... left, right, high, low... tap, type, tap, type...

Tech: *points to the screen* Ma'am, this is your baby.

Me: Okay?

Tech: Do you see this dark spot right here? *points to the middle of my baby's chest*

Me: Yes???

Tech: That's where a heart is supposed to be beating.

Me: Okay?????

Tech: There is no heartbeat.

Me: No heartbeat?

Tech: No, ma'am. I'm so sorry. Your baby's heart is no longer beating. Excuse me, please.

Tech walks out of the room

Me: ... ...

I couldn't breathe. I couldn't move. I couldn't...

I looked at my husband. His face was expressionless.

Tech returns: I just spoke with your doctor's office. You are to go immediately to see your doctor. He will give you the next steps. I'm so very sorry for your loss.

I stood up, and somehow walked to the car, got in the car, and we went to my OB's office. I'm so grateful he didn't let us stay in the waiting room... we were immediately directed to an exam room. Doctor walks in... I don't remember much of what happened or what was said during that conversation...

Dr: I'm so, so sorry! I'm... I'm just so sorry... you're too far along... need to wait until you go into labor on your own... we need to deliver baby naturally... go home and call me when you either start bleeding or you feel contractions...

Me: I have to deliver? I have to go through labor to deliver? I have to wait? I'm going to deliver???

Dr: This is the safest way to proceed...

Me: How long? How long until labor starts?

Dr: I wish I could give you a definite answer. I'd like for us to wait for your body to start the process on its own. Until then, stay off of your feet and call us if you have any questions.

And so, we went home. I went home knowing my baby, whose heartbeat I had already listened to many times, who was 20 weeks old, my baby had died... on MY watch! And here comes the guilt... what in the world did I do wrong??? This isn't supposed to happen!!! We were past the dangerous point!!! What did I do wrong???

It was November 2, 2009. My second daughter's 7th birthday was only three days away. How do I explain this to my kids? How do I tell them their baby sibling has died? How do I go on living when all I want to do is crawl into a grave and never return? How do I lay in bed knowing my baby is dead? The last time I felt baby move was... HALLOWEEN NIGHT! That was when I felt baby moving frantically. I thought it felt like dancing. What if baby was in distress? What if I did something to kill baby? Why? WHY? Why do I have not one, but TWO babies who were with me for such a short time and passed on before me? For the first time in my life, in my newfound freedom from emotional tyranny, I was allowed to feel emotions... oh BOY, did I ever feel emotions. My chest felt like a deep, dark abyss... like dark, black tar was filling my heart. Yeah, to say I was in a severe emotional depression would be like saying the Grand Canyon is only a creek. I didn't want to see anyone, I didn't want to talk to anyone, I didn't want to eat... all I could tolerate was a TV. On day 5, I called my doctor's office.

Me: I can't... I can't deal with this anymore. I can't continue with my dead baby in me. Please, please, can't we do something???

Nurse: I'm so sorry... let me talk to the doctor, and I'll call you back.

About 10 minutes... or was it 10 hours??? No... it had to be 10 minutes later. I got the call to be at the hospital the next morning. We would try to induce labor. I hoped knowing it would be over soon would help me sleep. Nope... I was wrong.

November 9, 2009, we arrived at the hospital at 6 am. They knew we were coming. They were expecting us. As we got off the elevator, we were directed to our labor and delivery room... directly across from THE NURSERY!!! It's not like the floor was full. During my stay, there were more than a handful of rooms available, and they chose to put me in the room closest to the nursery where I could hear babies crying AND I was next door to a mother who delivered a full-term and healthy baby. How do I know? I heard its first cries after it was born along with the few other babies in the nursery that was on the other side of my door... which was directly beside my hospital bed. Why in the world did they choose to keep me close to the other mothers rather than on the other side where I'd be less likely to hear those healthy babies' cries? I guess it's more important to make it easier on the nurses than to take into consideration the feelings of a patient who is about to deliver a dead child. So, ask me this... did husband do anything to try to help in this situation? Of course, not! No, he was far too busy not being there with me. He drove me there and promptly left. All of the kids were taken care of and headed to school, and yet he found every excuse in the book to not be there with me. Unbelievable? Yeah, but it was par for the course and so very indicative of the condition of our relationship.

The first task in this depressing delivery was to start an IV. After the 10th needle stick, and calling anesthesia, it was decided to bring in an ultrasound machine to help find a viable vein. Lovely! Finally, on try number 12, they were successful in starting an IV. I decided I wanted to go through this labor with no pain meds. I wanted to feel the physical pain more than the emotional pain. Call me crazy, yes. However, I felt like I deserved to feel that excruciating physical pain.

Deep down, I was convinced I had killed my baby. Why would I think that you ask? Well, as ashamed as I am of admitting this in black and white, I must anyway. The truth is, when I found out I was pregnant with my sixth baby at the age of 35, initially, I was not happy about it at all. In fact, I was pretty freaked out about it. We already had severe financial difficulties (thanks to my husband), and I was already tied to him for the rest of my life with my four living children. I didn't want to go through pregnancy, delivering, and raising another baby on my own with less than adequate money to do so. I didn't want this baby to endure what my other children had to, growing up in that household. So, I... I called an abortion clinic to find out what I needed to do to end my pregnancy. That's right... this loving mother of four living children, the woman who is a "pro-lifer," was making plans to end the life of her sixth child. At this point, the only people who knew of my predicament were me, God, and a wise, supportive, and kind friend.

Not to be outdone by Ryan Reynolds in Deadpool, I find myself with the need to break the fourth wall again. Please understand that it is not my intention to condemn, point a finger at, or chastise anyone who made this choice that I did not choose. I fully empathize with that decision. I cannot know exactly how you felt or what you were going through, but I now know first-hand the excruciating burden of the decision whether or not to have an abortion. There was a time that I could not do so. I couldn't understand how anyone could even consider voluntary termination of their pregnancy. I was one of those well-intentioned yet unwittingly reactive "pro-lifers". So, if you are someone who did choose abortion, please allow me to extend a sincere apology on behalf of those who have made you feel like a monster. You are not a monster! You are someone who went through an extremely difficult situation and did what you thought was best for you and your family in that situation. No one should condemn you for that! And if they do, they need to put a mirror in front of their own face and look at their own imperfections!

As for me in my own dilemma, I was making plans with my friend as to how I was going to keep all of this a secret from everyone. It was while talking through the entire situation that I realized there was no way possible I could ever voluntarily end my child's life. I believed all the way down to my toes, and finally concluded, once   life was created, I had no right to take the life that I had helped create, regardless of my circumstances. So,

I decided to keep my baby and that was the best choice for me and my family. Not only did I choose to keep my baby, I grew increasingly excited about this new life that I was given the opportunity, the absolute privilege, to love as I do my other children. I was grateful for my decision.

And now... now my sweet baby who I had contemplated taking its life a mere four months before was gone, and I felt completely responsible. So, yeah, in this severe emotionally depressive state, I had convinced myself that the mere contemplation of abortion is what took my baby's life. And, yeah, I wanted to go through this labor with no pain meds because I thought I deserved that physical pain for what I put my baby through. There is absolutely no logic when it comes to that level of mental and emotional pain and anguish.

I tried. Lord knows I tried to endure that pain without meds; however, the means by which we had to induce labor was beyond comprehension. It wasn't Pitocin this time. Nope... this induction made Pitocin look like getting a paper cut. This time they used an oral med as well as a suppository. We alternated between these methods of administration until we saw progress. When the first labor pain hit, and it was so intense I thought I was literally going to die. And given my mental state at that time, I felt that death would've been a welcome result.

About 10 hours into this ordeal, another very dear friend that I have been friends with since elementary school visited me. It was such a relief to see someone who I knew was concerned with how I was doing. She brought me the most adorable blue stuffed teddy bear in blue pajamas and prayed with me. That teddy bear, to this day, resides on a shelf next to my bed. To my sweet friend who blessed me with such a powerful gift, if you're reading this memoir, THANK YOU!

Husband had still not made another appearance at this point. At 4 pm, I hadn't made much progress in my labor, and the kids were getting off school and needed supervision. He did text to say he'd be back to the hospital in the morning. Wasn't that generous? The contractions had finally started, were coming every two to three minutes, and were even more intense than any of my other labor and deliveries. Thankfully, I had a nurse, after the shift changed, who was more compassionate than all of the other nurses put together. We had an extensive conversation about my pain and my reason for rejecting any pain meds. I spilled my entire sordid situation to her and revealed to her how I believed it was my cold heart that killed my baby because I contemplated murdering this precious human. She responded with, "REALLY??? You really think you are that powerful???" I have to laugh now because she was absolutely right. That amazing person, oh so subtly and gently, convinced me that I needed pain meds to navigate this torture of delivering my dead child. And so, I conceded to morphine. And, if I may, sweet nurse who talked me into allowing pain meds, from the bottom of my heart, THANK YOU!

My labor, despite the pain meds, was the most traumatic and painful labor I had endured up to that moment. The best part? With my tongue firmly planted in my cheek, I must admit, the "best" part of that situation was the fact that I could have any pain med I wanted. I didn't have to worry about the safety of my baby... so I could be as drugged up as I wanted. And, at that point, thanks to that wise nurse whose name I cannot recall, I asked for every pain med that I was able to have. I was hoping the pain meds would relax my body, physically, to help this process hurry up and be finished already! Nope... no such luck.

27 hours... yes, you read that correctly... after TWENTY-SEVEN hours of labor, my baby was born. That's longer than my other four labor and deliveries put together. Wrap your brain around THAT! And, how about we add insult to injury here. Brace yourself for this tidbit of information. I wasn't allowed to push because they were concerned with the integrity of the baby physically. At the risk of giving too much information here, my apologies to the squeamish, they were concerned that baby would not be intact. Being lifeless for as long as baby was as we waited for labor to start on its own, there was the possibility that limbs would not be in their proper place on baby's body. That's what was taking so long.

I know you cannot see me as I type this in my home office, so you have no idea that I needed to walk away from this for a while... that I'm having to stop and start A LOT. As you can imagine, this entire memoir is causing me to relive everything I've endured. So far, this portion has been the most difficult to relive. It is literally nauseating. Grief can be nauseating. And there is no time limit on grief! It is currently October of 2023. It has been almost exactly 14 years since this tragedy, and it feels like it just happened. The day-to-day grief has lessened, but the memories come flooding back so easily. Thank you for your patience with me. Anyway, deep breath, and I'm back. Now, where was I? Oh, yes...

So, finally after 27 hours, baby was born still and silent. The doctor and staff went through the same procedures with my baby as they did with my other babies, only this time, rather than a room full of congratulations, happy conversations, and the beautiful sound of a crying newborn, it was deafeningly silent. I was asked if I wanted to hold my baby. Husband had finally decided to show up, and he asked to hold baby as well. WHAT??? Yeah, I let that happen exactly 1 minute and 15 seconds. So, I held my baby for as long as they would let me. Baby was six inches long and weighed one pound and one ounce. Baby fit in the palm of my hand. How do I remember that? After the amazing nurse who convinced me to allow pain meds measured my baby, she gave me the measuring tape she used. They made a baby book for me with baby's footprint and handprint (I was able to have those prints tattooed on my back along with my other babies' names). They asked if I had a name for baby that they could write on the book. I asked if baby was a boy or girl. They could not give me a definite answer because there was too much decomposition. That was my breaking point... that is what opened the floodgates of my tears. I asked if there is any way we could find out boy or girl. They offered to do tests; however, I wouldn't be able to bury baby because they would send him or her to the lab instead. As I started to weigh the pros and cons of this decision, husband chimed in.

Him: We are NOT having a funeral!

Me: What? Why not???

Him: Because we're not. It's a waste of money, and we don't need it.

Me: I NEED IT! I at least want to have a memorial at church. This baby is my child regardless of age and deserves to be honored.

Him: It's not going to happen, and that's final! Doc, we're going to have you send it for testing.

Up to that point in our "marriage," there were many times I was INCREDIBLY angry with him. This was a turning point for me. This was the angriest I had ever been in the almost 16 years that I had known him. In that moment, I completely gave up. In that moment, my soul and spirit cried out in anger to God. In that moment, I declared to God that all of my efforts were in vain, that Proverbs 31 was a joke, and I was finished with Him. In that moment, I cursed God, I cursed this person to whom I had given 15 years of marriage. In that moment, November 10, 2009, I was just DONE.

So, let's recap the stats here... 27 hours. 27 hours of labor for the privilege of holding my baby who died before being offered a chance to experience anything beyond the womb, who was not given the dignity of a name or a memorial service to honor its life, whose father couldn't even muster the decency to acknowledge their precious life. Incomprehensible! My feeble mind just could not grasp any of it. All of this and I was still hearing the cries of healthy babies all around me. I just wanted to go home! I asked my doctor how soon I could leave. I couldn't go anywhere. Because of how long we waited for baby, I had developed a pretty significant infection. I had to stay on IV antibiotics, at least one day and maybe longer. The first time I tried getting out of bed, I was so weak I couldn't walk without help, so I guess it was wise to stay. Husband went home, and I was so grateful. However, before he left the hospital, he decided to let his severe insecurities shine bright for all to see. Oh, you're going to LOVE this part (no, that wasn't the sound of bowling balls rolling at the bowling alley... that was the sound of many eyes rolling).

Him: I guess I'm going home.

Me: Okay. BYE!

He starts to open the door when he notices my blue teddy bear that was gifted by my friend, who is a woman.

Him: What's this???

Me: That's a blue teddy bear.

Him: I can see THAT; how did you get it?

Me: [my friend's name] came to see me and brought it with her. She gave it to me.

Him: You're trying to tell me that some woman came to see you while I was gone?

Me: Yes, [first husband's name], she wanted to pray with me in person.

Him: You said you didn't want to see or talk to anyone.

Me: I didn't invite her; she knew I would be here, so she wanted to offer a shoulder.

Him: I don't believe you... you're lying to me!

Me: WHAT??? Why would I lie to you about that?

Him: You didn't tell me anyone came to see you.

Me: You didn't ask me. I forgot to mention it... I was kind of in the middle of something rather traumatic, so I forgot.

Him: Liar! Some man came to see you, didn't they? Some man that you're f****ng behind my back brought that up here... I bet that man is the baby's father!!!

Me: Seriously??? You're doing this NOW!?

Him: Yeah... that's gotta be what happened.

Me: You are out of your mind! Just go... LEAVE!

Him: So you can get your boyfriend up here??? ... yeah, I'm outta here!

Just when I thought he had hit his worst, he just had to one-up it, didn't he?

Finally, I was released to go home. Leaving a hospital after going through 27 hours of labor with no baby to love is indescribable. The black tar abyss was growing and taking over my entire being. This was the darkest place I had ever been. Luckily, I was given a six-week maternity leave off of work. I went home, went to bed, and wished death would hurry up and take over. The problem with that was, I was still married to someone who refused to do anything around the house or for the kids... the four other children that I had who needed me.

At this point, I find it necessary to chase this particular rabbit down its hole.

Yes, I know I had four other children to care for. Yes, I love those babies, and they needed me. Yes, I was, am, and always will be grateful for the gift of my four living children. And... not but... AND I had just been through the worst experience any parent could ever endure with a side order of a horrifically abusive marriage. Just taking the next breath was all I could muster during those days, weeks, months after the stillbirth. Every person I encountered who tried filling my heart and mind with their "wisdom" should have just beat me down with a jackhammer instead. It would have hurt much less than the words they spoke to me. Again, the platitudes of those who are uncomfortable and have no idea what to say are more destructive than anything. I think my "favorite" conversation was this one:

Woman that I don't know: Aren't you the one who just lost their baby?

Me: I guess I'm "the one"???

Woman: You know, you should be so grateful for your living children.

Me: Yes, I'm grateful for my living children.

Woman: That must be such a comfort to you.

Me: *blank stare*

Woman: You know... because you know you can always have another if you want to.

Me: *blank stare*

Woman: And, obviously, you weren't supposed to have this one.

Me: Excuse me?

Woman: *stammers* Well, I mean, you already have FOUR children.

Me: Um, ma'am, how many children do you have?

Woman: Two

Me: I tell you what, since you already have TWO children, what I'd like for you to do is choose which one you'd like to keep and which you'd like to lose.

Woman: *blank stare*

Me: You mean, you can't choose which of your children you'd like to die???

Woman: *blank stare*

Me: My baby, who I carried and delivered, who died at the age of 20 weeks in the womb, is just as much my baby as my other FOUR are.

Woman: Well... *stammers* ... I didn't mean...

Me: Excuse me, I need to go gather my four children that I was "supposed to have" ...

WHAT IS WRONG WITH PEOPLE???

CHAPTER 15

So Much Lost, and So Much Gained: *I'm an Orphan— No, Wait—No, I'm Not!*

It was the end of 2009. The nightmare no parent should ever endure, the death of my child, had come to fruition, and I was dreading the impending holidays. Somehow, I "zombied" my way through the next two months. After all, I had become a professional dissociative. Thanksgiving dinner was prepared, the family Christmas traditions were observed, gifts were purchased and distributed, New Year's Eve morphed into New Year's Day 2010. I had no parents, a miserable marriage, and had never felt so alone in my life. It was at this pivotal time in my life that I decided I wanted to find my birth father.

Over the course of the last decade, I had tried utilizing the recently developed technology of the Internet to find my birth father and had looked on search websites to find him. I knew his full name, the year he was born, and I knew he was career Air Force; that was all I had to go on. Unfortunately, I was having zero luck in finding him. My problem with all of the dead ends? I had to pay a good chunk of money to get more information... money that I did not have. Yes, I wanted to make that connection so badly. Even if, as I had been told my entire life, he genuinely wanted nothing to do with me, I needed to know him; I needed to meet him.

There was one time, it was in 2004 soon after my youngest living baby was born, that I thought I had found him. I had a last known address that was in south St. Louis city. I told husband what I had found and asked if we could please drive to that address. Where we were living at the time was only about twenty-five miles from that address. We printed off the directions from MapQuest and, no, that isn't a mistake. Young ones, there was a time when Maps was called MapQuest, those maps were sketchy at best, our cell phones were not "smart"... they only made voice calls... and the most advanced new cell phones at that time would allow you to create an extremely limited message using letters. We now call this text messaging. They were so fancy!

So, we piled all four of the kids into our truck and drove to the address. We parked on the street three houses down from the house that I was given as my birth dad's last known address. Husband got out of the truck, walked to that house, and knocked on the door. A man answered the door, but I couldn't get a good look at him because his back was to me. I thought my heart was going to pound straight through my chest. I tried to take deep, deliberate breaths as I watched husband walk back to the truck. My mind was going a million miles an hour. Was that my father? What if it is? Would he want to see me? What if he DIDN'T want to see me? What if it's NOT him? What then???

Husband sat back down in the driver's seat and shook his head at me. The man he talked with at that house bought the house from my birth father. I lost it! I started to weep... I couldn't tell if it was relieved sobbing or disappointed sobbing. Either way, I couldn't get ahold of my emotions that were pouring down my cheeks. I had to resign myself to the understanding that it was obvious I wasn't supposed to meet my birth father. Still, that longing to know who he is and put a face to a name continued to nag at me. As of January 2010, I was striving to find my new "normal." I had to go back to work and teach, the kids were back to school after our Winter break, and still I felt so lost... so empty. Until...

I feel the need to reprise my Golden Girl Sophia act here... picture it, St. Louis, Missouri, January 2010, it's a Wednesday evening. I was taking the kids to their mid-week church classes. It was a typical Wednesday, that is, until husband told me to meet him at a specific restaurant after dropping off the kids. There was someone I needed to meet... someone he's doing a heating repair for after work. Okay??? Why in the world would I ever need to meet someone whose home heating system you're fixing? Regardless of who I "needed to meet," I pulled into the restaurant parking lot and husband met me at my car. He was acting all nervous and weird... more weird than normal. "What is going on here? What's with you?" He responded, "Just come with me... you've got to meet this guy!" Okay, so at least I know it's a guy. I walk into the restaurant, and I see a man sitting with his back to me in a booth. Then, I see him stand, turn around, and look at me with tears in his eyes.

Him: Oh my... you look just like your mother!

Me: Wha...???

Him: You look just like your mother!

Me: My mother? WHO ARE YOU???

Him: It's me!

Me: It's you?

Him: I'm your dad.

Me: *realizing this is my birth father* [his name] Is that really you???

Him: Yes, daughter, it's really me!

Me: You wanted to meet me?

Him: Of course, I wanted to meet you... you're my DAUGHTER!!!

We stood there in a tearful embrace for a few minutes and sat in the booth together. I couldn't believe it... I was sitting at a restaurant with my birth father! AND he WANTED to meet me! How did this happen? How did he find me??? I asked him just that, "How did you find me?" But here's the thing, folks, he didn't find me... husband found HIM! Um, say again??? Yeah, the shock of the century... husband? How is that possible? How could he find my dad when I couldn't? Why in the world would he do something like this for me? What was the ulterior motive? Regardless of the reason, this was the most amazing moment in my life. Finally... FINALLY I could start getting some answers. Finally, I could hear HIS side of the story. Finally, I had the possibility of a positive daughter-father relationship.

That evening, we talked non-stop until it was time for me to pick up the kids. We exchanged cell phone numbers and decided to meet and talk again and SOON! So, two nights later, at a 24-hour restaurant, we met... just the two of us. And that's exactly what we did. We talked.

Walking into that restaurant less than 48 hours after meeting him, I felt like I was walking on a cloud. It was so surreal, so dreamlike, so WEIRD! I had spent a good amount of my entire life, 35 years... almost 36, dreaming of the day I would sit in front of my birth father. I was so excited and terrified at the same time. After the initial "I can't believe I'm sitting here with you" and "tell me about your family" and "I love Pink Floyd too!", it was time to bring out the big guns. I needed some real answers to some terribly difficult questions.

Me: I have wondered all my life about you. I've been told so many stories, so many excuses as to why I couldn't meet you. I want to hear YOUR side of things.

Him: I don't think you do.

Me: Yes. I really do.

Him: I don't think you realize what you're asking.

Me: I absolutely DO know what I'm asking. I want to know... I NEED to know why. Why didn't you want anything to do with me while I was growing up?

Him: WHAT? Who told you that?

Me: FPF did.

Remember that FPF was the female parental figure who adopted me as her own, under whose iron fist I was crushed.

Him: She WHAT? She told you I didn't want anything to do with you? *Looks down at the table, shakes his head, sobbing quietly.*

Me: That's not true? *Also sobbing quietly.*

Him: Daughter, I can tell you whatever you want to know from me, but I want you to really think about if you really REAL-

LY want to know, because once I tell you I cannot UN-tell you. There's a lot of answers I will give you that will be unpleasant to hear at best.

Me: I KNOW there will be ugly and difficult things I will hear, but that doesn't matter to me. I cannot go any longer wondering... wondering if all of the bad events I've survived is because of who I am or because of who THEY were.

Him: Why would you think the bad things are because of who you are?

Me: I just do... please believe me when I tell you, I. MUST. KNOW. EVERYTHING!

Him: Daughter, you have no idea just how much you're like me.

And, with that, looking in his eyes, I could see that he understood why I must know everything. He then proceeded to take me through his experience with my birth mother, their trauma, and how he was cut out of my life. That's right, he was cut out of my life without his consent. To the contrary, my dad WANTED to be my dad all of my life and he did everything in his power to stay not only in contact with me, but to stay in my life as my dad. When I heard that, I hoped that our new relationship would be at least a vindication of everything he sacrificed just to be a part of my life in some capacity.

Before I go any further, I need to offer this disclaimer regarding the following story. I have not asked permission of my dad to divulge all of the details as to what he told me that night as well as since that meeting. I will give generic information for highly sensitive occurrences, then maybe he and I can write one of my subsequent books. We shall see...

So, my dad... my dad was so young when he found out he was going to be a father. When I say young, I mean not-yet-out-of-high-school young. He married my birth mom and worked himself sick to try to be a good husband, provide for his family, AND finish high school. Taking responsibility for your choices, not backing down from the difficulties of adulting, and striving to do the right thing; that's what you did in the '70s... and that's what my dad did.

This is the generic part where I tell you that life happened, as it does to us all, and my birth parents divorced. This is NOT what my dad wanted AT ALL, and I'm positive he'd tell you the same thing and not be ashamed of it. He loved my mother with all of his heart, with all of his being. My dad doesn't do anything halfway. He gives his entire heart, soul, and energy into who and what he loves. That's something else I'm so proud to say that I got from my dad. He was absolutely devastated when they divorced, but what happened after that almost destroyed him.

It's no secret that FPF was a tyrant. And it wasn't just me that she controlled. It was everybody in the entire house that was under her rule. FPF expected you to know when to jump without asking her, and you were also expected to know how high to jump as well as to what length to jump, AND what gymnastics to perform in order to stick the landing. According to my dad, FPF ran the show, and my birth mother had no choice but to adhere to FPF commands. So, when FPF decided that my birth mother and my birth father should divorce, that's exactly what happened. At that point, my dad had no other choice but to follow FPF's every command. My dad was told that under no circumstances would I ever know who he was. Furthermore, he would only step foot on their property when he was given permission, despite the fact that he had legal authorization for visitation rights. Seems fair, doesn't it? You heard that correctly, folks, my dad had visitation rights authorized by a judge and was not allowed by FPF or the pedophile to visit me. Did that stop him from trying? Heavens, no! My dad told me the story about one instance in particular when he tried to visit me at the home where I was living, which happened to be FPF and the pedophile's home. He was met in the driveway by the pedophile and a shotgun and was told to immediately leave, or the County Sheriff would be called. When my dad produced the court document reminding them of his visitation rights, the authorities were called, and he was escorted off the property.

Another instance involved a special occasion at my home, and he was invited to it. If I remember correctly, it was for my birthday. When he arrived for the party, he was given the directive that he was to keep his distance from me, and that I was going to be told that he was just a family friend. He was also told that if he didn't like those stipulations, he could leave. And so, my dad stayed at the party. I cannot even imagine the heartbreak that must have caused him. To be in a hostile environment for the sole purpose of seeing my child, and then not being allowed to hug my child or to express my love for them as their parent? And yet, he did that for me.

After my dad lost his basic rights to have contact with his child, and because this was at a time in history where the Vietnam War was still a reality, my dad chose to join the US Air Force.

My dad served our country in several capacities, the most grueling was his time as a PJ, or more commonly known, Pararescue. My dad is one of the badass men who literally risked their life to save his brothers in combat. He jumped out of helicopters in the middle of active combat to not only rescue wounded soldiers, but he would also administer life support services to those soldiers, desperately trying to keep them alive long enough to get them to a medical facility in a safe location. He did this in every American conflict from 1972-1996. Dad, if you're reading this, I MUST say, again, THANK YOU for your service and your sacrifice!

There are probably some of you out there who are saying, "Hey, wait a minute! What about Chapter 4? Isn't this the same dad from Chapter 4 in this book who promised to see you when you were 14 or 15 years old, and he never showed up like he promised? Isn't that the situation where FPF reminded you that your dad wanted nothing to do with you?" Okay, first of all, you have an incredible memory, and I am thoroughly impressed! Second, yes, this is the same man; however, much like our current social media and news media, that was only a twisted and manipulated part of the story that was riddled with half-truths and lacking in facts. On the night of full disclosure and transparency, the night I finally got my answers, my dad filled me in on what truly happened that day.

He was still in the USAF and was given a two-week leave. That's military talk for a vacation. He decided to contact me and visit. He knew I was about 15 at the time and thought maybe he'd be able to see me because I was older. Yes, he did call. Yes, I did speak with him. Yes, he did promise to come and see me during that leave. Yes, he did have every intention of seeing me.

After our conversation ended, that's where the problem started. According to my dad, when I gave the phone back to FPF, she made it VERY clear to him that under no circumstances would he EVER come to see me. The same old song and dance again. It was not his fault he never showed. He, along with the rest of us, were merely pawns in FPF's sick game of ultimate control. It was not my dad's fault at all.

The truth of the matter here is, he DID want a relationship with me. He DID spend every last penny of his menial income as an enlisted pararescue on lawyers trying desperately to keep contact with me.

By the way, if you aren't aware, enlisted servicemen and servicewomen's income isn't even the equivalent of minimum wage. It wasn't then, and it isn't now. Wrap your brain around THAT! Please excuse my digression.

He DID want to know me. He DID want to watch me grow up. He DID want to attend my school concerts, my graduation, my wedding, the birth of my children. He DID want to be involved in my life. He DID! And it was all stolen from him, stolen from me. For WHAT? Control? Superiority? Selfishness? PRIDE???

Maybe all of what should-have-been was stolen from us by that horrible excuse for a human being, the FPF, for control, superiority, selfishness, and pride. That is probably true, but I believe there's more to it. I think it was fear. Fear is a powerful emotion and causes people to do inexplicable things. What was she afraid of? Maybe she was afraid of losing what she thought she had control of. Maybe she was afraid that what she wanted would have been denied. Maybe, just maybe, she was afraid that people outside of that prison (the house where I lived my first

18 years of life) would see her for who she really was, that they would realize the moral corruption, the disgusting degeneracy, the utter depravity, that SHE ALLOWED, going on right under their noses.

I'm sorry... I have to walk away and take a breath...

deep breath

Perspective is such an incredibly beautiful tool for regrouping when falling off the emotional deep end. So is a shot of Irish whiskey... oops, there I go digressing yet again.

I've become rather contemplative as I learn to how to be loved by a parent. Perhaps the best way to explain my thought process and the ripple effect this newfound relationship has within my family dynamic is this: I have a plaque in my bedroom that says "I heard your prayer, trust my timing. –God" and boy is THAT accurate! If timing had been different in meeting my dad before FPF died, how different would the relationships with my other family members have been? Would I have been able to break the family curse, I mean tradition, of no feelings allowed? Could I have been the one to show my children, my nieces, FPF, my entire family that feelings are a good thing? Could I have been the one to stand up and say it is absolutely wrong to prevent someone, especially children, to bottle up their feelings pretending that everything is hunky-dory-perfect at all times no matter what?

Maybe.

Maybe I already have.

I don't know if it's my age, or the confidence I've developed as a result of my dad's unconditional love that I had never experienced until meeting him, that has caused more of an indifference towards certain members of my family and closeness with others. What I do know is that I express my thoughts and feelings completely and unashamedly regardless of what they want to hear. I have learned to establish healthy boundaries that, when necessary, keep certain family members at arms-length. I no longer allow them to hurt me whether directly or through passive aggressive behaviors. What's the best part of this ripple effect? I have the privilege of watching my now-grown children with the same attitude and actions; they are creating healthy boundaries for the benefit of their own mental health. The bottom line here is, whether it's my age or my confidence, I've found something that I desperately wanted and needed, my voice. I found my voice as a result of finally having a positive, unconditional loving father-daughter relationship I adore my dad, and I'm so very grateful for the beautiful bond that we have developed.

Dad, I love you most!!!

CHAPTER 16

I Can't Live Like This Anymore! *Finally, I Found My Voice!*

One of my favorite movies of all time is, without a doubt, The Princess Bride. If you are not familiar, please do yourself a favor and watch the entire movie. For now, to the newbies and the seasoned Princess Bride followers alike, the scene I am replaying in my mind is when Prince Humperdinck is trying to marry Princess Buttercup... and marry her as quickly as possible. The scene happens in a church with what looks like a priest preparing to perform the wedding ceremony. We see the betrothed kneeling in the front of the church when the priest begins to speak. Also, if you haven't seen The Princess Bride, the priest had a speech impediment much like Elmer Fudd in the Looney Tunes cartoons.

"Mawwiage. Mawwiage is what bwings us togevah today. Mawwiage, dat bwess-ed awwangement...dat dweam wivin a dweam... and WUV, tuwoo wuv, will fowow you foweva... so tweasuh yo wuv..."

Westley and Buttercup were connected by tuwoo wuv... um, I mean true love. Prince Humperdinck tried, desperately, to end Westley's life, and almost succeeded, however... true love. Fezzik and Inigo Montoya take Westley to Miracle Max to see if anything could be done to bring Westley back to life. When Miracle Max asked Westley, who was "nearly dead" and unresponsive, why he was still alive then pushed on his belly, we heard him say "true love." Is there such a thing as true love? I had no idea... I didn't know if anyone truly loved at all. Remember the guy from Chapter 7? You know, my ex-fiancé who I now call "the felon." That wasn't love, that was manipulation, much like the boy from Chapter 6. Then, there's the husband.

I feel the need to reiterate we were both still children when we made the adult decision to marry. At that point in my life, I truly believed I wasn't worth anyone's time, so when I was given any positive, at least what I considered positive, attention, I would convince myself that they loved me... that it must be TRUE love! In my defense, there is no way I could've known the difference between love and manipulation. I was taught by example that manipulation IS love. So, I began a marriage in 1994 at the age of 20 thinking that was as good as I would ever have it. And, as the years progressed, as you've already seen, I slowly realized that my marriage was not a marriage at all. I watched my married friends at church interacting as loving Christ-centered families, and I longed to have that as well.

In 2010, I finally realized that, despite my best efforts, it would never happen with the person I had married 16 years before. I was so alone in that marriage! I was expected to do everything necessary to keep the household running smoothly and raise the children, and the icing on that crumbling cake was that I was expected to turn a blind eye to his money squandering (doesn't every family have every single toy the man decides he has to have despite the lack of income and being above their heads in debt?) as well as his infidelity. Remember in Chapter 14 when I alluded to the fact that he was unfaithful? Well, not long after he found my dad, early in 2010, I found proof of my suspicions, proof that he really was cheating on me. Any other woman would have had the strength at that point to end the marriage, but not me. I was still convinced I would never be good enough for any other man, so I decided to bury my head in the sand even deeper. The problem with that choice is that the fighting became exponentially worse. By the time we got to the end of the summer, I was at a breaking point. Husband agreed to seek marriage counseling. Now, before you think "at least he was trying," au contraire, mon amie. It was obvious after the second session that his mission was to get the counselor on his side as much as possible and then, as we would leave the session, I was asked, "Did you hear what she said to you? Why don't you do that to fix this?" Why don't I??? Really??? The truth was crystal clear; I was expected to take care of everything, and he was responsible for absolutely NOTHING.

Husband decided the marriage counselor I was paying for wasn't helping, so he sought the pastor of our church for help to "fix" me. At one point while meeting with that pastor, I suggested a trial separation. After all, absence makes the heart grow fonder, right?

Whoops! I have to go catch my rolling eyeballs...

The church had a condo that was used when traveling missionaries were in town. It was currently not being used, so he offered one of us to stay there for a couple of weeks while the other was at home taking care of the house and kids, then switch. And so, we tried that. After that month of trial separation, we tried the marriage one more time. Since this is reality and not a fictional fairytale, most likely you already know what happened next... or do you?

The end of 2010 was quite similar to the end of 2009. I, once again, "zombied" my way through Thanksgiving, Christmas, and the New Year's festivities. Autopilot is an acquired skill, my friends. So, there we were, January of 2011. Husband was becoming more and more angry every day, which turned into the worst abuse he could muster without leaving visible bruises on me. Let's see, his favorite behaviors were launching his giant keyring full of keys at my head and grazing my ear, throwing a punch with his fist at my face and punching holes in the wall instead, and picking up a TV and hurling it at me... back when TVs weighed about 500 pounds. Every bit of this occurred in our bedroom. Why is it that fighting parents believe that the walls and doors of their bedroom miraculously become soundproof? All 4 of my babies heard us... heard every horrible curse, scream, insult, things being thrown, and at the end of the altercation, my hysterical sobbing and screaming, "I CAN'T LIVE LIKE THIS ANYMORE!!!" I was starting to hear my voice of confidence taking shape. The event that brought my voice of confidence from deep inside my brain to my audible voice was the absolute last straw for me.

Husband and I decided to take the kids for dinner at one of their favorite places to eat. It was about 5 miles from our house. While we were finishing the meal, something was said... I cannot remember the exact dialogue that started this particular fight. Husband was starting to get loud and call me those favorite "pet" names of his... my "absolute favorite" name he called me was f****ng c**t b***h. I told him I wasn't going to listen to him anymore, told the kids to go home with dad, and I started walking home. And, at that, I stood up and started walking out the door. I had gotten to the parking lot of a church a few buildings down from the restaurant, and husband came speeding down the street and skidded into that parking lot right in front of me, dangerously close to hitting me with his truck. He demanded that I "get the f**k in the truck NOW!" To which I replied, NO! And tried to keep walking. He got out of that truck and stormed towards me. I took my cell phone out of my pocket and told him to leave me alone, or I'm calling the police. He immediately stopped, turned around, got back in that truck WITH MY CHILDREN IN IT, and peeled out of the parking lot, speeding down the street. All I could do was keep walking. I didn't know what to do. I felt like I had no other place to go, so I walked the rest of the way home. When I finally walked in the front door, all of the kids were in the living room trying to pretend they were okay. Husband yelled for me to go into the bedroom, so I did. He got in my face and started screaming at me every expletive known to man, and some that I think he made up. He then proceeded to take me by the arms and shake me violently. I fell to my knees sobbing, and then it happened. I was on my knees, and he took me by my arm and dragged me into the living room where my 4 precious and innocent children were sitting on the couch with their eyes as big as hubcaps. Husband dragged me to the middle of the living room floor where he proceeded to tell my children, "Do you see what your mother makes me do to her??? Don't EVER be like her!!!"

I couldn't believe what I just heard. What I make him do to me???

In that moment, it was as if time froze, and the fourth wall had broken in my brain. I could hear my voice inside my head saying "Why are you allowing this to happen? Dad would be so angry if he knew you continued allowing this abuse! You are better than this... you are stronger than this... you deserve better than this... your children deserve better than this!" I felt a spring of strength begin to well up from deep in my gut. It stood me up. I squared up in front of him.

Me: What did you say to MY children?

Him: You f****ng heard me!!!

Me: What I MAKE you do to me???

Him: That's right, you f****ng b***h, what YOU make ME do to you!

Me: That's it, I'M DONE!!!

Him: What do you mean, you're done?

Me: I'm DONE! I'm done with your name-calling, I'm done with your cheating, I'm done with your apathy, I'm...

Him: My WHAT?

Me: Your APATHY!

Him: Are you calling me STUPID?!?

He loved to ask me if I was calling him stupid when I'd use words that he had no idea what they meant.

Me: Yep! That's what that means... I'm calling you STUPID! Maybe I should get you a Webster's dictionary so you can look up all of the "big words" I use. Although, you'd have to know how to spell them, so I guess that won't work either... APATHY MEANS YOU DON'T CARE WHAT HAPPENS!

I'm done with your STUPIDITY! I'm just DONE! GET OUT OF MY HOUSE!!!

The second week of January 2011 is when I told him to leave. I had no idea how I would survive being a single mother of 4 children, but I didn't care. I could not allow that monster another day of showing my daughters that it's okay for a man to treat them like a worthless piece of garbage just because they're women. AND I couldn't allow that monster another day of showing my son that it's okay to treat a woman with utter disrespect, contempt, and abhorrence.

As much as my heart was broken because of my irreparable marriage and knowing how much this was going to hurt my children, what was even more heartbreaking was how the people who I thought were my friends turned their backs on me and chose to believe the lies being told about me and the events leading up to the end of my marriage. I was having a conversation with someone, who shall remain nameless, and when I called to tell them that Husband and I were getting a divorce, I was met with judgment and disdain.

Me: I know I made a covenant to God and to husband when we got married; however, I just cannot stay married to him.

Them: But marriage is for life! That's scripture!

Me: Yes, I know in most circumstances, divorce is not an option. However, there are stipulations given by God in scripture that give permission for divorce.

Them: No... marriage is for LIFE!

Me: Infidelity. That is a stipulation. When someone chooses to cheat on their spouse, they have broken the covenant, and that is grounds for a biblically allowable divorce.

Them: No... once you're married, you stay and fix it. You made your bed; you lie in it!

Me: Even when there's abuse? You want me to stay in a marriage where there's physical, mental, and emotional abuse on a daily basis?

Them: YOU MADE YOUR BED; YOU LIE IN IT!

As much as I love this nameless person, they are wrong. Abuse is WRONG, infidelity is WRONG! When infidelity occurs, and every means to mend the broken marriage has been exhausted and that spouse is still not willing to change their ways for the betterment of the marriage, divorce is the only option. And so, Husband and I started the process of getting a divorce.

PART 4

Confusion

CHAPTER 17

We See What We Want to See: *Operation Love Bomb*

When I was young, back in my high school days, you could find most of us on any given evening and weekend at "The Mall." Ah, yes, the mall. That ubiquitous destination wasting our time and money while simultaneously establishing the social hierarchy of the teenager. It was a much simpler time. It was a time when parents dropped off their teen at the mall without a care in the world. There were no cell phones to track anyone's location, no means to confirm meeting locations between friends, and the way "mom and dad" knew to pick us up was when we'd use the pay-phone to make a collect call home. When the home phone would ring and someone picked up, the message that person at home would hear went something like this: computer-sounding voice, "You have a collect call from…" and the next voice finishing that sentence would be a familiar one saying, "I'm ready mom, come pick me up." They didn't have to accept the charges, and we got a ride home for free; a win-win situation for all involved. It was during this time in pop-culture history, in the early 1990s, that there was a fad involving wall art. 3-D magic eye posters, to be exact. I don't know anyone who had one of these posters on their wall at home, but they were all over the mall kiosks. If you're unfamiliar with 1990s 3-D magic eye posters, I encourage you to Google it and look at the images. We would stop and look at these 3-D posters and go cross-eyed trying to figure out what the picture was supposed to be. I don't know that I ever truly saw the intention of those pictures, nor am I sure there ever truly was a distinct picture to be seen. We would say what we "saw." It's the Space Shuttle Challenger! No, it can't be... it has to be a Lisa Frank unicorn. No WAY! I see Madonna! We all saw what we wanted to see. Isn't that true in most ambiguous situations? We see what we want to see, especially when we're at our most vulnerable place in life.

It was the last week of January 2011. I was only 2 weeks into my new single-mom-hood. It was a Monday morning. There had been a lot of snowfall the week before; in fact, we already had several snow days off of school that winter. I was a teacher, and I hated, despised, and loathed snow days. Mostly because they added those missed days to the end of the school year. So, it's Monday morning, and I had just gotten the call that my school district would be off again because of the snow. My kids' district did NOT call a snow day that day. I was livid! So, there I was, alone in that big house. All the kids at school, and me at home wallowing in fear and sadness. I decided to scroll Facebook to see if there was anything that would distract my terribly overwhelmed and terrified mind. There was a post that caught my eye. A local radio DJ had posed a question regarding suggestions from his listeners for apps to add to his new iPad. The first comment under that post said: "I suggest staying away from the <competitive local radio station> app." That was rather clever, so I "liked" that comment, had a brief chuckle, and went along scrolling on my merry way. Just a few minutes later, I received a notification in my Facebook private message inbox. It seethed gooey smoothness... like melted Cool-Whip. It was from the guy whose post I liked about the iPad app. The message from that guy said, "Red hair, likes my comment, likes karaoke... I think I'm in love!" I didn't recognize the name of the person who sent me that message, so I stalked his Facebook page. Now, it is my mission to keep the identity of everyone else involved in my story anonymous, so I'm going to call this person Voldemort—he who shall not be named.

I was at the beginning of a divorce, I was at home during the day because of a snow day, so I decided to respond to this message, and a conversation began.

Voldemort: Red hair, likes my comment, likes karaoke... I think I'm in love!

Me: Do I know you?

V: No, but I WANT to know YOU!

Me: Okay... so, tell me about yourself.

V: I'm pretty boring. I work, I go to culinary school, I go home. That's about all... what about YOU?

Me: Wait... are you attached to anyone?

V: I'm attached to my 3 kids, my work, and school. That's it.

Me: Wow, you sound like a devoted dad. Where's their mom?

V: ... ...

Me: Did you leave?

V: No... sorry. Needed to answer nature. So, where were we? Oh, yes... you were telling me about yourself.

And that, my literary friends, was the beginning of the worst decision I've ever made in my life. And boy, have I made some super-doozy-horrible-mistakes in my time! Our Facebook conversation continued the rest of the afternoon off and on until I was told he had to pick up his kids from school, would I give him my cell phone number? We exchanged numbers and continued texting, and then he called, and we talked on the phone until the wee hours of the morning. I was lavished with so many compliments about my beauty, my intelligence, and my sense of humor... normal people would have started questioning motives. Me? Question a man who was my age, okay, a year younger than me, who was complimenting me and pouring it on thick as molasses outside in the winter? Nope. I ATE IT UP! Hook, line, and sinker.

V: So, Ms. Teacher, when do I get to meet you in person?

Me: Hmmm... I have no idea. I'm a teacher, so my hours are pretty solid Monday through Friday 7:30-3:30. And, you live almost an hour away from me.

V: It's only 45 minutes. I looked on MapQuest.

Me: Okay, 45 minutes away. The only way I could accommodate your schedule is to use a sick day.

V: Okay, so what's the problem?

Me: You want me to use a sick day to see you in person?

V: That's the only way you'll be able to see me.

"... the only way you'll be able to see me." Really? Now THAT should have been another "say, whaaa???" moment, but

I blew it off as a joke and gave a little chuckle and didn't think another thing about it. And, despite the start of red flags that I did not notice, or had no idea what to look out for, a relationship began. I couldn't afford to take a sick day, so I figured a way around that. I made the plans, I paid for the meal the first time we met because I needed to accommodate his sacrifice to meet me. I jumped into this relationship way too fast and overlooked the head-scratching moments because he was so generous with his love bombing. In case you aren't aware of this narcissistic tactic, buckle your seatbelts, my friends.

Love bombing is an abusive tactic used by a narcissist. "Love bombing is a form of psychological and emotional abuse that involves a person going above and beyond for you in an effort to manipulate you into a relationship with them... the love bomber's ultimate goal is not just to seek love, but to gain control over someone else. Over time, those grand gestures are an effort to manipulate you and make you feel indebted to and dependent on them... love bombing is most often associated with people who have an anxious or insecure attachment style or narcissistic personality disorder (NPD)."[1] This is exactly what happened to me. I was ecstatic when husband showed me attention, but he was never THIS "nice" to me! I thought all of the extravagant gifts for me, the over-the-top compliments, the extravagant toys and gifts for my kids, the planning our future together was because Voldemort was truly in love with me and my children. I had absolutely no clue what was really happening.

At the risk of jumping ahead in the story, I want to help anyone who is in a similar situation as I was to avoid the unneces-

---

1   https://www.medicinenet.com/what_is_love_bombing/article.htm

sary heartache of falling victim to this manipulative doorway to abuse. The first time I heard the term "love bombing" I had a hunch this was something I had experienced. I only wish I had learned of this narcissistic tactic before I met Voldemort.

Recently, as I was researching love bombling, I found information that was as if they had an invisible person with me and Voldemort everywhere we went every minute of the day for the next 7-plus years of my life. According to the Cleveland Clinic website, "And while they spend the early days over-extending themselves to win your favor, when the honeymoon phase ends and real-life kicks in, a person who love bombs may resort to more manipulative tactics like gaslighting or domestic abuse in order to keep their partners around."[2]

"Love bombing is a situation that can be hard to get out of because you may not know how genuine someone is until it's too late," says Dr. Tiani.[3]

Ladies and gentlemen, hear me and hear me well! If it looks too good to be true and you can feel in the depths of your soul that something is deeply wrong with how someone is over-extending themselves to win your favor, run... run far, run fast, and don't look back! Do not pass "Go!" and do not collect 200 dollars. That advice is not just for Monopoly players. If you're not sure whether the person's expressions of affection are genuine or manipulative, here is yet another sign that demonstrates what manipulative rather than genuine looks like. We, Voldemort and I, had been dating about six weeks at this point. We were pulling

---

2   https://health.clevelandclinic.org/love-bombing/
3   https://health.clevelandclinic.org/love-bombing/

into the parking lot of a local karaoke bar for a fun night of singing and this was the conversation:

Him: Ready for a fun night of singing?

Me: Absolutely!

Him: I love you so much!

Me: *smiling*

Him: I said, I love you so much!

Me: *nodding and smiling*

Him: Aren't you going to tell me you love me?

Me: *panicked smiling*

Him: Well... aren't you???

Me: *panicked and nervous smiling*

Him: *angrily yelling* What the f**k? I tell you that I love you and you're just sitting there with a dumb smile planted on your face and you won't even tell me that you love me back?????

Me: *panicked and no longer smiling*

Him: This is bullsh*t! What the f**k is wrong with you? Thanks a lot for nothing! I've spent all of this money on you AND your kids, and this is the thanks I get? You can't even say you love me back? Unbelievable!

Me: *sheepishly speaks* I love you too.

Him: There, now was that so difficult? You're so adorable! Now, let's go have a fun night of singing!

Now, before you say "Uh... DUHHH! Of course that's manipulative behavior!", check out this research and you might understand where I was coming from. He was deep in the throes of The Idealization Phase.

Love bombing tends to occur in three phases. The first phase is called The Idealization Phase: "During this phase, your partner bombards you with excessive love and affection to draw you in and convince you to let your guard down. At first, it may seem too good to be true or easy to be swept off your feet."[4]

This is exactly what happened to me, and I chose to see what I wanted to see. I wanted to see my knight in shining armor come to my rescue, pick me and my children up, put us on the back of his white steed, and ride off into the sunset. Voldemort told me, more times than I can count, that I was his broken porcelain doll that had been shattered and he was my broom and dustpan; that he was sweeping up all of my broken pieces and putting me back together again. Isn't that so sweet!?!

No? It isn't?

Well, NOW I know that!

---

4   https://health.clevelandclinic.org/love-bombing/

CHAPTER 18

The Biggest Mistake of My Life: *RED FLAGS! RED FLAGS EVERYWHERE!*

That Dr. Tiani from the Cleveland Clinic sure is one smart cookie. I didn't know that what I chose to see rather than the reality of what was actually happening was forcing me into a situation where I saw no way out, where I felt completely stuck in the mess of my own making. I met Voldemort at the end of January 2011. My divorce was in process and far from over. Husband made it very clear that because I kicked him out of the house, I would never see "one red cent" of money to help pay the mortgage, you know, the mortgage for the house where his children were staying, and it was my responsibility to refinance the mortgage. Well, the problem with that, genius husband, is that I had to have my final divorce papers in order to refinance, and husband was dragging his feet in completing every requirement we were given to get that divorce final. He couldn't wrap his precious little mind around that fact, and so, we went into foreclosure. I was about to lose my house because of him and had no earthly idea what I was going to do. It was the middle of May 2011, and my children and I were about to be homeless.

During the process of love-bombing me, Voldemort was also love-bombing my 4 children. He had them convinced that he was the best thing since sliced bread and, "It isn't just a coincidence that I met you and your mom at this time in your life. I was meant to rescue you all from homelessness." My poor, innocent, and defenseless children were hoodwinked just as much as I was. Voldemort decided he had the perfect solution to our foreclosure problem. How about we buy a house together? It's okay to let that old house go because by the time the bank takes possession, we'll already be in our new home together. Never mind that the kids will have to change schools. It will be a new school year! New home, new school year, new start to life. It will all be completely perfect and wrapped up in a new-home-size bow. And so, that's what we did. We had to apply together because neither one of us had good enough credit to be approved for a mortgage on our own. Yes, I know, that's yet another red flag.

In early July, we moved into our new home together. It was a huge house with an even bigger mortgage payment. Voldemort justified that this particular home was the home we just had to buy because we needed the room for all 4 of my children as well as all 3 of his children when it was his weekend with his kids. That made sense. He also assured me that with his $95,000 a year job, it would be no problem to pay the mortgage. Please don't ask if he really had a job that paid him $95,000 a year because you know the answer to that. He did not.

We were still in the Idealization phase of the love-bombing, so I continued in my oblivion, convinced that he was going to take care of me and my kids for the rest of our lives. And that was despite the figurative "elephant in the room." What figurative "elephant" am I referring to? That would be his children's mother. You know, the woman he was still married to that I didn't know he was still married to? The one who Voldemort told me about two weeks into our relationship, "Oh, yeah... I'm at the beginning of a divorce too."

RED FLAG, RED FLAG, RED FLAG!!!

What he did NOT tell me, that I found out much later from his mother, was that the marriage he was still in when we met was, by all intents and purposes, a good marriage with no problems. When he asked his then-wife for a divorce, she never saw it coming. I had absolutely NO idea about any of that at the time; how could I know? I took everything he told me at face value. I also didn't know that his family called me "home wrecker" behind my back and despised me. Something else that came as a shock to me was that Voldemort was in a horrible legal situation with his cousin over a truck that he had sold to that cousin without a legal title. He was trying to find an escape hatch out of that situation when he first sent me that Facebook message. So many, oh so many lies!

So, this is where we are in this dumpster fire... I mean, this part of the story...

My divorce was final on May 30, 2011. Voldemort was still in the process of getting his divorce finalized when we moved into our new home that July. We were starting to find our new norm, and then the new school year started. My poor children were already devastated by the divorce, and now they had to change schools. We were still living within the boundaries of the same school district, but not in the same buildings within the district. I was in a home with the king of justification and finagling. He had convinced me that this was a good move for the kids. That this is the best thing that could have ever happened to them and that they would be happier in the long run. That was farther from the truth than the east is from the west. My babies were miserable, struggling, deeply hurting, and none of them would tell me anything except that they were all okay and happy. And so, my oblivion continued.

Summer turned to fall as it does every year. In October, Voldemort and I had planned on attending a fall festival with some friends. As we were getting ready to leave, he approached me in the bedroom with a little box, got down on one knee, and asked me to marry him. I was so happy. I thought to myself, "Finally, someone loves me enough to give me a REAL proposal!" My ring was a $20 knock-off from Overstock dot com, but I didn't care. I decided it was wise to be so careful with our money. I really want to insert the eye-rolling emoji at this point, along with the smacking my head emoji because, really? Yep, we were officially engaged before his divorce was final. The kids seemed excited for us, but not as much as I had hoped. It seemed they were not as happy as they had been all summer. I had no idea why that was.

We blinked, and it was the end of November. This Thanksgiving would be the first Thanksgiving that I would not be with my children; they would be with their dad. I was devastated by this. Voldemort decided it would be wise to go ahead and get our marriage license since we decided to have an early December wedding, so the day before Thanksgiving, we did just that. Why did he decide on that particular timing? Because the Tuesday before Thanksgiving was when his divorce was final, and we had to wait 24 hours before applying for our marriage license. That's right, 24 hours after his divorce was final, we got our marriage license. Isn't that SO romantic?

The kids were with their Dad from after school the Tuesday before Thanksgiving until the following Monday. Voldemort informed me that getting our marriage license the Wednesday before Thanksgiving would be a good way to help my heart be happy. Wasn't that just so sweet? He was always thinking of me... at least that's how completely clueless I was to the manipulation that continued. The problem was, the Devaluation phase of the love-bombing was evolving right under my nose, and I still didn't smell the stink radiating from the entire situation. What's the Devaluation phase, you ask? According to the Cleveland Clinic, it is "...once you've let your guard down and get comfortable in the relationship, red flags start to appear. Your partner may try to exert control over you in a variety of ways. They may become more demanding of your time and get upset when you make plans without them. They may also try to limit access to your friends and family, and gaslight you into thinking nothing is wrong with their behavior. In the most severe cases, they may use fear and intimidation to get you to behave differently than you normally would and even resort to physical violence."[5] Looking back on the events over the course of the fall of 2011, I can see that devaluation so clearly.

Yeah, yeah... hindsight, 20/20, blah, blah, blah.

I'm quite ashamed of the fact that I allowed all of this to happen, so let's get to the big turning point that was the mark of the beginning of devaluation.

It was the beginning of November, and we knew that Voldemort's divorce would be final any day. On this particular Thursday, the kids were with their dad, so we decided to celebrate the

---

5   https://health.clevelandclinic.org/love-bombing/

impending joyous occasion by going out of town. We went back to Voldemort's old "stomping grounds" to stay in a hotel and sing some karaoke. On our way to check in to the hotel, I started getting a really deep, dark feeling in the pit of my chest as if I knew something bad was going to happen... it felt like a scary premonition to me. I couldn't explain it.

Okay, time-out...

Before I go any further with this explanation, you need to know a few specific important details. The cell phone that Voldemort had was purchased by me and was on MY cell phone plan. He was "so grateful" to be away from his ex's cell phone plan and thanked me profusely when we put him and his new phone on my plan. He even went so far as to make sure I knew all of his passwords: his phone, email account, and any other password he had. I was told that because that phone was technically MY phone, I had permission to look at it at any time I deemed necessary.

Okay, time-in...

Voldemort and I arrived at the hotel we were going to stay in that night after karaoke. He had parked in front of the hotel and went inside to get us checked in. He had left his phone on the charger in the car. I proceeded to open his phone, and the first thing that popped up was a text conversation between him and one of the girls in the friend group he was a part of. She was married to someone who was also a part of this friend group. It was NOT a group conversation at all. It was just between him and her. As I read through the messages and looked at the pictures that they had exchanged with each other... forgive my crudeness, but they were dick-pics and tit-pics along with other parts of her that I cannot unsee, the dark pit in my chest grew bigger and enveloped every part of me. The things he said to her in those texts were identical to the intimate things he had said to me on many occasions in our relationship. I felt like I had been punched in the gut, but I tried desperately to keep my emotions in check and not say anything to him about it. He got back in the car and started to drive us out of the parking lot to the karaoke bar where we were going to meet with some of his friends. I was silent and unsuccessfully tried to push myself into the car door to get as far away from him as possible.

Voldemort: Baby, are you okay? What's wrong?

Me: Nothing... I'm fine.

V: Now, you know you can tell me anything that's troubling you.

Me: Remember when you said I had every right to look at your phone at any time I thought necessary?

V: *His face promptly morphed from Dr. Jekyll to Mr. Hyde* WHAT DID YOU DO?

Me: And you gave me all of your passwords to everything and told me I had free reign in all of your accounts?

V: WHAT THE F**K DID YOU DO?

Me: Why are you texting with [that woman's name]?

Voldemort, who was driving MY car, whipped into the nearest parking lot, grabbed his phone, jumped out of the car, and started SCREAMING at me.

V: WHAT THE F**K DID YOU DO, YOU F****NG B***H???

Then, he proceeded to launch that phone as close as he could to me on the concrete beside my foot, and it broke into a million pieces. He then charged at me, grabbed me by my arms, picked me up, and screamed at me while shaking me with all of his strength.

V: WHO THE F**K DO YOU THINK YOU ARE, GOING THROUGH MY PRIVATE PHONE? WHO THE F**K DO YOU THINK YOU ARE, READING MY PRIVATE TEXT MESSAGES???

Then he threw me to the ground and started pacing around me.

V: You worthless piece of SH*T! Don't you EVER go into MY phone without permission again, DO YOU HEAR ME, B***H???

I was stunned; I was in utter shock. I didn't see this coming a mile away. After a long pause, I heard something from him that shook me to my core.

V: Baby, I'm sorry… but you know this is your fault, don't you? You got into MY phone without my permission, and because of that, you made me hurt you. Why would you do that?

I couldn't believe what I was hearing.

Me: But… but you said…

V: What? What did I say?

Me: You said that was… that I could… that any time I …

V: I don't know what you're talking about. Look, you made a mistake. It happens. How about we forget all about this silly cell phone stuff and get to karaoke? I love you… and I can't wait to hear you sing for me, baby!

I didn't know what to do. I was too terrified to move. I felt my world come crashing down around me, again, and yet I was convinced it was my fault! I tried to just ignore the screaming voice in my head saying, GET OUT! GET OUT NOW!!! But I couldn't get out. I had bought a house with this man. I had already uprooted my kids once; they didn't need that to happen again. And, besides, this was all my fault. I thought to myself, "I should have ignored that deep, dark feeling I had in my chest telling me that something wasn't right. I'm sure this was a fluke, that this will never happen again. I just need to be more careful with my actions, that's all." So, I stayed in that relationship. I felt trapped, like I had no other choice. All of the strength, the voice I had found, the way I was able to get away from such abuse before, was gone. The love bombing built up this creature, Voldemort, to a place that I felt indebted to him no matter what actions he chose. Remember, in the devaluation phase, once you've let your guard down and get comfortable in the relationship, this is when they gaslight you into thinking nothing is wrong with their behavior, use fear and intimidation to get you to behave differently than you normally would and even resort to physical violence. This is exactly what happened to me. Day by day my newly discovered self-worth was eroding into non-existence at the hands of Voldemort. His web of love bombing, and now this added layer of devaluation, made breaking free from him that much more difficult.

Back to Thanksgiving week, 2011. It was the Wednesday before Thanksgiving, and we had gotten our marriage license. The next day, Thanksgiving Day, he had to work the morning shift, so after he was off work, we went to his family's Thanksgiving dinner on his mom's side. They didn't know we were engaged. I know, now, that's how he planned it. He didn't want them to know, despite the obvious ring on my finger. The rest of the week, that Friday and Saturday, were rather uneventful, and then came that Sunday. Voldemort was at work. His shift ended at 2 pm. He decided that was the perfect day to get married. He told me to call my dad, my best friends (a married couple, and he was an ordained minister), and we should meet at a specific police department/courthouse where a friend of his was working, and we should get married on that day. I did as I was told that day, and I married Voldemort at that police station/courthouse. My kids had no idea what was happening. Voldemort convinced me they would be so excited about our surprise. I probably don't need to tell you, but they were NOT excited about it AT ALL. They were completely devastated that they were not a part of the wedding. There was nothing that I could do to change what had happened. I just did my best to convince them that we would all be one very happy family. I couldn't even convince myself.

CHAPTER 19

No, She Doesn't!
How Did Charlie Brown's Teacher Get In Here?

One of the few escapes I had as a child was during the holiday season, the end of October through Christmas, because CBS would show three of my favorite cartoon specials: It's The Great Pumpkin, Charlie Brown; A Charlie Brown Thanksgiving; and A Charlie Brown Christmas. In every Charlie Brown (also known as Peanuts) cartoon, there would be a scene where Lucy would hold a football on the ground, much like for a field goal, and she would convince Charlie Brown to kick that football. At first, he would say no because she would always move the ball before he could kick it, and he would always end up falling on his back. Lucy would give some excuse and then a convincing argument as to why she WOULDN'T move the football this time. Charlie Brown would reluctantly agree, he would run towards the ball to kick it, and at the last second, Lucy would move the ball AGAIN, Charlie Brown would end up on his back AGAIN, and Lucy would explain why she moved the ball AGAIN. As a young child, what I didn't understand about the Peanuts cartoon is why we would never see an adult, and when there is an adult portrayed, it was usually their schoolteacher. All we would see is their legs and feet, and their voices would be indistinct and muddled... that famous "wah WAH wah" sound. You remember that sound, don't you? It sounded like a softly muted trumpet that just said "wah, wah, wah" over and over. I just could not wrap my little girl brain around how these Peanuts kids could have a complete conversation with their teacher and understand them despite the wah-wah voice.

All right, I've avoided this chapter long enough. Here we go…

As soon as Voldemort's divorce was final in November, his child support payments started. I was happy to make sure that payment was made; however, it was becoming more and more difficult to make ends meet despite his supposed exorbitant pay-checks he was earning at his job. I had no idea where the money was going, and he made it a practice to convince me that it was my fault. Didn't I remember spending all of that money getting drunk at the bar? Because, as he told me, I was a drunk.

I wasn't a drunk!

He was taking my money out of my purse and taking it to the boat to gamble, or to play slots when we went to karaoke. And I was required by him to attend karaoke every night it was available. He had us on a weekly regimented karaoke bar rotation.

All I wanted to do was to make sure our monthly bills were paid and there was enough food for the entire family and fuel for the cars to get us back and forth to work. Oh yeah, I forgot to mention, his child support payment was more than our mortgage, which was more than I'd ever had to pay for housing in my entire life. We had continued attending the church I was taking my kids to since my youngest was just a toddler, and when we would go, Voldemort would try to hit up the pastor and deacons for finan-cial help. He would convince me to help him beg the church to pay our bills, which I did despite my extremely overwhelming embarrassment. He would sit in the sanctuary of the church, and he would weep and moan, crying out, "Lord, why won't you help us, your humble servants? We know your timing is perfect, so please would you see to it that the leadership of this church will help us by paying our bills?" Of course, he would wail this loudly where he thought the men of the church would hear him. Then, when they'd tell us NO, he'd badmouth the entire leadership and every adult in that church all the way home. Gee, I wonder why they wouldn't help us. Could it be they had a gift of discernment? Maybe?

Somehow, we had survived up until the end of the first week of December 2011. We had no money for the kids' Christmas gifts, no money for Christmas dinner, and no money to pay our bills. We were overdrawn to the maximum overdraft protection amount and barely had enough fuel for the cars to get us to work until we got paid again. I was at the point that I didn't think I could handle any more crises.

The first Friday of December 2011, I was finishing up my last class of the day when I received a call from the nurse at my 3rd child's school.

Nurse: I need you to pick up [3rd child] as soon as possible.

Me: But it's the end of the day. Can't she just ride the bus home?

Nurse: No, ma'am. I'm really concerned. In my professional opinion, she should not put any weight on her right leg. Please come pick her up and have her seen as soon as possible.

Me: Okay?

And so, I did just that.

When I got to her school, her right leg looked like she was trying to smuggle a giant softball inside her jeans at the knee. It really did look bad, like we were going to have to cut her jeans, otherwise they would be stuck on her. She didn't seem to be in a lot of pain. According to her, at recess, a little boy knocked her down on the concrete part of the playground. She said she knew it wasn't on purpose and he felt really bad about knocking her over. I wasn't surprised at how easily she fell. 3rd child was a tiny little girl. She was so light, if she had an umbrella, a good wind could pick her up and carry her away like Mary Poppins. I rushed her to the pediatrician's office. Luckily, they were able to fit her into their evening schedule.

When we arrived at the doctor's office, we were quickly taken to a room and then we were promptly directed to take her to the X-ray office around the corner, that they are expecting us, and to bring the disc with the pictures back to the office... ASAP. It was a Friday, so First Husband would be taking the kids for the weekend anyway. I texted him to let him know what was going on and that we might be late to the exchange location where we'd always meet to trade the kids. Where we did the kid exchange was a neutral public location, and I felt safer there than at my, or his, house. I told First Husband, if he wanted, he could meet me at the Dr's office when he got off work.

At the X-ray office, the tech called 3rd child's name. My baby girl was beside herself in panic. She was terrified of the X-ray. I told her it doesn't hurt at all... that all they do is take a picture. She didn't care. She had no idea what was happening to her. My poor baby was in panic mode over getting X-rays. She found her courage and went with the tech. Within a matter of minutes, 3rd child was finished, and we were given a disc and told to immediately go back to the pediatrician's office for further information. I didn't think anything of what was going on. It was a simple hematoma; I was sure of it. Maybe the growth plate was affected. Maybe they'd need to do surgery to fix the growth plate. That's all it could be, right? No biggie!

When we arrived, again, at the pediatrician's office, it was the end of the workday, and the nurses were going home. Weird! Why couldn't this wait until the morning? I wondered. We were taken back to one of the exam rooms and we waited... and we waited, and waited, and then waited some more. After what seemed to be 2 days' worth of waiting, the doctor FINALLY walked into the room.

Dr: [3rd child], I need you to find your siblings in the waiting room. I need to talk to Mom for a minute.

Wait, what? That's weird. I've never had a doctor do that before. What's going on here?

Me: Is that really necessary? *nervous giggle*

Dr: *after 3rd child closed the door... sits directly in front of me and takes my hands with tears in her eyes* I'm sorry... I'm so very sorry.

Me: Dr [doctor's name], what is wrong? Has the growth plate been damaged? What is going on here?

Dr: I'm so sorry, but... your child... [3rd child] has CANCER.

Me: No, she doesn't.

Dr: Yes, I'm afraid she does. Your daughter has cancer. We can see it on the X-ray.

Me: No, no, she doesn't have cancer! You cannot see cancer on an X-ray... no, it has to be something else. What else could it be? No... NO SHE DOESN'T!

Dr: *Wah WAH... wah, wah, wah, WAH... WAH wah...*

At this point, I started to wonder... why do I hear Charlie Brown's teacher, and where did she come from?

Me: I'm sorry, but I need you to go get my husband. I can't understand you... and I'm not going to remember anything you say. Please go get my husband and he can tell me what you're saying...

The doctor left the exam room then returned with Voldemort, who then sat and listened to what the doctor had to say. I couldn't understand anything. All I could hear was static and the sound of Charlie Brown's teacher. At this point, first husband walked in the room and, again, I had to hear those horrific words again... "your daughter has cancer." I just could not wrap my brain around it. No, she doesn't! She CAN'T have cancer. THIS CAN NOT BE HAPPENING!

I heard some of the important things the doctor was saying. Be at Children's Hospital in the morning... pack a bag... she could be there weeks... full battery of tests... biopsy... orthopedic surgeon... good luck...

I watched myself walk out of that room, through the waiting area, get in my car, and drive to my house. We gathered the children in my living room along with first husband and his new wife to tell all of the kids that the doctor believes 3rd child has cancer. We formulated a plan, the kids went with first husband, and about 12 hours later, we all would be at St. Louis Children's Hospital.

Remember back in Chapter 6 when I talked about my bad life choices? Well, as embarrassing as this is, I promised myself that I would tell my story with truth and full disclosure to the best of my ability. That means, you deserve to hear all of it... the good, the bad, and the oh-so-very ugly. Well, here's the reality of what happened the night my daughter was diagnosed with cancer.

When first husband took the kids to his house, I was left in my living room alone. I was alone, I was panicked, I was in shock, I was terrified. Voldemort was in our four-seasons room adjacent to the living room and as usual, he was smoking. I absolutely hated cigarettes. I hated the stink, I hated the cost, I hated everything about smoking. I walked into the four-seasons room and, according to Voldemort, I looked like a green ghost. I started trembling; it was more than that. I would say it was an equal mix of trembling and shaking, much like a magnitude 10 earthquake, and I couldn't stop. It was obvious I was literally going into shock. Voldemort ran a warm bath with lavender to try to calm me. All that did was turn my plain old bathtub into what looked like a jacuzzi tub. He told me to stay there, that he'd be right back. When he returned, I was still in full shock mode. He took a large McDonald's cup and filled it with Jim Beam bourbon and walked back out to his smoking area. I chugged all of that Jim Beam in one gulp. It was almost a fifth of bourbon and it did absolutely nothing to calm me. I was getting scared. I climbed out of the tub, put on my robe, and shook my way back out to where Voldemort looked like a chimney in the winter. I told him I was getting scared, that I needed to go to the emergency room. He stood from his seat, walked to me, and handed me his cigarette.

V: Take a drag of this.

Me: *still shaking* No way! I'm a singer, I'm a teacher. There is no way I'm going to do that!

V: TAKE. A. DRAG!

Me: FINE!

What Voldemort did not see or hear was the internal shouting match that ensued. In my mind's eye, there was a boxing ring with what appeared to be 2 versions of me: one in each corner. One side screaming about what a mistake smoking is... how it's a disgusting habit... how it would make me a hypocrite to start smoking as I had been one of those who loudly criticized anyone who chose such a repulsive habit. The other side was screaming about how we couldn't afford an emergency room visit... that it was just one cigarette... how important it was to pull myself together because there was a much more dire situation I was facing so if that meant trying to calm myself through the means of a cigarette, it needed to be done. I probably don't need to tell you, that fight was over faster than when Mike Tyson bit off Evander Holyfield's ear.

I inhaled, I exhaled, and when I did, it's like every trembling nerve exited my body along with the smoke. The world slowed

down, I sat down, and finished that stupid God-forsaken cigarette. From that point on, I couldn't survive without them. I was
so disgusted with Voldemort for introducing me to such a disgusting habit... I hated myself even more because of it. Did I finally
calm down enough so that I didn't have to go to the emergency
room? Yes. Did I sleep at all that night? Not at all. The trembling
stopped, the terror did not.

Bright and early, we were at St. Louis Children's Hospital. We
had absolutely no idea what we were about to experience. No
one can have even a bit of a clue about what we were about to
experience; not unless you've been thrown into "the club." When
you are a cancer parent, you are immediately and without your
consent forced into one of the worst "clubs" known to man and
womankind. Hey, I had already been chapter president of the
I-survived-childhood-sexual-abuse club, the I-survived-a-near-fa-
tal-miscarriage club, the my-baby-died-and-was-born-still club,
why not work my way up the ranks in the my-baby-has-cancer-
and-might-not-live club as well? For the record, I would happily
give every one of those club-president meeting gavels back from
whence they came; they are not all they're cracked up to be.

Our entire entourage slowly walked into the main entrance of
St. Louis Children's Hospital. We looked like tourists' sight-see-
ing in a foreign country. We didn't know where to go, we didn't
know the "language," we had our packed suitcases and no clue
what to do next. We were greeted by a security guard who had
obviously been there way too long already. We were rudely asked
why we were there. Luckily, I had my paper with all of our ap-
pointments listed. I showed it to the guard, and she pointed down
the hall, grunted something about the elevator and a different

floor. We nodded and, like a band of zombies, we found the elevator. We walked into a room and a kind woman with a sympathetic face greeted us. My baby was poked, prodded, IV'd, and examined like she was a science experiment. For a nine-year-old little girl, she showed such bravery and courage. The rest of us, not so much. At the end of the day, we were told that the biopsy would take 7 days... SEVEN days before we would have a result.

SEVEN DAYS? With all of the medical advancements, it still takes 7 days for biopsy results. And so, we were told they would call us as soon as they had the results, and they sent us all home. We tried to keep our minds occupied with anything else, but that's difficult to do when you have no money. Christmas was less than 3 weeks away, we had no money, and I was quickly running out of hope. Maybe, just this once, I'd see a miracle?

CHAPTER 20

Permanent Options:
Could I Get a Compass, Please?

I remember, back in the day, when arcades were all the rage. In one room, there were multiple video games just waiting to be conquered. We would spend every quarter we could find for just one more shot at breaking the score record. In kid-world, putting your initials at the top of the leaderboard was as prestigious as winning the Super Bowl. Nowadays, we as a culture have evolved into a more personal and complex game: Escape Rooms. What is an escape room? I'm so glad you asked. According to "Professor Google," an escape room, also known as an escape game, is a game in which a team discovers clues, solves puzzles, and completes tasks in one or more rooms in order to accomplish a specific goal in a limited amount of time. The goal is often to escape from the site of the game. Now, I've never been to an escape room; I'm not so sure that my complex PTSD would serve my team well in that situation. From what I've heard from those who have tried this newfangled game, there isn't much information to go on in order to escape. Clues are found, puzzles are puzzling, tasks are undertaken, and hopefully, before time is up, the team can find their way out of the challenge. If that's your thing, you do you. This is a no-judgment zone. For me, I've had about 5 lifetimes full of attempting to navigate through difficult challenges trying to escape not for the fame, but for my survival.

We waited those 7 days to hear something, anything, about the biopsy. All we knew at that point was to not allow 3rd child to put any weight on her right leg until they could give us more information. Finally, FINALLY, I received a call. The name that came up on my cell phone said StLChildren's. I prayed one last time, "Please, PLEASE don't let this be cancer!" only to hear from the voice on the phone, "We have confirmed, your daughter has cancer. It is Osteosarcoma." Once again, I watched myself writing the information I was given... bone cancer... oncology... 9th floor of the hospital... more tests... treatment plan... orthopedic surgeon... chemotherapy...

What they didn't give me was a compass. Over the course of the last few months, my divorce from first husband was final, I lost my home, I bought a new home with the man who, at the time, I thought was the man of my dreams, then married that man less than a month before finding out my daughter has cancer. What would have been helpful at this point? A life-directing compass, please? My fear of the unknown is epic, so to me, it felt like I had been dropped in one of those escape rooms, it was completely dark, and I had no directions, no flashlight, no information. Nothing! My baby was looking to me for help and answers, and I had no idea what to say or which direction to go. All I could do, all any of us could do, was go a day at a time and allow the doctors to lead us.

The day after we received the confirmation of Osteosarcoma, we were back at Children's Hospital to meet the oncology team. It was me, Voldemort, first husband, and first husband's new wife in a meeting room facing a team of doctors. They were all extremely kind to us and so accommodating. We were then given a giant binder. I'm talking about a 6-inch binder. In that binder was a roadmap, a compass if you will, containing everything you need to know about what my daughter was about to go through as well as stuff I really didn't want to know, but they were legally obligated to inform us. A plan was already in place as to how they were going to save my daughter's life. They had already been in contact with the orthopedic surgery department from Washington University, one of the most prestigious institutions in the United States. It is renowned for being among the world's leaders in teaching, research, and patient care. It is also adjacent to St Louis Children's Hospital. My child would be the patient of a doctor out of Washington University who is one of the best orthopedic surgeons in the nation AND he is also a professor at the university. He teaches at the university... HE TEACHES THERE! He teaches orthopedic surgery students how to do their job! If anyone was going to be my daughter's surgeon, I wanted it to be someone who had to know their craft forwards and backwards well enough to be able to teach it.

So, the plan of attack to get my daughter cancer-free was a two-part process involving chemotherapy and surgery. Step number one was two-fold. We needed to have her Broviac surgically inserted, as well as remove the metastatic cancer from her lung. Wait... what? Metastatic cancer? Yep. Apparently, the impact of her fall caused part of the Osteosarcoma to break away from the original tumor and ended up in her lung.

And, not to be overlooked, what in the world is a Broviac? It's a fancy kind of central line. "A central line is a catheter, or soft flexible tube, that is placed into a large blood vessel near the center of the body. Central lines are used to give fluids, medications, blood products, nutrition and to draw blood for labs. A Broviac is a type of central line that allows for long-term access to blood. There is an entry site where the catheter enters the blood vessel and an exit site where the central line comes out of the body. The Broviac has a cuff under the skin near the exit site. The cuff is a thick fabric ring that circles the catheter line. As healing takes place over the first few weeks, skin will grow around the cuff to help hold the line in place. This also helps to keep germs from entering into, or around, the line. The central line, the Broviac, is placed in the operating room while the child is under general anesthesia. There would be a small cut in the neck for the entry site. It is usually covered with a steri-strip. Stitches may be placed at the exit site to help hold the catheter in place and is covered with a sterile dressing." My baby girl would have a 2-line Broviac, which we would be required to care for daily to try to keep her from getting any infections. The bad news is this was her first surgery ever. The worse news is this was only the beginning of a many-years-long string of surgeries. The good news is that having this Broviac kept her from being stuck with a needle for every blood draw, IV, and non-oral medication.

There are so many things I absolutely adore about St Louis Children's Hospital. On the top of that list is the fact that these doctors don't play around at all. As soon as the biopsy was confirmed, they were on it. The plan of action set, the timeline set, and it would all begin the week after Christmas. They wanted her to have the most normal Christmas possible before our reality was shaken for the rest of our lives.

Our next big meeting was with the surgeon. We were all put in this tiny exam room waiting to hear the surgeon's plan. Any time the 4 of us (me, Voldemort, first husband, and first husband's new wife) had to be together, it was extremely awkward at best. Add a heaping helping of stress, a gallon of worry, and a dash of resentment, and you've got yourself a smorgasbord of "get me the hell out of here!"

Finally, the doctor walked in.

Dr: Sorry to keep you waiting.

Me: No worries / First Husband: We have been waiting a very long time! / First Husband's New Wife: We thought you forgot about us. / Voldemort: It's about time!

Dr: Well, I'm glad you're all here. There's a decision you have to make, and I need to give you all of the necessary information for you to make an informed decision. You don't need to make this decision today. I want you all to think it over and talk about it together.

Me, FH, FHNW, V: *biggest eyerolls in recorded history*

Dr: So, there are 4 options I'm going to cover today... *opens several tabs on his computer.*

Dr continues: Option #1: We do a complete amputation of her right leg. As you can see points to the CT scan on the computer monitor the cancer goes all the way from the patella to about 2 inches below the hip socket.

FH: The patella?

Dr: That's the kneecap.

FH: Oh

Dr: The problem with this is it would leave nothing to attach a prosthetic, so option #1 really isn't an option.

He paused

Dr: Option #2 is we remove the cancerous femur and replace it with a cadaver bone. The problem with this is that as she grows, and she's still got A LOT of growing to do, we'd have to do another surgery to replace it probably every year, if not more, for the length of her right leg to keep up with the length of her left leg, so option #2 really isn't an option either.

Dr continues: Option #3 is we remove the cancerous femur and replace it with a metal rod. The problem with this is that as she grows, we would have to do another surgery to lengthen it probably every year, if not more, for the length of her right leg to keep up with the length of her left leg. Over time it would end up pushing out her hip and that would cause a whole lot of other problems for her, so option #3 really isn't an option either.

FH: Now, wait a minute Doc, you told us we have 4 options and now you're saying 3 of the options aren't really options??? What the fk, pardon my French.

Dr: *opens iPad video* Well, option #4 is this...

We then watched a short video from the Mayo Clinic describing the procedure that Dr wanted us to choose. The procedure is called Rotationplasty. If you go to YouTube and search Mayo Clinic Rotationplasty, you might find the video that we saw. The best way to explain Rotationplasty without any visual aids is this: Rotationplasty is a surgery for bone cancer at the knee. A surgeon removes the cancerous part of the leg, including the tumor. The lower leg is reattached at the sight of the amputation, but it's rotated 180 degrees. The ankle joint functions as the new knee joint. The result is to wear a prosthesis, or artificial limb. Rotationplasty is a more functional alternative to an above-the-knee full leg amputation.

The video has an animated depiction of the surgery showing how the cancerous portion of the leg is removed, then the healthy portion of the leg, from below the patella to the feet, is turned 180 degrees (backwards) and attached where the cancerous part was removed. This leaves the patient with a backwards foot.

A backwards foot? Yes, a backwards foot.

As I watched this video, I was struggling to comprehend what this doctor wanted to do to my child. This is our only real option? Permanent disfigurement??? As I started down a rabbit hole of utter despair, I heard my 3rd child shout out from behind me.

3rd child: I'm gonna have a backwards foot??? THAT IS SOOO COOL!!!

Ah, the wisdom of a nine-year-old!

Dr: You are so right... it IS cool! And it's the best... really, it's the only option we have.

Me: Doctor, if you believe this is what's best for 3rd child, I say do it. We don't need to think about it.

FH: Now, wait just a g*d**m minute here. Don't I get a say in this???

Me: You really need to argue this?

FH: I think we should at least look at this from all sides. We got time to decide, don't we doc?

Dr: Yes, you have a few weeks before we need to do any surgeries. We're hoping the chemo shrinks the tumor to the point that it kills the tumor completely before we do anything else.

FH: Ok, then. Let's not be too hasty... let's talk about this.

I was dumbfounded. What was there to talk about? The option for the best quality of life for this little girl was Rotationplasty. Why does everything have to be a fight with that man?

The new year came and went... it was January 2012, and my daughter was beginning the literal fight for her life. We were given a regimented schedule of chemotherapy treatments that would all be done in-patient. The schedule was almost 10 months of high-dose Methotrexate, along with Doxorubicin, Cisplatin, Ifosfamide, Cyclophosphamide, Etoposide...

... and a partridge in a pear tree!

The chemo schedule started January 2, then on March 16 we would pause the chemo and have the surgery that we chose, then after recovering from that, go back to the chemo treatment. Easy-peasy, right? Now, all I needed is to have someone take a stick or a rock or a sledgehammer of some sort and knock some ever-loving sense into first husband.

Our follow-up appointment with the orthopedic surgeon was when we had to give him our final decision. This probably goes without saying, however, the nurses almost had to call security because first husband wanted to have a knock-down-drag-out fight in that little exam room. Although, looking back, his issue wasn't just about the surgery. He was extremely concerned about such a drastic and permanent change and how 3rd child would be viewed by everyone she would encounter. She was barely 10 years old, and he knew the most formative years were on the horizon. No one wants to watch their child live the rest of their life with a decision that was made on their behalf that could potentially alter everything beyond just the physical: their social, emotional, and mental health. Parents already worry about the most difficult years of their child's life, the teenage years. He didn't want any added undue stress to be put on his child. I know it didn't sound like it to him, but I agreed with him. His point was valid. The problem was, there were no other viable alternatives.

FH: What if we make the wrong decision?

Me: I know what you mean, but what other choice do we have? Do we really want to put her through surgery after surgery after surgery each of which might not be successful? Do we really want her to go through life missing an entire leg with no possibility of a prosthetic? Or do we want to give her a fighting chance at life with this strange procedure so her ankle can be a knee joint, and the prosthetic will make mobility 85% easier on her? This is the only choice that gives at least a sense of normalcy.

That. That was his breaking point. I watched first husband crumble into a ball of hysterical crying. I wanted to lose it like that too, but I knew I had to be strong for everyone involved.

FH: This is so unfair! I don't understand why? Why our little girl? How can she grow up looking like a freak? She did nothing to deserve this. Why? WHY HER??? Once this is done, that's it. Nothing will ever be normal for her again.

Me: Actually, the change of "normal" happened when that little boy knocked her down on the playground. I want to hug that little boy. Who knows how long we would have gone without knowing about this cancer? That little boy saved her life! And you're right. Nothing will ever be normal for her again.

CHAPTER 21

Long Sleeves? In the Summer? *It's Fine. I'm FINE.* *EVERYTHING'S FINE!*

I've liked the band Aerosmith since I was in 7th grade. The hip-hop group RUN-DMC did a cover of "Walk This Way" by Aerosmith. It was both mind-boggling and groundbreaking when these two groups collaborated. It changed the face of music, in my opinion, for the better. Aerosmith subsequently released seven of their own studio albums between 1987 and 2012. Of those albums, my favorite is Pump. It was released in 1989 and it has my favorite Aerosmith song: "What It Takes." There's a lyric in that song that says, "Girl before I met you, I was F-I-N-E fine." Now, I've been told that F.I.N.E is an acronym describing what fine really means. This acronym explains why most men in the world shudder uncontrollably when they hear their significant other, their woman, say "I'm fine, it's fine, everything's fine." That's their signal to run for the hills. So, pray tell, what is the acronym for fine? Well, F is for f**ked up, I is for insecure, N is for neurotic, and E is for emotional.

My new mantra had become "it's fine, I'm fine, everything's fine." I had no other choice. My daughter was in the throes of chemo treatment for her metastatic osteosarcoma, she had a life-saving surgery (Rotationplasty) that had disfigured her for the rest of her life, Voldemort decided to quit his stable job because

"God told him to" and he decided to work as a contracted 1099 employee as an ad salesman for a local tiny radio station working only for about 5% commission, we had used all of my only summer's paycheck to pay enough of the mortgage to keep us in the house and not be foreclosed, and first husband decided that summer was the perfect opportunity to sue me for full custody of all 4 children as well as full child support. The icing on this disaster cake? Voldemort was in full-love-bomb-devaluation-phase mode, and we were in the worst form of it... gaslighting and physical violence. So, why didn't I leave him? Or at the very least, why didn't I kick him out of my house? Feels like déjà vu all over again, doesn't it? Boy, I sure know how to pick'em, don't I? This was 'First Husband 2.0... the next level of domestic abuse'.

As long as I didn't question anything he did, didn't inquire as to his whereabouts, and basically just kept my mouth shut and agreed to every whim, every idea, every choice of his, then I'd be ok. What I couldn't fight was that nagging, dark pit that overwhelmed me constantly. It was the same dark pit in my gut that first appeared back in chapter 18. It was a frequent guest of mine that ended up taking permanent residency.

Voldemort just might be the most appropriate name for a real-life person in the history of naming people. If you are a Harry Potter fan, you totally understand. If you're not, Voldemort, in the Harry Potter world, is "he who shall not be named". Voldemort in the Harry Potter world is the most sinister, most evil, most powerful and hated villain EVER. It is possible that this Voldemort is just as sinister and evil.

Was Voldemort stealing from me? Yes. Was he lying to me? Daily. Did I know what was happening? Nope! At least, not at that time. And, as much as I tried to be a supportive spouse, I had no idea that this creature I was married to, who parallels the Voldemort from the Harry Potter world, had such evil ulterior motives.

Some might argue that I had to have known what was going on, that I was under a cloak of willful ignorance or worse, self-deception. So, what's the difference? "Willful ignorance occurs when individuals realize at some level of consciousness that their beliefs are probably false, or when they refuse to attend to information that would establish their falsity... self-deception occurs when individuals believe false things with complete conviction." Either way, the chaos brought on by this Voldemort damaged me in so many ways, as well as my children. What I truly did not know at the time is that, when I was not at home, he was abusing my children as well. To this day, I have not forgiven myself for that. My precious and amazing children were going through that much more mental and emotional abuse (they hold fast to the admission that he never physically abused them) because of my choices. Now that we are much more removed from that timeframe, my children and I had conversations at length as they danced around the specifics of what happened when I was not there. I have apologized and sought their forgiveness on numerous occasions, and every time their response has been nothing but sympathy, kindness, and forgiveness. They have each told me they understand I was doing the best I could in such a dire situation and, given the circumstances, they do not blame me for any of it. For that, I am eternally grateful!

Because 3rd child was in the hospital most of the year 2012, I had to choose between taking care of her while she was in-patient and being at home taking care of my other three children. Voldemort didn't have a real job, so he was home. This is one of the reasons I felt completely stuck in that marriage. I felt that I had no other choice but to stay with him so I could have an adult at home taking care of my other children. Contrary to the Super-mom creed, I could not be in two places at once and my crystal ball to keep an eye on things at home was in the shop, so I continued to live in oblivion.

I will not speak for my children and what they endured at the hands of Voldemort, so I'll just give you a taste of the absolute hell I crawled through while married to him. Let's see, where shall I start? The infidelities (yes that's multiple), the gaslighting, the name calling, or the bruises he left on my body? How about I tell you about one of the nights that involved all of the above? As I said before, I was required to fulfill his karaoke expectation almost every day of every week. Yes, I was still working but that didn't matter. HE wasn't working and had no morning obligations, so what was the problem? The problem was, I was expected to stay until the bar closed, I was expected to drink A LOT because he would tell me "you're so hot AND sexy when you're drunk!" This particular event, the culmination of abuses, started about an hour before I had to be ready to leave for the bar. That nagging feeling, the dark pit in my chest, was darker and deeper than normal, so I waited for him to get in the shower, and I investigated his phone. As I read through countless messages between him and other women, women I did not know, and the pictures exchanged, I felt gut-punched to the point of wanting to vomit. I took pictures with my phone of as much as I could. When he walked out of our master bathroom into our bedroom, I asked him if he knew <the name of one of the girls he'd been texting>.

Voldemort, without a flinch, without a pause, without even a hint of concern turned to face me.

V: Do I know who?

Me: [the name of one of the girls he'd been texting]

V: Hmmm, no. I've never heard that name before.

Me: Are you sure?

V: Yes, I'm sure.

Me: *opening my phone* So, then who is this? *shows the pictures of his texts*

V: I don't know what this is, but it's not me.

Me: I took these pictures of YOUR phone. This is on YOUR phone!

V: What the fk are you doing in my phone again? Huh? He pushes me down to the floor.

Me: standing back up Why are you texting these people? Am I not enough for you?

V: I DIDN'T SEND THOSE TEXTS!!! YOU F****NG B***H! YOU ARE OUT OF YOUR F****N MIND. *He picks me up and shakes me as hard as he can and throws me against the wall.*

I stand up, again, desperately trying to control my hysterical crying.

Me: If you didn't send those texts, how did they get on your phone?

V: *raises his fists like he's going to hit me in the face* I told you I didn't send those texts, DUMBASS! Now stop your f****ng crying and get yourself ready, we're leaving in 15 minutes.

My arms would be riddled with his handprints. You could see the outline of his hands on my arms. I was beyond embarrassed by this, so I would have to wear long sleeves. It was the worst during that summer because St Louis summers are miserably hot and humid. I decided I'd rather suffer the heat than have to explain to everyone why there were giant handprints on my arms. The saddest part about this scenario is that it happened more often than not. And this was just the beginning.

CHAPTER 22

You'd Think I'd Be Used to This By Now: *That's Two, Two, Two Cancers at Once*

I was a child of the 70's and 80's. There are many iconic earworm commercials from the 70s and 80s. Maybe you remember one of these: "Don't squeeze the Charmin," "Where's the Beef," "I've fallen, and I can't get up!" Ah, so many memories. The one that came to mind as I was thinking about this chapter was a Certs breath mint commercial. "It's two, two, two mints in one!" You might be thinking, "What in the world do Certs breath mints have to do with cancer?" Typically, I'd agree that those two subjects do not match, however as you've probably realized, my life story is anything but typical.

The year 2012, chockfull of so many traumatizing events, was finally in its last months. 3rd child's last chemo treatment was the last week of October. My poor baby endured a lung thoracotomy to remove metastatic Osteosarcoma, two months of chemotherapy, a permanent life-changing Rotationplasty, then another 7 months of chemotherapy. All of the tears, the sleepless nights, the recurring nightmares, the worry, the financial desperation, the custody battle, the overwhelming helplessness of watching my poor baby suffer through wave after wave after wave of vomiting, losing her hair, losing too much weight, struggle to eat anything to regain at least a little strength, all of this came to a culminating end as I watched my baby, my warrior, my brave little girl ring the bell signaling she was completely finished with her cancer treatment. At a follow-up appointment 4 weeks later, we were told 3rd child is officially cancer-free! And, for just one moment, there was joy, laughter, and camaraderie among all of us: the kids as well as the adults. I decided we needed to celebrate this milestone, so I hosted a cancer-free party for us. We had my in-laws over and combined that side's family Christmas celebration along with the cancer-free celebration. Finally... FINALLY we would be able to find our new normal and get on with our lives. We did it... we survived!

We had about three weeks of "normal." Christmas day came and went quickly. We were so grateful to the amazing organization Friends of Kids with Cancer. They made sure all of the kids had Christmas gifts as well as provided us with Christmas dinner. I'm convinced that every person in that organization hides their angel wings and halo because they are all absolutely angels on earth.

The week after Christmas, just before the new year, I noticed a rash had developed on 3rd child's cheek. My first reaction was panic, but I didn't want her to see that. I made an appointment for the next day and took her to our pediatrician, the one who first told us about 3rd child's cancer, to find out what they thought this rash was.

Me: Hey, Dr [pediatrician's name]! It's so good to see you.

Dr: Hey! Congratulations on being cancer-free! I can't imagine how difficult it has been for you all.

Me: Thank you... so, we're just wondering what's up with this rash on her face.

Dr: Well, vitals are all good. No fever. Does it itch?

3rd child: No. I can't feel it at all.

Dr: Have you eaten something new?

Me: Not that I know of.

Dr: Did you change laundry detergents? Or use a new soap? Anything new that you've used?

Me: No, nothing new... same ol' same ol'.

Dr: It's probably a viral infection. We'll need to let it run its course. If it isn't any better by next week, let me know. Until then, Tylenol for pain, Hydrocortisone for itching.

Me: Will do. Thank you, doctor.

But the rash did not get better. It did not go away. The rash stayed exactly the same. Still no itching, still no fever, and still there. The next week, we're in January of 2013 now, I took her back to the pediatrician. She was puzzled by this, so she set up an appointment with St Louis Children's dermatology department just as a precaution. And so, back we went to the place I loved the most and hated the most all at the same time. After 2012, I could have driven to that hospital with my eyes closed. There were several occasions that I just about did. Walking into the main entrance of the hospital from the parking garage, we were greeted by the security guards. Yes, the grumpy one we first met was still there, but we were quite familiar with each other at this point. I had to ask which floor of the hospital is the dermatology department. The doctor who saw us seemed concerned about the rash, knowing 3rd child's history. It was decided that, in order to rule out the unthinkable, we needed to do a biopsy of the rash.

Another biopsy? Yep. It is common practice to start with the most concerning possibilities and get them ruled out before exploring any others. And so, 3rd child had a skin sample taken and it was sent to be biopsied. And, you guessed it, another 7 days of waiting had to happen. Lovely! I did my best to forget about that biopsy. I tried focusing on cleaning house, my six grade level curricula, ANYTHING but that biopsy.

On January 30, 2013, I was at work and was preparing for my next class, 2nd graders, after my lunchtime. For the record, elementary music teachers usually don't have time to sit down and actually eat lunch. We usually inhale our food like a Dyson vacuum cleaner while continuing to work. I was about to go use the restroom when my phone rang. It was 3rd child's oncologist at Children's Hospital. This was not the nurse... this was the DOCTOR calling. THE DOCTOR! The only time the doctor calls instead of the nurse is when it's bad news.

Me: Hello???

Dr: Good afternoon, I need to speak with you for a moment.

Me: Ok, what's up?

Dr: We have the results of 3rd child's biopsy.

Me: *I sit down at my desk.* Yes? And?

Dr: I'm so sorry, but the biopsy shows that 3rd child has secondary Acute Myeloid Leukemia.

Me: ....

Dr: Are you there?

Me: *choking back tears* Yes, I'm here.

Dr: If you remember, the first time you met with our team, we gave you a large binder full of information. There was a section where we showed you the possible side-effects of chemotherapy treatment. It was in three categories: common, not as common, and rare. In the rare category, we see only about 4% of our patients present those side effects. One of those rare side effects is secondary cancer. Sometimes the chemo drugs can cause other cancers. Well, 3rd child is one of those rare cases. The chemo drugs have caused her to have secondary AML. I need you to bring 3rd child back to the 9th floor ASAP. Like, today, as fast as you can get here. Do not pass "Go," do not collect 200 dollars. How soon can you get here?

Me: Um, uhhh... I'm not sure. I'm at work. I need to let my administrators know that I need to leave... I need to find coverage for my classes, I need to get home, pack a bag, and go get her from school... how do I... how do I tell her? What do I do? I don't know what to do!

Dr: I suggest, when you tell her, make sure she's surrounded by caring and supportive people, so she knows she's not alone.

Me: Ok. My next class is on its way. I will call 9th floor when we're on our way to you.

I put the phone down and somehow walked myself across the building to the main office. I passed my class of 2nd graders and their teacher. I don't remember saying anything, or even looking at them. I had to get to the office... just get to the office...

I walked in and asked for the whereabouts of my assistant principal.

Me: Where can I find [assistant principal's name]?

Administrative assistant: Oh my, what's wrong? You look like you've seen a GHOST!

Me: I need to talk to [assistant principal's name] as soon as possible please.

AA: I'm on it!

I was directed into the assistant principal's office and that was my breaking point. I fell to my knees and sobbed hysterically.

Assistant principal: Oh, my goodness, what's happened?

Me: I can't believe this! It's NOT POSSIBLE! I just talked to 3rd child's oncologist.

AP: The DOCTOR called you?

Me: The doctor called me to tell me my daughter has secondary AML!

AP: Oh, NO! Oh, I'm so sorry. How can we help you?

Me: I think I passed my 2nd grade class on the way up here. What should I do? I have to go get [3rd child] and get her to Children's as fast as I can. I need to find class coverage, I need to pack her a bag, I need to tell her...... HOW AM I GOING TO TELL

HER? I don't know... I don't know what to do. I can't... I just can't go through this AGAIN! What... what do I do???

The people at that school are some of the most kind, caring, helpful, selfless people I've ever known. While I sat on my AP's floor having a complete mental breakdown, they had called Voldemort, found class coverage, shut down my laptop, gathered all of my personal belongings, brought them to the office for me, AND brought me a bottle of water. They helped me formulate a plan. First, I contacted her school and set up a meeting in the principal's office with 3rd child, her teacher, the school counselor, the principal, me, Voldemort, and her best friend. I got myself calm enough to drive home, packed a bag for the hospital and picked up Voldemort, drove to her school, and in the calmest way possible, surrounded by kind and supportive people, told my daughter that she has been diagnosed with secondary Acute Myeloid Leukemia. Then, I called the 9th floor and let them know we were on our way to them. She was admitted and they started the same barrage of tests they had done back in December of 2011 and boy am I glad they did. Yes, it's standard procedure, and I'm so grateful for standard procedures.

The next day, all of us parents were shuffled into the same meeting room as when we received our first big binder. We were given another binder... a new, improved, and BIGGER binder. In this meeting with the oncology doctors and just us 4 (me, Voldemort, first husband, and first husband's new wife), we were told that 3rd daughter has secondary AML, AND they found the metastatic osteosarcoma again in her lung. My child had two... TWO cancers at the same time!

AT THE SAME TIME!!!

How can this be possible? HOW??? How, when only 2 months ago, we were told she was cancer free? This can't be happening! But it was. So, we were given the new plan of attack to get my baby back to full health. First priority was getting the Leukemia in remission.

The best choice in this situation was for 3rd child to have a bone marrow transplant. They would test her siblings first to see if they were a match. The odds of a sibling being a match were not favorable, but they wanted to start there. I asked if her dad and I should be tested for a match, but they said it was virtually impossible for a parent to be a perfect match. I was quite surprised by that. Later, I did some of my own research on the subject and this is what I found.

"When it comes to finding a match for a bone marrow transplant, it's all about the HLAs: Human leukocyte antigens. HLAs are proteins, or markers, found on most cells in your body. Your immune system uses these markers to recognize which cells belong in your body and which do not. HLA typing is complex because you have many HLA markers. Half are inherited from your mother and half from your father, so each brother and sister who shares the same parents as you have a 25% chance (1 in 4) of being a close HLA match. Extended family members are not likely to be close HLA matches. About 70% (7 out of 10) of patients who need a transplant won't have a fully matched donor in their family. Research has found that a donor must match a minimum of 6 HLA markers. Many times, a closer match is required. A best match is found through detailed testing. Because some HLA types are more common than others, some patients may face a greater challenge in finding a matching donor.

The best bone marrow transplant outcomes happen when a patient's HLA and the HLA of a registry member or cord blood unit closely match. This is much more complex than matching blood types. There are many HLA markers that make a person's tissue type unique; however, matching certain markers is what is critical to a successful transplant. What makes a close match? The Be The Match Registry® is a listing of potential donors and cord blood units and their HLA types. When people join the Be The Match Registry, they provide a sample of their DNA by swabbing their cheek. This cheek swab is tested for a minimum of 6 basic HLA markers. A patient's doctor will usually choose several donors who appear to match the patient at a basic level. The doctor will ask that these donors have additional tests. These detailed tests will show which donor's HLA most closely matches the patient's HLA markers. These tests are usually blood tests or additional cheek swabs. About 8% of members who complete additional testing will go on to donate. If a member is asked to donate, that means they are the closest HLA match to the patient, they are the best donor."

Step number two in this multi-faceted plan was for another thoracotomy to remove the osteosarcoma from her lung.

Step three was, after recovering from the thoracotomy, to start an intensive chemo regimen until a matched bone marrow donor was found. Once the donor was found, 3rd child would have the most powerful chemo treatment to completely annihilate her immune system to prepare for the BMT (bone marrow transplant). It was too much… too much information to take in all at once. After the doctor gave us the plan, he suggested we all go to 3rd child's hospital room together and break the news to her about what's going on and how we're going to fight this killer disease.

We all walked to her room together, at least I watched myself and the entourage walk to her room. My dissociative muscles were getting such a great workout during these years, weren't they? Hang on, I got sarcasm all over my laptop.

So, we all walk into 3rd child's room and closed the door. She was quite engrossed in watching Say Yes To The Dress on TLC and had no intention of turning it off until that episode was finished.

Dr: [3rd child's name]?

3rd child: Yes? *She doesn't take her eyes off the TV screen.*

Dr: We need to talk with you about what's going on.

3rd: OK? *Still doesn't take her eyes off the TV screen.*

First Husband: <3rd child's name> We need you to pay attention to your doctor.

3rd: *Pushes TV to the side.* Ok. Fine. What's up?

Dr: You know how you had all those tests again?

3rd: *Rolls her eyes* Yes?

Dr: Well, since we found that Leukemia, we thought we better check on the rest of you to be sure there's nothing else going on.

3rd: Ok? *Showed a more serious look on her face.*

Dr: The thing is, when we looked at your scans, we saw the Osteo is in your lung again.

3rd: Ok?

Dr: That means you currently have 2 kinds of cancer that we have to fight.

3rd: I have 2 cancers?

Dr: Yes

3rd: 2 cancers?

Dr: Yes

3rd: *She's silent but we can see her wheels are turning.* So, what's the plan?

Dr: We're going to take out the cancer in your lung, and we're putting you on the BMT list immediately to find someone for a bone marrow transplant.

3rd: Ok. *She paused with a contemplative look on her face* So, we've got a plan. Can I finish watching my show now?

Me: Yes, sweetie, you can finish watching your show.

And that's exactly what she did.

Some may say my child is the bravest child they've ever known... that she wasn't afraid at all. I agree to an extent. If you talk to her now, she'd tell you that at the time, as a 10-year-old, she really didn't understand the extent of danger she was in. Her sweet little mind couldn't comprehend all of it. How could she? How many 10-year-olds do you know who have faced their own mortality not once... TWICE! Inconceivable! And yes, Inigo Montoya, I DID use that word and I DO know what it means.

Over the next 6 months, I watched that little girl fight for her survival while trying to navigate life with a backwards foot and a prosthetic leg AND finish 4th grade successfully. She truly was, and is, a Superhero!

CHAPTER 23

Another diagnosis???
It's Like Déjà Vu All Over Again!

Yankees Hall of Famer Yogi Berra is remembered as much for his classic sayings, "Yogi-isms," as he is for his career. Was he being serious? Was he just trying to get a laugh? I can't tell you for sure. Nevertheless, some of my favorites are some real head-scratchers. Here are just a few of them:

- It ain't over 'til it's over.

- You can observe a lot by watching.

- Baseball is 90 percent mental. The other half is physical.

- When you come to a fork in the road, take it.

- I never said most of the things I said.

- You should always go to other people's funerals, otherwise, they won't come to yours.

- He hits from both sides of the plate. He's amphibious.

- Pair up in threes.

Poignant, aren't they? None of them can compare to my all-time favorite Yogi-ism:

It's Déjà Vu all over again!

Allow me to catch you up in our timeline. From the end of January until the beginning of July, my 3rd child was at St Louis Children's hospital. Her BMT was successful and, despite a few glitches in the process of getting my baby girl in remission and cancer-free, she was released under a truckload of restrictions. Us parents literally had to take a class on what to do and especially what NOT to do for the first 100 days post-transplant. She started her 5th grade school year that August, but not in-person. We followed every rule, watched over her like a hawk, gave her every medicine prescribed, and she was finally cleared to go back to school January of 2014. Finally, some sort of normalcy, RIGHT? Oh, wait… this is my story so, you guessed it, there's no normalcy to be found.

We sailed into the year 2014, more like skidded sideways into 2014, and we thought all was finally going to be right with the world. Right around that time, my 2nd child, my son, was starting to deal with some back pain. I thought it was because his backpack was just too heavy and told him he needed to unload most of those books. That didn't fix the problem. I had him go to a chiropractor. That didn't fix the problem either. We tried Ibuprofen, we tried muscle relaxers, we tried seeking the advice of our pediatrician who referred us to an orthopedic specialist. No fix, no fix, and no fix. And his pain was getting worse by the minute. He was to the point that he could not stand up straight. Something was terribly wrong.

The orthopedic doctor was out of Mercy hospital in St Louis. He referred us to get a series of bloodwork tests, but nothing was showing up as an issue. The next step was to have an MRI done. If you've never had the privilege of having an MRI, the most challenging aspect of this test is the need to be completely still as the test is happening. My boy was in so much pain, he could not stay still for an MRI! He had to be sedated for it. What they found was a mass. They could not tell us what the mass was, they just knew it was a mass of some sort. It was decided they would pull a sample from that mass and have it biopsied. Oh, boy... here we go again with a biopsy! They did that biopsy, we waited the 7 days, and they had no answers. They did a 2nd biopsy, we waited another 7 days, and they had no answers. Then they did an invasive exploratory biopsy, they sent that to Washington University, we waited the 7 days, and they STILL had NO answers. This momma bear was getting to the point of "this is ENOUGH already!" After being told even Washington University didn't have any answers, and they had exhausted every other avenue, the doctor requested the insurance to cover a PET scan. He had requested it before all of the biopsy surgeries, and it had been denied by the insurance company. Since they had exhausted all of the other tests, that's when they approved a PET scan. What exactly is a PET scan? I'm so glad you asked!

PET stands for positron emission tomography. A PET scan produces 3-D, color images of the body. It helps reveal the metabolic or biochemical function of the tissue. The PET scan itself took all of about 10 minutes and we had results about an hour later. It was June of 2014, and my 15-year-old son was diagnosed with cancer. They didn't know what specific cancer it was, but they knew for sure it was cancer.

If I may, I feel the need for a brief rant here. A PET scan revealed what we needed to know the same day it was done, BUT insurance forced my baby to go through three grueling surgeries, with a week in between each, just to be told they didn't have answers? My baby suffered an extra month before they finally approved the one test that gave us answers the same day? Sounds to me like Yogi Berra came up with that plan!

The same week, we were given an official diagnosis. My son, my 2nd child, was diagnosed with Anaplastic Large-Cell Non-Hodgkin's Lymphoma. That's just a fancy way of saying cancer. As my feeble mind wrestled with the fact that we had to travel this pediatric cancer road, for the THIRD time, I decided to call 3rd child's oncology doctor.

Me: Hey, doc. I got a question for you.

Dr: Ok. Whatcha got?

Me: If your child were diagnosed with Anaplastic Large-Cell Non-Hodgkin's Lymphoma, which hospital and which doctor would you take them for treatment?

Dr: One of your other children was diagnosed with Anaplastic Large-Cell Non-Hodgkin's Lymphoma?

Me: Yessir.

Dr: Seriously?

Me: Yessir. Where would you recommend for the best treatment?

Dr: They need to go to Mercy hospital's pediatric hematology-oncology and see Dr [2nd child's doctor's name].

Me: No kidding? That's exactly where and who we were referred to!

Dr: He's the best with this particular Lymphoma. Best of luck to you all.

Well, at least that was some good news. That week, my son went through the same series of follow-up tests as 3rd child. Luckily, there were no other cancer issues to be found. Here's the eerie part. When my son was at Mercy hospital having a bone marrow aspiration done, at the exact same day and time, my daughter was having HER bone marrow aspiration at St Louis Children's hospital. Voldemort and I were at Mercy while first husband and first husband's wife were at Children's. We texted back and forth that day to keep the other side updated as to what was happening.

Seriously, people, you just can't make this up!

2nd child had the right kind of lymphoma if there is such a thing. In this case, yes, it was the right kind. Why, you ask? Because the research doctors in the pediatric hematology and oncology department of Mercy hospital were in the beginning phase of a research study. They were needing to test a specific treatment for Anaplastic Large-Cell Non-Hodgkin's Lymphoma. This treatment is a targeted chemo that goes after that specific cancer cell. I absolutely wanted my son to be a part of that study, so we signed all the necessary paperwork, and he was a part of that study. Along with this targeted therapy, he had to complete the standard protocol of chemo treatments. His chemo cocktail was very similar to 3rd child's: cyclophosphamide, vincristine, doxorubicin, and methotrexate. Although, rather than the partridge in a pear tree, we decided the targeted treatment would be much more beneficial. In fact, that targeted treatment was so beneficial, my son was already in remission after his 2nd round of treatment! Finally, some happy news! I'm so proud of my baby boy! And, in case you're wondering, he is now, at the time I'm writing this, a happy and healthy 25-year-old man who has been completely cleared from needing to see the hematology/oncology clinic ever again.

CHAPTER 24

You've Got To Put the Oxygen Mask On First: *That's Not a Belt— That's My Back*

The first time my children were ever on a plane was when we took our "Make a Wish" trip for 3rd child's Make-a-Wish. We (me, Voldemort, and the 4 kids) had the privilege of going to New Jersey, Jersey City to be exact, and we went to Carlo's bakery where we met and made a cake with Buddy Valastro. That's right, folks. We spent an entire day with Buddy the Cake Boss. It was amazing. What was more amazing for me was watching my children experience their first time in an airplane. They were mesmerized by the speech given by the crew regarding safety and what to do in an emergency. They talked about the seat belts, the emergency exits, and the most intriguing portion of the safety speech: oxygen masks.

"If needed, oxygen masks will be released overhead. To start the flow of oxygen, reach up and pull the mask toward you, fully extending the plastic tubing. Place the mask over your nose and mouth and slip the elastic band over your head. To tighten the fit, pull the tab on each side of the mask. The plastic bag does not need to inflate when oxygen is flowing. Be sure to secure your own mask before assisting others."

That last part... be sure to secure your own mask before assisting others... yeah. THAT!

Moms are notorious for taking care of everyone and everything around them and leaving their own needs for last. Needs... schmeeds. Who's got needs? I'm a mom... moms don't have needs, right? That's what we, as moms, have been conditioned to believe. I'm the poster child for this anomaly.

After I had recovered from my stillbirth, and my body tried going back to normal, I noticed a few strange things surrounding my monthly cycle. By the way, if you're a guy reading this, I'm hoping this isn't too uncomfortable of a subject for you.

Before 2009, my monthly cycle was so regular, I could practically set a clock with it. After 2009, not so much. I had no clue when and where it would appear out of nowhere. That, I could handle. What I struggled with was the terrible pain that came along with it. I'm not talking just the normal, everyday cramps women get on the monthly. No, this pain was in a class all by itself. At first, it would last 3 or 4 days. As time went on, the length and depth of the pain became longer and so much worse.

As much as I hated to, I went to my OB/GYN. This is the same doctor who delivered 3 of my healthy babies and was there for my losses. I went to him for answers. He had an ultrasound done and they found cysts. He said that it looked to him like the cysts were bursting and that was causing my pain. I asked what could be done? Is there a medication that can shrink the cysts? Is there a procedure? What can be done, Doc?

His answer was ... drum roll please... have a hysterectomy. That's the only thing that would stop the pain. Major surgery, down for a minimum of 6 months, then about a year until full recovery? There is no way I had any time for THAT!

The first time this pain was truly debilitating was in 2010. Remember back in chapter 16 when I told you about the trial separation? Yeah, it was in the middle of that. I couldn't stand up, I couldn't walk, I could barely move from my fetal position. I called first husband to see if he would help me get my stuff into my classroom so I wouldn't miss work. Lo and behold, he DID help that day. I guess he was in a good mood? Regardless, that was the first time it was that bad. So, in 2010 during the separation, I did not have the time nor the money. Then through 2011, as it got worse, I was going through the divorce, the foreclosure, marrying Voldemort, then 3rd child's diagnosis.

As the end of 2011 rolled around, just before the cancer diagnosis, I begged my doctor to schedule the hysterectomy during spring break 2012. I didn't care if I had the time or money. I couldn't deal with this every month. So, we scheduled my hysterectomy for March 16, 2012. Does that date sound familiar? That's right! That was the day 3rd child had her Rotationplasty surgery. Ain't coincidences fun?

So, I left my "oxygen mask" dangling as I struggled every month just to survive that horrific monthly pain, too busy to take care of myself because I was surrounded by multiple fires of different sizes, shapes, and colors, I was trying to put those fires out first and then maybe I'd try having that surgery. And, as each month passed, the pain got worse and lasted longer than the month before.

All through 2012, 2013, 2014 as I spent day and night in hospital room with one of my children, my back pain would rear its ugly head. I tried pain meds, muscle relaxers, heating pads, ice pads, Icy Hot cream. If it was an option to try, I tried it. I was desperate. As 2014 turned into 2015, I was to the point where every month I might have had 4 or 5 days where I could stand and not cry out in pain. I would beg Voldemort to help relieve this pain. I showed him where it was the worst. The first time I asked him for help...

Me: I can't take this. Please, please help me. I need counterpressure.

V: I guess.

I lifted my shirt and pointed to my low back right at where the pelvis starts.

Me: Do you see it.

V: Do I see it? *He put his hands on the spasming part and grabbed it.* I can FEEL it! It looks like you have a giant belt around your back. It's as big as my HANDS!

Me: Yeah, that's not a belt... it's my back. *Then I broke down in tears.*

And he was right. That's how big, bad, and ugly it was. I handed him a piece of 2x4 wood and asked him to put it in the middle of the biggest part of that muscle spasm and push. He did and for the first time in a long time, I felt relief. That is, until he stopped. Then I was immediately back in the same pain. On and on this went. Why didn't I have the surgery at that point? Well, let's see. It's the spring of 2015. Remember the house that Voldemort said he HAD to have? We were in foreclosure. AGAIN. The sheriff was going to be coming to the house and removing us from the premises. We had no place to go. We were going to end up living in the minivan. I was overwhelmed with gratitude when a dear friend and his wife offered for us to live in their home for a reduced monthly amount. They had just moved out of it because they had bought another house and hadn't decided what they were going to do with the first house. They were my heroes for sure. Arrangements were made for the kids to stay in their school because, technically, we were homeless. We moved into that house, my pain was an issue I was still dealing with, and my 3rd child decided she didn't want to live with me at all anymore. She didn't want to say it, but it was because of Voldemort and what he was doing when I wasn't around. Soon after that, we lost both of our cars to the repo man. I was putting out fires EVERY-WHERE! Why? Voldemort was destroying everything around me. And, still, that elusive oxygen mask kept waving at me to put it on. I couldn't! I didn't have time to take care of me. But here's the problem with that line of thinking, and I learned it the hard way. When we don't make time to take care of ourselves, our bodies FORCE us to take care of ourselves. That's exactly what happened to me.

It was the last week of December 2015. Christmas was a success, I had all of my kids with me at home, and we were playing one of the board games they got as a gift: the Game of Life. I had a pain hit me rather hard. It was like all the other pain I had been surviving, except this time it was exponentially worse. I was sitting at the kitchen table, and I bent over from the pain.

Voldemort: What's happening?

Me: *whispering* I can't... it hurts.... so much worse...

V: Ok? *He rolls his eyes.*

Me: I need to go to the emergency room. Like, NOW

V: Now???

Me: Yes, NOW!

And we got in the van and drove to the emergency room. It was about a 10-minute drive. We had to stop twice for me to throw up from the pain. Now, I had been through 5 labors. Five times I experienced the pain of labor and delivery. Not once during those 5 occurrences did I ever vomit from the pain. 2 times I needed Voldemort to pull over so I could throw up... because of the pain.

I didn't want to be at this particular hospital, it was the same one I delivered my stillborn baby, but it was the closest emergency room, so I didn't have a choice.

When I arrived, after the triage portion of the trip, we were put in a room and told the doctor would be with us shortly. Yeah, shortly in emergency room talk is about 4 hours minimum. I was doubled over in that hospital bed begging for death when a nurse FINALLY walked in and asked why we were there. I had zero capacity to speak so Voldemort gave a brief description of why we were there. I was too busy crying and dry heaving in pain. I was asked on a scale of 1 to 10, what is my pain. My response was 153. The nurse giggled. I looked her square in the eye and said 153... do I look like I'm kidding??? She immediately stopped giggling and walked out of the room. It was decided that they would give me IV Dilaudid. If you're unaware, IV Dilaudid is one step below general anesthesia. This stuff should knock out any normal person. Apparently, I'm not normal because the IV Dilaudid did absolutely NOTHING for me. About another hour went by and the nurse returned.

Nurse: On a scale of 1-10, 10 being the absolute worst, what is your pain level?

Me: *gasps, then whispers* Well, the last time you asked I was at, what, 153?

Nurse: Yes

Me: *still whispering.* Now? I'm about 153. *I continue to dry heave*

Nurse: ....

Voldemort: You CAN see she's still suffering, right?

Nurse: *nods*

And so, they gave me another dose of IV Dilaudid.

What did that do for me? Well, besides the fact that I was in the most excruciating pain known to woman, it made me not care that I was in that much pain. Did it stop the pain? Not even a little.

There was only one positive result of that 2nd dose. I finally stopped throwing up. Although, at that point there was nothing left to vomit.

About 2 hours later, we were informed that my doctor was NOT on call, and they released me to go home. No medications, no follow ups. Just a "nice to see ya, come back if it gets worse." So, we went home. That Dilaudid lasted for a while, almost 24 hours, but once it wore off, "bam—ZOOM to the moon!" I begged Voldemort to take me back to the ER. I just couldn't take it anymore. The pain was just too much to bear. Back we went, and this time, my doctor WAS on call. After my first dose of IV Dilaudid, I was told I was officially NPO. My doctor called and said to keep me overnight. Tomorrow would be my hysterectomy. I tried to do the Snoopy dance, but the pain was just too much.

We were told the surgery would take 2 hours MAX and that they'd call with messages to keep Voldemort posted as to what was happening in the surgery. We had decided on a full hysterectomy which means they would take my ovaries as well. The only thing that would be left of my girlie innards would be my cervix.

My 2-hours-max surgery turned into 4 and ½ hours. There's something they did not anticipate... the reason for all of the pain in the first place. I had Adenomyosis. What is THAT? Well, basically, my uterus was trying to kill me. My doctor had quite a difficult time getting that thing out the normal way. My uterus was not only the texture of a large kitchen sponge, but it was also the size of a 4-month pregnant uterus. YIKES! I guess you could say I gave birth to a 4-month-along uterus? YUCK!!!

And so, I was FORCED to put on my "oxygen mask." I was finally released from the hospital to recover at home. I was so grateful that I was given 6 weeks off of work to recover. It wasn't enough by any means, but it was nice being able to take 6 weeks to try to find some kind of new normal for my body. Full disclosure, it took a full year to finally feel fully recovered. And while it did take what felt like FOREVER to get back to the place where I could feel like a woman again, I am grateful to say that my back-belt, you know, the muscle spasms caused by the Adenomyosis, are NO MORE! And there was great rejoicing!

CHAPTER 25

I Deserve Better Than This: Me, Voldemort, and the Deathly Hallows

I'd like for us to go back ever so briefly in time. Back to chapter 12, when I was a full-fledged Stepford Wife catering to every whim of first husband, doing everything I could to fulfill the Proverbs 31 woman's creed, when all I knew was self-deprecation and subservience, teetering on the fence between full-on legalism and true freedom. That's right, kids, back when I adhered to every tiny detail and facet of what was preached to me. I'm talking about the summer of 1997 and beyond. A now-beloved character was introduced to children and adults alike in a book that soon became a series of 7 books. I was told from the pulpit that Harry Potter and the entire series was purely demonic witchcraft, and its sole purpose was to destroy children's minds along with destroying the family unit as a whole. For the record, I do not agree with this opinion at all. This book series took us through the life and times of one Harry Potter and the harrowing adventures and challenges that he faced along with his friends Hermione, Ronald, Neville, Hagrid, and a cast of others. The biggest obstacle, the biggest villain, was Tom Riddle, also known as Lord Voldemort. Now, I've been using that name for my 2nd husband throughout a good portion of this book. It is now time to put that name, that character, that evil narcissistic humanoid to rest.

After my hysterectomy in January 2016 and my subsequent recovery time, I was back to teaching, my children were back to schooling, and Voldemort was continuing in his quest to financially and socially destroy everything I had ever attempted to make good. That summer, at the end of June 2016, 3rd child and I were invited to a fully paid week in Montana for cancer kids and one of their parents. That week of glorious adventures will forever be blazed in my memory. Both 3rd child and I were given a solid week of making connections with others who knew exactly what we were going through with everything pediatric cancer related. I cannot emphasize enough just how grateful I am for that brief calm before an incredibly stressful storm on the horizon. The day after returning home from 7 glorious days of stress-free living, I received notice that if I did not secure and offer proof of residency within my kids' (2nd and 4th child) schools, they would no longer be permitted to attend their school. We had been living at my friends' house for a full calendar year and our time was up. I had been operating under the wrong information that we had 2 calendar years to get back on our feet. I was WRONG! I literally had 2 weeks to find a new home, secure that home, and provide the school district with proof of living within school boundaries. I had only two weeks to accomplish this, or I would lose my children for sure.

TWO WEEKS!!!

I immediately began a non-stop effort to find a place for us to live and get a lease signed ASAP. I didn't care what the place was; all I needed was a place that had 3 bedrooms and was within the school boundary line. Mobile home, apartment, home—it could've been a 3-bedroom ROCK for all I cared. I was down to the last 3 days when a dear friend texted me that there was a house in town that she saw someone putting a "For Rent" sign in the yard with a phone number. I immediately called that number and met an elderly lady at this tiny, slab, 3-bedroom, 1-bathroom house. The monthly rent was just barely in my price range, and she did not require a credit check. We signed the lease that evening and, voila, I was able to keep my kids in their schools. At the end of July 2016, we moved into that tiny little miracle house. All Voldemort could do was complain, complain, complain about EVERYTHING. Nothing was ever good enough for him. I tried to make that tiny little miracle house a home, but it was never good enough. Even when 1st child had my grandson, it wasn't enough to be happy. Never mind that Voldemort refused to keep any job longer than 2 months. I found out later, from HIM, that he'd quit a job as soon as the state caught up with him and started garnishing his wages for the child support he owed. Gee, what a good father. Excuse me while I vomit!

I had been struggling with obesity my entire life. Even though I had lost enough weight that I was able to fit in "regular" clothes, I was still overweight. And, at this point, I'd had enough of everything. I'd had enough of Voldemort, my size, struggling with money, feeling like I was the only adult making any contributions to keep our home above water. So, December 2017, when it was announced at my school/work that anyone who wanted to participate in the building-wide Biggest Loser competition, we'd start at the beginning of the new year, January 2018. This was IT! This was what I was wanting, what I was needing, to kick-start my road to "health". To be clear, by medical standards, I WAS healthy barring the number on the scale, but I still hated what I saw in the mirror and decided that meant I was "unhealthy".

I was so excited to start this journey. Our first day back to school after the Winter break and New Year's holidays, we had our first weigh-in. As per the rules of the competition, we would weigh-in every Friday morning and the last Friday before Spring Break would be the final weigh-in. The person who had lost the most body weight percentage, not number of pounds, would be the winner. There was real money involved. And so began my quest for weight loss.

I decided I wanted to figure this out on my own. We couldn't afford any outside help like personal training or dietician. I just decided to track and limit my daily calorie intake to no more than 1800 calories a day and would have a decent cardio and/or strength training session at the gym every Monday through Friday after work. As with any new health plan, the first few weeks I didn't see any change, but then the scale started to shift. I didn't win the biggest loser competition for work that time around, please don't get me started on the woman who absolutely cheated her way to "winning" that competition, but I did notice something else more significant. The more weight I lost, the more confident I became. And the more weight I lost, the more confident I became; the more abusive Voldemort was to me. He was still imposing the same rules of our social calendar. I was still expected to be his karaoke-ho. The problem was, as I lost weight, the more of a "light-weight drinker" I became. I was still expected to drink as much as I always had, but I wasn't able to tolerate the alcohol nearly as much as I had been able to before I lost any weight. That was bad enough, however, the name calling, the physical violence, the gaslighting was becoming more severe as I continued gaining confidence. Voldemort was losing his control of me and that did not bode well for me AT ALL! Nor, did it bode well for my 4th child. She was the last one at home with me. 1st and 2nd children were out of high school, 3rd child lived mostly with her dad, so the fall of 2018, it was me and 4th child living in the house with Voldemort.

He was constantly threatening to leave me. For the first 7 years, I would fall apart in tears and beg him to stay. That's exactly what a narcissist wants. This is how they are validated, by getting those around them to desperately admit they are needed to survive, and that's what I had done. Usually, I ended up sobbing on the floor in a pool of blood begging him to stay to which I would hear "Now that's all I needed you to say... of course I'll stay because you need me so much!"

Our financial issues were getting worse every day, the violent behaviors were getting worse every day, Voldemort was stealing from me and my bank account daily, he had tried to convince me I couldn't survive without him, and 4th child didn't want to stay with me anymore (I couldn't blame her). It was December 2018 and I had lost 88 pounds since January that year. I was so proud of myself for reaching a goal I never thought was possible. I was a completely different person physically and mentally. Now, a real MAN would have been encouraging and maybe even complimentary. Unfortunately, I wasn't married to a REAL man. I was done making excuses, done with the drama, I was just DONE! I decided that I deserve so much better than this... that I would be so much better alone than with this daily abuse.

I finally started fighting back.

As I reflect back on that time, I liken the situation to Harry Potter and the Deathly Hallows. It was Harry Potter that had to destroy Voldemort, but Harry Potter had to die first for him to be able to accomplish the task of destroying Voldemort. There was a piece of me that had already died long before this final confrontation, and because of that death, I was able to rise as a new me and finally rid myself of Voldemort.

It was February 24, 2019. I was meeting a dear friend for lunch after a chiropractic appointment. We had just gotten word that one of Voldemort's uncles had passed away. I offered to drive him to the wake and the funeral to pay respects. He refused. He said "no, we don't have the gas money to get there and back." I insisted we go, he loudly shouted "NO, WE DON'T HAVE THE MONEY AND THANK YOU VERY MUCH FOR RE-MINDING ME!!!"

O...K...

So, I went to the chiropractor and then to lunch with my friend. I was so grateful for the time away with my friend. She had a way of helping me gain perspective in such a kind and loving way. She helped me see what I needed to do and never once judged me in the process. I guess I had been gone too long because I received a text from Voldemort saying he was going to his uncle's wake. I offered to meet him to put fuel in the car, even though it would put us further in the red, but he refused that as well. I shrugged and said "whatever!"

Later, when I arrived home, 4th child was in the front room. I asked where Voldemort was, she shrugged her shoulders. I didn't think anything of it. About that same time, he comes barreling into the driveway, tires squealing to a halt. He jumps out of the car, storms into the house, goes straight to the bedroom and starts packing his stuff. Now, he had done this exact theatrical production numerous times before. You remember, when I'd always end up on the floor in a pool of blood begging him to stay? Well, not THIS time. I didn't follow him into the bedroom to ask what I had done wrong again, I didn't cry, I didn't flinch. I was stoic... I was apathetic. He was slamming things around in the bedroom, and I still didn't move. Voldemort then screamed "Will you get in here???" I calmly walked into the bedroom.

V: I've had enough of your sh*t! I'm leaving and I'm NOT telling you where I'm going.

Me: Ok

V: I MEAN it this time. I'm done with this; I'm done with YOU!

Me: Ok

V: What do you MEAN ok???

Me: Well, in doing my research, I've come to the realization that YOU, sir, are a textbook narcissist!

V: I'm a WHAT?

Me: Narcissist... shall I spell it for you? N-A-R

V: *Interrupts me* I know how to f****ng spell it, dumbass. Who the f**k do you think you are telling me what I am???

Me: Look, are you leaving or not?

V: *He pauses* YES, I'm leaving you, and you CAN'T STOP ME!

Me: Ok

At this point, I begin helping him put his stuff in the bag. And, thus, began the love bombing phase known as the Discard Phase. This happens when the love bombing narcissist is confronted about their harmful behavior, or when there is an attempt by the 'love-bomb-ee' to reset healthy boundaries. The 'love bomber' will avoid accountability by refusing to cooperate and compromise or by abandoning the relationship.

I walked into the front room with 4th child, who had the biggest grin on her face. Voldemort stomped out the door with one bag, stomped back in the house, then stomped out the door with a 2nd bag, got in the car, slammed the door, and sped off again, tires squealing, again, and left.

All I had left to say to this monster was "Buh-bye."

The next morning was a Monday. I arranged for a sub and took my last personal day so I could get my situation figured out. It was my pay day. I was waiting at the bank before it opened. They knew me and Voldemort, so before their day officially started, they asked how they could help me. I withdrew the entire amount of my paycheck down to the penny and promptly drove across town and opened my own account at a different bank, then I went to a different cell phone provider and opened a new account with them for me and 4th child. Then I got my own car insurance on just my car. The last step was talking with the landlord to get the locks changed and the lease only in my name. This is where I had a bit of a hiccup.

You see, when we moved in, I paid with cash and got a receipt. An agreement was made that I would pay half of the rent twice a month, because I got paid twice a month. Voldemort insisted... INSISTED... that he be the one to deal with the landlord and pay the rent. What I didn't know was that Voldemort was only making partial payments. We were a total of 4 months behind in our rent. The landlord was starting the process to have us evicted. I begged and pleaded with him to give me mercy, and then I told him the entire story of Voldemort and what had happened. By the grace of God, that landlord had pity on me. I made a deal to continue paying half the rent twice a month in cash, but with each payment I would add an extra $100 until I was caught up. I made sure that I was on time every single payment and it was always with that extra $100. And, he had the locks changed as well as created a new lease with only me and 4th daughter allowed to live there.

Now, you didn't really think that was the end of the Voldemort saga, did you? On my side of things, absolutely YES it was. On his side? Oh, he tried A LOT to convince me to take him back. It was getting to the point of harassment. Yes, I had made it to where he could no longer live in that house. Yes, the locks had been changed. This did not stop him from trying to weasel his way back into my good graces. And to be completely honest here, I was afraid of him. I knew what he was capable of, and I was scared. So, I did two more things to ensure my freedom:

It was the beginning of July 2019. My first big move was securing an ex parte order. That's right, my friend. I took my strength, my resolve, and myself to the county courthouse and filed an order of protection—a restraining order. Voldemort was not allowed to be within 500 feet of me or my house for the next year. That was the easy part. The not-so-easy part was my next step: filing for divorce. I, obviously, could not afford a lawyer to represent me. Instead, I did my research. I discovered that, because Voldemort and I did not share any real estate property and because we did not have any children, I would be able to file for divorce pro se. That means I represented myself in the process without the assistance of an attorney. Also, I was able to dissolve the marriage because I lived in a true no-fault state. I did not care that I had to pay for everything, that I had to hire someone to find him because I had no idea as to where he was living at that point. I jumped through every legal hoop and finally, September 25, 2019, exactly 7 months to the day after I started my new life of independence, I was no longer married to Voldemort.

PART 5

Now You Know the Rest of the Story...
Thank You Paul Harvey

CHAPTER 26

Karma, Anyone? *The Greatest Revenge Is No Revenge... Move On and Be Happy*

If you've never seen the movie, the original 1996 movie, not the TV series, First Wives Club, it is, as you can probably imagine, about disgruntled divorcees seeking vengeance for their husbands dumping them for much younger new wives. It stars Bette Midler, Goldie Hawn, and Diane Keaton whose characters were the reason their husbands were so successful in their careers. These first wives willingly sacrificed themselves for many years in their marriage so their husbands could achieve their career goals and become wealthy only to be blindsided, drop-kicked, and left behind while these ungrateful excuses for men moved on with their lives having 20-somethings as their new relationship toys. The end result was, in these victims' eyes, justice and being the "winners" in this plot of revenge. Yes, it was just a movie, and it was hilarious. But there is one problem I can see with this sort of "feel-good" movie. Looking at the big picture, does that sort of revenge truly result in joy, happiness, and peace? If you had asked me this question on February 25, 2019, I would have said "You bet your sweet bippy it does!" I also would have been wrong. Looking at the big picture, seeking revenge is not about getting even in order to achieve joy, happiness, and peace. When a person feels justified in seeking revenge, it's more about an expression of hate rather than seeking peace.

But isn't the opposite of love hate? No. "The opposite of love is not hate, it's indifference." This quote comes from a man who could very well be the personification of love versus indifference. Elie Wiesel was a Romanian-born American writer, professor, political activist, Nobel laureate, and this is, in my humble opinion, the foremost of his accomplishments: a Holocaust survivor.

In this day and age, and as I'm writing now it is the end of 2023, I've watched as all platforms of social and news media have been a highly negative influence on our culture, to the point that people are attempting to change history. I don't mean taking what happened in history, learning from it, and trying to make our world a better place. No, I mean there are people who are trying to deny specific events in our world's history.

Now, stay with me here while we briefly chase this rabbit...

The most significant event of the 20th century is one of those examples of people trying to deny it ever happened. Yes, there was a Nazi regime led by a man named Adolf Hitler. Yes, he led an oppressive, dictatorial government. Yes, he gave the order to annihilate the entire Jewish population not only in Germany, but in the whole world. According to jewishvirtuallibrary.com, "The two most reliable sources for Holocaust data are the U.S. Holocaust Memorial Museum and Yad Vashem. Though this is the best information available, it is based on estimates and cannot take into account the unknown number of victims whose bodies were never recovered or for whom there were no records. The Nazis kept detailed records of the people who passed through the camps; nevertheless, we do not know how many Jews may still have been unaccounted for in the many places where they were murdered. In addition, as the Allies began to close in on Germany, the Nazis began to destroy their records. We also don't know the precise number of Jews in any of these areas. The population data ranges from 1937-1941 so, for example, the countries where the figures came from 1937 may not accurately reflect the number of Jews at the time the war began. Though the two institutions have different estimates, if you average the total number of Jews each says were murdered, the result is the commonly used figure of six million."

SIX MILLION!

This isn't even counting the people trying to help their Jewish family and friends escape death or the people merely suspected of helping Jewish people escape and survive. And this is an average estimation! The definition of genocide, according to Sergeant Google-Bing, is "the killing or mistreatment of a large number of people from a particular national or ethnic group with the aim of destroying that nation or group." According to Merriam-Webster, genocide is "the deliberate and systematic destruction of a racial, political, or cultural group." Anyone that tries to say the Nazis were not proponents of genocide, they are a LIAR!

Now, imagine knowing that you and your family are on the list to be murdered, you are all taken captive and sent to a place where you are forced into heavy manual labor, where vicious and inhumane "medical tests" are being performed for the sake of "research", where you're limited to barely one meal a day, where you watch innocent men, women, and children beaten and murdered only because they, YOU, were born into an ethnic religion. I would venture to say you would have seething, dark hatred for those imposing such an awful event as genocide against you. This was the experience of Elie Wiesel. He survived this real-life trauma, this real-life HORROR. Now, I have no idea what brought him to the understanding that the opposite of love is not hate, it is indifference. What I DO know is that the majority of people would completely understand him living with hate and wanting the murderers to be destroyed in the ultimate act of vengeance. Yes, we are human and can understand this line of thinking. The problem is that hate, which is in close relation to unforgiveness, destroys the person hanging on to that hate and unforgiveness. These strong emotions cause a strong response. Love, as well as hate, causes a strong response. Indifference, on the other hand, is much more neutral and does not beg for any response whatsoever. Let's check out the definition of indifference. "Absence of compulsion to or toward one thing or another." And, Professor Google-Bing, what say you? "Indifference is a lack of interest, concern, or sympathy."

When we could not care any less about a person or situation, THAT is the opposite of love.

Okay, thank you for following me out of that rabbit hole. Let's dust ourselves off and get back to my original point, which is how wrong I was in February 2019 to think that getting revenge on Voldemort would bring me joy, happiness, and peace. If you listen really carefully, you might be able to hear February-2019-me asking "okay, if revenge won't bring me joy, happiness, and peace, then for the love of God, tell me what will!!!" Simmer down February-2019-me. You will learn the answer to that sooner than you realize.

I absolutely cannot blame February-2019-me for those feelings. That poor woman had been through so much more than should be given to 25 people combined. I cannot fault her for wanting revenge on everyone in her past. I cannot fault her for the 6-foot wide and 100-foot-tall walled fortress she had built around her beyond-wounded heart. I cannot fault her for anything and everything she was feeling and experiencing at that time. She wasn't wounded, she was defeated. Much like the example in the 90's sitcom Friends that Rachel gave in season 2 episode 1 after she realized she had missed her chance with Ross, "But today, it's like there's rock bottom, then 50 feet of crap, then me." And that's exactly where I was. Did I miss Voldemort? Now, that's a loaded question. This might help explain why...

One of my favorite bands during that time was Halestorm. Lzzy Hale has a powerful voice and writes some pretty amazing songs. One of her songs that was hitting way too close to home:

"I Miss the Misery". Here's a little bit of those lyrics:

I miss the bad things, the way you hate me.

I miss the screaming, the way that you blame me.

Miss the phone calls when it's your fault

I miss the late nights—don't miss you at all

I like the kick in the face and the things you do to me

I love the way that it hurts... I don't miss you, I miss the misery

Ah, yes... the domestic abuse paradox at its finest. Unless you've been there, you simply cannot understand why anyone chooses to stay in that situation. But that's not the point of this chapter whatsoever.

Poor February-2019-me… I want to hug her.

So, there I was… I was wallowing in a cesspool of absolute terror. Why? Why in the world would I be living in so much fear? Well, my friend, let's put February-2019-me under the psychology microscope.

- For the entirety of the almost 45 years that I had been on this earth, the people in my life who were supposed to be the most supportive made it very clear that not only was I worthless, but I couldn't do anything right. I had been second-guessing my every move (I still do) and trying, desperately, to win their approval, to no avail.

- For the entirety of the almost 45 years that I had been on this earth, I had always been with someone. Until age 18, obviously with FPF and MPF. In college, I had roommates. I married first husband after my sophomore year of college. Less than two weeks after first husband left, I had Voldemort in my home.

- I was struggling with Complex PTSD. Of course, I didn't realize it at the time, but PTSD is NO JOKE, and I was trying to survive with it. People with PTSD… especially those with C-PTSD (remember chapter 3?) do not do well when the future is not clear. Fear of the unknown is debilitating. C-PTSD causes the need for complete control of everything. I know, I know that having complete control over everything is not only impossible, but it is laughable… but even the façade of control is soothing to the C-PTSD soul.

- I was convinced there was no way I could make it on my own, even though I was putting up a good front with my children... at least I thought I was. It's pretty difficult to have a good, strong game-face on when every single night you are hysterically sobbing yourself to sleep. I. Was. Terrified!

February 25, 2019, was absolutely Independence Day for me and my children. Freedom from Voldemort, freedom from abuse, freedom from inhumane expectations from my abusers... it was definitely Independence Day in my home. I was the one in control of my life and no one else could tell me what to do, where to go, or when to be where. I could come and go as I pleased. More important, I could finally figure out what I really wanted and needed for my life. It was during this time I became even more close with my dear friend who had been through very similar circumstances as a child as well as their first marriage to another Voldemort. This is the same friend I was with on the day before my Independence day. We had so many long talks, often very late at night. She and her husband helped me see my value; they helped me see what I deserve. I embraced the fact that I was so much better alone rather than in a violent and abusive relationship with a narcissist. To that friend and her husband, I must say:

THANK YOU and GO TEAM S!

From my Independence Day, February 25, until around the end of June, I was a hermit of sorts. I went from being required by Voldemort to participate in his high karaoke-life expectations (remember I was required to be out and closing bars almost every night of the week, otherwise I would regret it), I went from daily social frivolity to zero social life in a split second, and I was LOVING it! Time at home without expectations; without expectations to "look hot" for Voldemort while we were out so that men would talk to me and try hitting on me... and then go home for abuse to ensue because men talked to me and were hitting on me. Yeah, how do ya like THOSE apples? As we would be on our way to the bar, Voldemort would talk about what a "turn-on" it was to see men looking at and trying to pick up HIS woman, and then on the way home, I would be shamed for being a "f*****g drunk wh*re" for talking to those men, then I would be tossed around our bedroom like a pinball because I would ask him to explain why he was so angry at me for doing what he told me to do. Wow... digression alert! Sorry about that...

Anyway, back to the beauty of being a homebody without any others' expectations...

You know, the funny thing about not going out every stinking night of the week? Money becomes less scarce... especially when there's no one else stealing your money and then gaslighting you into thinking you spent all of that money on alcohol when, in fact, they were feeding it into slot machines and buying drinks for other people... ooops. Sorry, was about to digress again...

During those 4 months, I decided I didn't need social interaction ever again. My kids and my job were the only social anything I would need. Well, Facebook was in the mix as well, but I didn't consider that TRUE social interaction.

So, what brought me out of my hermit status? A dear long-time friend from college (I refuse to use the term "old") reminded me that he, his girlfriend, me, and Voldemort were supposed to be going to a concert in the city. I tried getting out of it, but they did what good friends do. They convinced me it was time to get out and try to breathe on my own in a social situation. They also agreed they would keep a close eye on me and if I needed to imbibe a bit, they would be sure I got home safely. And that's exactly what they did. I cannot even begin to describe the catharsis I experienced that night. My attitude shifted. No, I did NOT need to be a hermit and never explore outside the safety of the 4 walls of my home. I realized that, deep down, I'm an extrovert and I love to be with people, on my own terms of course. So, from June until around the beginning of September, I dated. Until school started, I could go out whenever I chose because it was still summer break from school. Once school started in August, I would only date Friday and Saturday nights... and the occasional Sunday evening. If it was during the week, I was sure to be back home early because of work the next day. I was so excited about the prospect of dating!

First, I dated myself. Yes, you read that correctly. I took myself out on dates. Dinner, a movie, going to Barnes and Noble to read a book I didn't intend to purchase, a long drive to nowhere in particular... I enjoyed my own company, my music, my choices and really thought A LOT about if I ever did choose to date guys again, what would that look like? First of all, they would be required to check off every box on my mental list. If there was one box not checked, or if I was sensing even the slightest hint of a red flag, BUH-BYE... NEXT! I'll get more into that process I experienced a little bit later; probably in the next chapter, so, to be continued.

Anyone who has been through a divorce knows that the marriage isn't over when the divorce is final. No, the marriage is over

LONG before that. I had been officially married to Voldemort, according to the courts, from November 2011 until September 25, 2019. For me, the marriage was over years before that. As of July of 2019, I had filed the restraining order, I filed for divorce, I did everything necessary to rid myself of Voldemort. I was so full of hate for Voldemort, for what he had done to me and my children, and I wanted to prove to Voldemort, to my children, and to myself that I didn't need him. Furthermore, I didn't need ANY man to complete me because I was completely complete on my own.

To July-2019-me, YOU GO GIRL!

Yes, there was still a ginormous part of me that desperately wanted to see Voldemort experience the all-too-true adage "what goes around comes around." I wanted to know where that beautiful "karma" was and what was taking so long to show up? That part of me wanted to see and know that Voldemort was suffering more than my children and I combined. What I hadn't discovered as of yet was a quote that, once I found it…thank you Facebook, I eventually started incorporating into my every choice. It is a quote credited to the 17th century English poet George Herbert: "Living well is the best revenge."

The first time I read that quote, living well is the best revenge, I remember rolling my eyes and saying "whatever!" But then, I re-read it again… and again… and again. It started to lift my soul. It lifted kind of like how an elevator lifts us. Ever try getting on an elevator at the busiest time of the day? It's especially challenging at the hospital, and I would know. Only so many people fit on one elevator and, it never failed, there was someone who needed to stop at each floor before arriving at YOUR floor. That quote, at about the 25th reading and contemplation, lifted me to the next floor of a 30-story building of sorts.

Reading 25: Ok, so this means when I'm living my best life, Voldemort will suffer for what he did to me and my kids. Evil laugh

Elevator stops, I unload a little bit of my emotional baggage, I read it again, elevator lifts.

26: When I'm living my best life, Voldemort will suffer for what he did.

Elevator stops, I unload a little bit more of my emotional baggage, I read it again, elevator lifts.

27: When I'm living my best life, I won't think about how Voldemort will suffer.

Elevator stops, I unload a little bit more of my emotional baggage, I read it again, elevator lifts.

28: When I'm living my best life, I won't think about Voldemort.

Elevator stops, I unload even more of my emotional baggage, I read it again, elevator lifts.

29: When I'm living my best life, I won't care about what will happen to Voldemort.

Elevator stops, I unload most of the rest of my emotional baggage, I read it again, elevator lifts.

30: When I'm living my best life, I won't care about Voldemort at all. Remember, the opposite of love is indifference.

Ding, ding, ding! The elevator finally goes to the top.

Please forgive my hint at a self-deprecating pejorative.

It's usually a long and tedious process to get to the point of indifference. That 30th floor is a beautiful place, however, there's a much more magnificent place above the 30th floor. That magnificent place is what I like to call the Forgiveness Penthouse Suite. Will Smith once said, "There is no revenge so complete as forgiveness." True forgiveness is a process; it is a daily choice we make to prevent the actions of others from dictating our emotions and choices. That brings us to the questions of the hour... um, I mean the questions of the chapter. First of all, did Voldemort ever have his karma appointment fulfilled? I cannot answer that because once I made it to the 30th floor, the place of indifference, I stopped that information highway and created the healthy boundary for myself so if anyone tried giving me an "update" on anything Voldemort related, I stopped them, thanked them for trying to help, and politely asked they not tell me anything at all. THAT was liberating!

The 2nd question of the hour and chapter: had I truly and fully forgiven Voldemort? Would you believe me if I told you, absolutely YES, as of September 25, 2019, when the divorce was final, I had truly and fully forgiven Voldemort?

No? You don't believe me? You don't believe that, at that time, I had truly and fully forgiven Voldemort???

Sarcastic gasp

I was trying to sound shocked, but I have a feeling there's a bit of my sarcasm that was lost in the translation. Of course, I hadn't truly and fully forgiven him. I was still trying to learn how to forgive, so at that time I was not in the mental or emotional state to be able to muster any semblance of forgiveness. There were individual days that were better than others. At first, those better days were few and far between, but as time continued, thanks to George Herbert and Will Smith, the number of better days were beginning to outnumber the bad ones. And so, I stayed stuck on the 30th "floor" at the level of indifference in regard to Voldemort. I had not yet made it to the Forgiveness Penthouse Suite. Oh, I wanted to OWN the Forgiveness Penthouse Suite, but in order to do that, I needed to allow my soul to be lifted one more time to that next level beyond the 30th "floor" of indifference. For that to happen, I had to forgive...truly and fully.

Yes, I needed to forgive Voldemort, but it wasn't just about forgiving Voldemort. I needed to forgive MPF and FPF, to forgive first husband, to forgive every person who had so egregiously hurt me. And then, I began to realize something that I hadn't even considered until another dear friend brought it to my attention. Forgiving these people from my past would be a walk in the park, a piece of cake, easy-peasy... forgiving them would be an easy-peasy walk in the park with a piece of cake, compared to forgiving the most difficult and important person that I hadn't acknowledged. I needed to forgive myself. Forgiving myself was the necessary forgiveness that, to this day, is my greatest struggle. Have I taken ownership of the Forgiveness Penthouse Suite yet? Nope. Am I working to try to achieve that elusive rainbow in the sky? Absolutely I am. And one day... maybe soon... one day, I will sign that deed, move into, and take residence in the Penthouse Suite of Forgiveness. I smell yet another book on our horizon... oh, how I love the smell of books!

CHAPTER 27

We Plan, God Laughs: *No One Can Check Every Box... Right???*

Parenting is NOT for the faint of heart. It is fascinating to me how at every stage of parenting, I believed THAT was the most difficult stage. As I am writing this, all four of my "babies" are officially adults. I truly thought that once my kids were at the adult stage, I could take a step back and enjoy how my parenting is complete. Just then, you might have heard the sound of my belly laugh. See, this is the stuff about parenting no one tells you. Why? I believe it's because either a) people truly believe that once a child is the age of 18, they are considered an adult and their parenting job is finished or 2) there has been an evil plot since the beginning of human life where parents of their adult children take a solemn silent oath keeping the harsh and tumultuous re-alities of this parenting stage a secret from any aspiring parents because there's a probability that if people knew the truth, there would no longer be procreation and the result would be the com-plete extermination of the human species.

Yes, I am still my children's parent regardless of their age, thus I am still and ever will be in a stage of parenting; however, the job description is completely different from our responsibilities with pre-adult age children. The good news is, I'm no longer their authority and cannot truly control my children; I can only offer advice to hopefully guide them with the wisdom I've gained and then stay in the background and watch as their choices unfold their life in front of them. The bad news is, I'm no longer their authority and cannot truly control my children; I can only offer advice to hopefully guide them with the wisdom I've gained and then stay in the background and watch as their choices unfold their life in front of them. I've already experienced the absolute elation and the absolute terror of having my adult child seek my advice, make the opposite choice, and suffer the consequences. It's like watching a train wreck in super slow motion.

I believe this scenario parallels the old Yiddish proverb "We plan, God laughs." For many years, I thought I had life and all of its intricacies all together and completely figured out. Much like my adult children, all too often I thought "I got this… I don't need help at all" or "I'm positive this is the right choice!" only to find out I DIDN'T have it, I DID need help, and the choice was absolutely the WRONG choice. In my defense, I was basing these decisions on my limbic system rather than my cerebral cortex. What is the difference between the limbic system and the cerebral cortex? According to psychologytoday.com, "A great deal of our moment-to-moment experience results from the interplay of these two parts of the brain. When you understand this interplay, you will understand a lot about how the mind works. The prefrontal lobe of the cerebral cortex performs the functions of logical analysis, planning for the future, and self-control. The limbic system is responsible for motivation and emotion, with one particularly important part, the amygdala, playing a key role in the fight-or-flight response and feelings of fear and anger." This isn't just psychobabble. Having survival mode set up mental camp in my limbic system and living in survival mode literally my entire life up to the year 2019 prevented me from having the ability to think logically. Of course, I didn't make the best decisions. The cerebral cortex operates slowly and is logical and precise, while the limbic system works fast and is dominated by emotion and impulse.

As of July 2019, I was beginning to transition to a new mental place where I could FINALLY give my limbic system a much needed and much deserved rest. Oh, that limbic system hasn't gone anywhere as demonstrated by my C-PTSD; however, I was finally able to slow down and start thinking logically. I had allowed myself to be alone, I had allowed myself to date myself and get to know ME. I discovered that I'm completely complete and content alone and I was completely complete and content in social settings as a single person, so what was missing? I decided I wanted to find a fun companion to experience social events and dates, and then I wanted to go home, by myself, and enjoy being single and independent. This wasn't what I needed; this was what I wanted. Before you stop me with the legitimate "Wait just a cotton-pickin' minute... what do you mean that's not what you needed???" question, allow me to clarify.

I no longer had unmet needs because my needs were already met by ME. I was slowly digging myself out of the financial hole that Voldemort put me in and was not only making ends meet, but I was also able to put a little money back for emergencies. I was able to grocery shop without a calculator adding every item and its tax down to the penny praying my card would not be declined AGAIN. My utilities were no longer on the verge of being shut off. Every bill was on-time with no extra fees or penalties. I was able to fill my car with fuel when it was at half a tank without worrying that I had over drafted my account AND giving myself the guarantee that I would not run out of gas; I would not have to walk or beg for enough gas money to get me back and forth to work. I was able to pay for my children's lunches at school and they no longer had to take the same PB&J sack lunch every day of the week. I was meeting my and my children's needs without stress or worry. It was liberating, it was beautiful, and it was AMAZING!

Because my needs were met by me, I was able to focus on what I wanted out of life. I could decide who I would allow in my life and who I would not give any attention whatsoever. I had complete control.

Insert maniacal laugh.

I allowed myself to look into the various dating websites and apps. I probably don't need to tell you, but the dating "pool" is an absolute cesspool out there, especially for a single woman in her 40's. I quickly learned that the sites that required a fee were for one thing and one thing only. I believe the kids today call it a "booty call." Those sites, at least in the year 2019, afforded the opportunity to create a profile on their site for free without the ability to message any other members, and those with paid memberships were able to message whomever they wanted. I refused... REFUSED to pay anything for these apps, so I was limited to only receiving messages. As soon as my profile was created, I was already being "pinged" with messages from desperate men of ALL ages. I didn't keep my profile on any of those sites for long because after reading their messages (many with pictures of body parts I truly did NOT want to see nor did I want to be in any contact with them in ANY capacity) I would feel like I needed to take a scorching hot shower to get the sickening full-body-shudder-gross-out-nasty feeling off of me. Reading all of that garbage

I would ask my empty bedroom, "Isn't there any man between the ages of 40 and 48 out there not just looking for a one-and-done-hit-it-and-quit-it experience?" All of the creepers who were hitting on me via these sites/apps were not men, no they were merely BOYS trying to pretend to be a man. It really was so sad. I shifted my focus from those shallow-end cesspools to a more tolerable platform: Facebook Dating.

Facebook Dating was much more palatable. Whomever came up with the format and guidelines of Facebook Dating was a GENIUS! After creating my profile, I was able to see suggestions of possible connections based mostly on the answers to my preferences and specifications for who I was looking for in a companion. The best part of that was there would never be a suggestion of anyone on my main profile page friends list. It was much more anonymous, and I felt so much safer. Now, I did have male Facebook friends who would message me privately and reveal their desire to take me out... that they had wanted to take me out ever since we had met, but I was either with First Husband or Voldemort. When they found out I was single, they were grateful for the chance to get to know me as more than just a friend. That was weird to me, but I was so flattered! And, while they were my friends, they still had to pass my rigorous screening process before I'd agree to go out with them.

If you remember back in chapter 26, I alluded to my scrupulous mental checklist if I were to ever consider dating anyone besides myself, and if only ONE of the requirements were not met, I'd move on to the next candidate. That list was comprehensive, extensive, and vast. That list covered everything from financial responsibility to respect, from music genres to sports teams, from past endeavors to future dreams, from personal experience to social ideals. I'm not going to take the time or word space to detail every individual criterion, but I will give you a few of the big points that were usually the first deal-breakers when a dating candidate was on the list of potentials. They had to:

- Be single... either divorced or never married I didn't care, but they HAD to be single.

- Fully respect me and my children in their speech and language AND in their actions.

- Have a job.

- Be fiscally responsible and financially stable... they had to be on top of their monthly bills AND not living paycheck to paycheck.

- Have their own residence... renting was acceptable, owning a plus.

- Have a car... a truck, SUV, or van would be acceptable as well. The point is, they had to be able to provide transportation to and from without my help.

- Be a US veteran. I didn't care which branch. Air Force would've been a plus because of my dad, but that was not a deal-breaker.

- Have none of their own children, unless those children were adults and on their own. I was not going to attempt to blend my family with theirs and be a stepmom to anyone's children again. Hypocritical? Maybe, but that's what I wanted. My rules, my choices.

- Love music... music HAD to be a huge part of their life and had to be eclectic in their music preferences; whether that mean merely having a love and appreciation for music and concert-going or the ability to sing well or play an instrument proficiently, OR all of the above.

That is quite the list of expectations, isn't it? And that's only the tip of the expectation iceberg. Why in the world would I have such a list of expectations? As I think back, I realize now it's because I believe, deep down, I did not want to be in a relationship with another man for the rest of my life and this was my way of protecting myself. That was my cerebral cortex doing its job. Just the thought of allowing myself to be in a position of potential disappointment, hurt, and more trauma was enough to make that 6-foot-thick and 100-foot-high impenetrable wall thicker and higher. Good luck to anyone attempting to scale THAT wall. And so, once I chose to open myself up to the world of dating, it was game on. Yes, Facebook Dating was much more safe and much less icky; however, there were still plenty of creepers out there and they were some sneaky old cusses! Due to the high level of creepiness, I found it necessary to, in addition to the above criteria, create an initial prerequisite screening deal-breaker checklist.

I had created my Facebook Dating profile and was rather surprised at the number of "likes" and private messages I received. The creepy factor wasn't nearly as dry-heave provoking as the other pay-to-play sites and apps, but there was definitely a creepy element among the predators. Usually, my screening process involved three levels.

Level 1-Any initial message involving "YOU ARE SO FN HOT, what they want to do to me, a dick-pick, or even a HINT of degradation, that warranted IMMEDIATE blocking.

Level 2-They passed level 1, and their initial message was respectful; however, if their response to my reply involved anything remotely in the vein of Level 1, that warranted IMMEDIATE blocking.

Level 3-They passed level 1, and they passed Level 2 with initial conversation that was respectful; however, if subsequent conversation via the Facebook Dating messaging started to sound like Level 1, that warranted IMMEDIATE blocking.

If anyone made it past Level 3, I would be willing to exchange cell phone numbers and would continue conversation via text. If that continued in a respectful manner, I would agree to speak over the phone and subsequently, I would agree to meet them in-person for a date. At this point with the prospect, I would only operate under the first six deal breakers listed above. I decided if a man had passed the first 3 levels, they deserved a chance to meet in person and I would continue the screening process. I would only agree to meet in a crowded public location and would drive myself so I could get away if necessary.

I created my Facebook Dating profile the beginning of September 2019. Between then and the middle of October, I agreed to go on 12 dates that had made it through levels 1, 2, and 3 of my screening process. I knew within the first 5 minutes of meeting them in person if I would allow another date. Of these 12 dates, can you guess how many were successful? If you guessed zero, you are correct. NONE of them were granted a second date. That was discouraging because 1) they all made it through my initial three levels of rigorous screening and the subsequent conversations, 2) I couldn't understand how I missed any of their red flags, and 3) it supported my theory that there were no good men left who were in my specifications.

That 12th date is one I will never forget. It was October 17, 2019, and it was the most important day of my new and improved life. Why, you ask? Patience, grasshopper. Stay with me...

I can't remember the guy's name or what he looked like. I can't remember his occupation or what he wore. I can't remember most of the conversation, but what I CAN remember is the last words he said to me and the last words I said to him. We met for dinner at a Mexican restaurant. He offered to pay when we arranged the date, so I thought this guy had potential. We had just gotten our food when...

Him: Oh, I forgot to tell you, I'm so excited today because I'm officially 6 months out of prison.

Me: You're 6 months OUT of prison?

Him: Yes, ma'am... it's six whole months today that I've been out of prison.

Me: ....

Awkward silence for what felt an eternity

Me: *I looked at my Smart Watch.* Oh, NO! *I opened my cell phone and pretended to look at my text messages.* That's my daughter... her ride ditched her, and I need to go pick her up. I'm so sorry, I have to leave.

Him: Are you serious?

Me: *Standing up from the table.* Yes, I'm so sorry. Thank you for dinner.

Just for the sake of clarification, my daughter did NOT text me, I did not have to leave because I needed to pick her up. That was my standard get-me-the-hell-outta-here getaway excuse.

I quickly walked out of the restaurant and, when I knew I was out of his view, I RAN to my car praying he didn't follow me out. I drove to a parking lot that was a few blocks away from that restaurant and called my dear friend, the one from chapter 26. Her husband was playing in a softball tournament that night and the games were being played less than 5 minutes from where I was parked. Coincidence? Not at all. I put the address of the ballpark in my phone and headed to the safety of my friends. It was a chilly October evening.

Me: That's it... I'm DONE! There are officially no more good men out there.

Her: Oh sweetie, you're going to have to kiss A LOT of frogs before you find your prince.

Approximately 2 minutes after she uttered those words, my cell phone pinged a text notification. It was this guy I had been texting back and forth with for about a week. Now, I need to give you a bit of background information on this guy.

Obviously, he had made it through level 1. His initial message to me via Facebook Dating private messaging was "I see you went to the Flogging Molly and Dropkick Murphys concert. I'm so jealous because I was supposed to go to that show and missed it."

Say WHAAAA????

Up to that point, I hadn't received an initial message anything remotely like that. So, I looked at his Facebook Dating profile. He lived about 20 miles from me. He was an I.T. guy and a US Navy veteran. And he answered one of the canned questions Facebook Dating offered as a choice to answer: what is the last song you sang? His answer? Kashmir by Led Zeppelin at karaoke. Now, you might be thinking UH-OH, stay away from those karaoke guys because remember that LAST one??? Nope... at this point, I was not allowing Voldemort to affect my future. I was intrigued by this Navy veteran who lived near me, who obviously liked concerts AND had similar taste in music. There was only 1 problem. My preferred age range that I had chosen was between 40 and 48 because, at that time I was 45 years old and thought that was a good age span. This guy was 50 years old. He didn't LOOK 50 in his pictures, so I decided that was close enough and he deserved a shot. This guy had passed level 1 with flying colors, so I sent him a response. I don't remember what I said to him, but I do remember his next message continued our music themed conversation and he quickly sailed past level 2. As our back and forth continued, he flew through level 3 on a beautiful flying-colors-rainbow. Phone numbers were exchanged, and the texting commenced. Not once did he allude to anything inappropriate whatsoever. He was a wonderfully nerdy, intelligent, perfect gentleman. We texted about music, books, our jobs, likes, dislikes, and all other things superficial. It was so refreshing being treated like a person and not an object.

Now, back to our regularly scheduled story already in progress...

My friend said, "You're going to have to kiss A LOT of frogs before you find your prince," two minutes later my phone pings a text message notification and it's this man who I had yet to speak to over the phone. The text message said, "Hey, I'm at the Brewhouse for karaoke. I've saved a seat for you. Will you be joining me?"

In-ter-esting!...

Me: Hey <my friend's name>, how far are we from Brewhouse?

Her: I'm not sure... not far?

Me: *I Googled "Brewhouse".* Hmmm... according to Maps, we're about 7 minutes from Brewhouse......... I'm going to karaoke!

And that's exactly what I did.

I was quite familiar with Brewhouse. Brewhouse was the Thursday karaoke bar that I was required to frequent with Voldemort. It had been almost a year since I had stepped foot in Brewhouse. Before I opened that door, I thought to myself "Please, PLEASE don't let this guy be a psycho-douchebag!"

As I opened the door and walked in, I heard a collective shout "FIREBALL!" Fireball was my karaoke name. I saw a lot of familiar faces, many who knew what I was going through as well as many that did not. Those who did not know I had gotten rid of Voldemort asked about him.

Them: Where's your guy?

Me: My guy? Oh, you mean [Voldemort's name]? We split up. Our divorce was final September 25. I'm almost a whole month [Voldemort's name] free!

Them: Oh, thank GOD! I HATED that guy!!!

Me: Really?

Them: Hell yeah... what a douchebag! He did not deserve you AT ALL!!!

Me: You hated him?

Them: HATED him! We hated what he was doing to you.

Me: You knew???

Them: Everyone knew.

Me: You knew!

Them: Yeah... we hated him... but we LOVE you!!!

That conversation happened, almost verbatim, at all of the weekly rotation karaoke bars where Voldemort and I had been regulars.

As I made my way through the crowd, I noticed a guy at the bar waving at me and pointing to the empty seat beside him. I waved back and eventually made it to where he was sitting.

Me: [The guy's name]? Is that you?

Him: Yes, ma'am, it is. Krista?

Me: Yessir. *I held out my hand to shake his.* Navy vet? Thank you for your service!

Him: *He shook my hand.* Well, thank you for your support!

Me: *I took a 5-dollar bill out of my wallet and tried to get the bartender's attention.*

Him: What are you doing?

Me: I'm buying myself a drink. Do you want one?

Him: Uh, no thank you… and you put that money away! I asked you here so I'm buying! What'll you have?

Me: Wow, seriously? I'll have a bourbon and diet. This is new!

Him: What is new?

Me: Having the guy volunteer to pay for my drink when on a date.

Him: You would have to pay for your own drinks???

Me: Sometimes I had to pay for theirs.

Him: *He shook his head* That is the most ridiculous thing I've ever heard. The woman should NEVER pay for ANYTHING on a date!

Me: Welcome to the 21st century… and, by the way, isn't dating a veritable cesspool nowadays?

Him: Boy, you ain't kidding... I'll drink to that.

I arrived at Brewhouse at approximately 9:30 that evening. It was a Thursday, but I was on Fall break, so staying out late wasn't an issue. That man and I talked... and talked... and talked. We would only pause the conversation for 1 of 2 reasons, either a) to answer nature or 2) when it was our turn to sing. I think I blinked twice and suddenly it was last call. What? Already??? We talked for almost 4 hours. It was as if we were the only two people in the bar, well besides the karaoke host and the bartender of course.

As we were being directed out the door because "you don't have to go home, but you can't stay here," he asked if I would be interested in a REAL first date. Based on that 4-hour conversation, I discovered that he was checking every box on my mental checklist. The only unmet criteria, which I decided could be flexible, was the age difference. A five-year difference wasn't a big deal to me, so I agreed.

Him: So, would you like to go on a real first date?

Me: I think that's definitely do-able.

Him: How about tomorrow night?

Me: Oh, no... I can't tomorrow night.

Him: Are you free Saturday?

Me: Yes, I'm free all day.

Him: Saturday it is. I'll text you tomorrow.

In case you're wondering, yes, he kissed me that night. I could tell he was rather nervous, which I thought was adorable. To be honest, I was nervous as well. What impressed me most at that point was there was no offer to go home with him. Such a gentleman!

As we texted back and forth the next day, it was decided that he would pick me up around 11am on his motorcycle. We would go for a ride and see where it would take us. I hadn't been on the back of a motorcycle in a very long time, and I was a tad bit uneasy at the thought, but wanted to look like a tough badass who didn't fear anything. I must have put on a great front because later he told me he didn't have any clue as to my fear of riding.

Finally, the time came, I heard him pull into my driveway and I did my best to get on the back of that bike as gracefully as possible, which was no easy feat especially after he had to help me secure the helmet that, thank goodness, fit me. It was a beautiful autumn day that Saturday; the weather could not have been more perfect, and the leaves were changing color. And then, I remembered it is terribly difficult to have a conversation on a motorcycle.

Him: *shouts something to me*

Me: WHAT?

Him: ... WOULD......EAT?

Me: WHERE WOULD I LIKE TO EAT???

Him: WHEN???

Me: YES!

Him: WHAT???

Me: WHAT???

Him: OK!!!

We had the opportunity to take a ferry across the Mississippi river during our ride. As we turned onto the road leading to the ferry, he pulls the bike over, stops, gets off the bike, and tells me he'll be just a minute. In absolute awe and amazement, I watched this man walk to the middle of the road, pick up a turtle, that I hadn't noticed, and carry it about 10 yards off the road into a grassy wooded spot. He almost had to pick up my jaw from the road as well. I couldn't believe what I was seeing. Realizing my astonishment, he suddenly seemed embarrassed, and he quickly said "Well, I couldn't let the little guy get killed," and got back on the bike.

I felt like I was in a dream. I thought to myself, "This guy is just too good to be true! If something seems too good to be true, it IS too good to be true." I was preparing myself to tell him BUH-BYE because I just KNEW the love bombing was about to commence. So far, I hadn't seen any red flags waving at me, there was no creepy feeling, and he was quickly checking off every one of my requirements. How can this be possible???

- Single (Divorced)—CHECK

- No children of his own—CHECK

- Owned his own home—CHECK

- Owned a truck AND a car—CHECK

- Both the car and truck were fully paid for so no monthly payment, showed his financial responsibility—CHECK

- I.T. career with the USDA—CHECK

- Veteran—CHECK

- Spoke respectfully to me and about my children—CHECK

- Music was an important part of his life—CHECK

- And, he added a criterion that I didn't realize I wanted on the list: showing respect for life, both people and animals—CHECK!!!

I don't know how, but my impossible list, you know the one that I thought that no one could ever check every box? Well, THIS guy was quickly and systematically knocking out each criteria like knocking out targets at the shooting range! I decided I needed to try scaring him away. That's the only way I could see just how real he was. So, I proceeded to tell him the overview of my life's story. Surely, SURELY this would make him run fast and run far away from me. Well, it DIDN'T make him run away and don't call me Shirley (ok, you are correct, that's much funnier when you hear me say it rather than reading it). We were in line to get on the ferry, so I had just enough time to drop the baggage bomb on him from the 30,000-foot view.

He didn't even flinch, except when I saw him choking back tears. His empathy was obvious when he said to me "I'm so very sorry you've had to endure all of that." He didn't try making it about him, he didn't try to one-up my story like it was a competition, he didn't try to belittle me, he didn't try to love-bomb me. He was so kind... so very kind!

We made it to the other side of the river and we rode a short way further before he pulled into the parking lot of what looked like a "hole in the wall" kind of place where we had lunch. The food was good, but the conversation was superb. We were jumping from one topic to another and back and somewhere along the way, the movie Deadpool was mentioned.

Me: I've never seen it.

Him: You've NEVER seen Deadpool???

Me: No, I was never really interested in movies like that.

Him: We must rectify this situation. Do you have Prime on your TV?

Me: No

Him: Well, that settles it... we'll go back to your place, I'll add Prime to your TV, and we're going to watch it. That ok with you?

Me: Sure?!?

And that is what we did. What I didn't tell him is how violence on TV or movies affects me. My C-PTSD makes watching any kind of scary or violent shows or movies rather difficult and tumultuous. When I watch something and the characters are physically hurt, I physically hurt as well. I literally feel pain when I watch violence, so I have to shut my eyes and cover my ears. If you've seen Deadpool, you know the very first scene does not involve teddy bears, unicorns, or sparkly rainbows. I was convinced he thought I was putting on a show when I buried my face in his arm while covering my ears. I found out later he didn't think that at all. I was especially shocked when he didn't make fun of me or belittle me for my low violence tolerance level. Who was this masked man? If you would ask him, he'd say, in complete honesty, "I haven't done anything special, I just treat people the way you're SUPPOSED to treat people."

We watched all of Deadpool, we went for Mexican food for dinner, and by the end of the date, I knew I had found one of the few remaining of an endangered species. I had found a good man.

Remember, my original plan was to never again allow another man into my figurative fortress of heart protection. Instead, I was hearing the faint sound of a giggle... we plan, God laughs.

CHAPTER 28

Am I Little Red Riding Hood, or Cinderella? *Is He the Big Bad Wolf or Prince Charming?*

As an elementary music teacher, I was given the opportunity to teach my kindergarten students nursery rhymes, so I would also read them fairy tales from children's books. In doing a bit of research, I learned that the Disney-type-renditions-with-only-happy-ending fairy tales were not originally all cute and sweet. The Grimm Brothers' fairy tales were actually quite dark and usually ended with someone being served as a meal or dancing themselves to death in hot iron shoes. For example, let's look at Little Red Riding Hood. The first print of this classic fairy tale was in 1697 by Charles Perrault. In his story, the big bad wolf gobbled up Red's grandmother, then he successfully disguised himself as Red's grandmother, and at the end of this rendition, Red is gobbled up by the big bad wolf. So, we see a rather unhappy ending for Red. On the other hand, we have Cinderella. The original telling of Cinderella dates back to Greek and Roman times. The evolution of this story brings us to the most familiar version, the Disney version. Of all the modern renditions of the Cinderella story, Disney's is my personal favorite. The poor abused girl ends up with a fairy godmother who gave her what she needed to attend the prince's ball, met the prince, danced with the prince, left at midnight, lost one of her shoes, was found again by the prince, married the prince, and lived happily ever after. After my first date with this man I found on Facebook Dating, let's refer to him as "Facebook Dating guy", I was rather concerned as I attempted to process what was happening in my life. Was I going to end up like Little Red Riding Hood, or Cinderella? Am I dealing with the big bad wolf, or prince charming? I kept my red flag radar on full blast and decided when he showed his true colors, I would give him my emergency "buh-bye" that I kept tucked away in my back pocket, then I would move on to the next prospect.

Facebook Dating guy (I will refer to him as FBDG) and I agreed that the purpose of our relationship was purely for companionship. Having an intimate relationship would NOT be on the table. We would enjoy each other's company and then at the end of the day I would go to my home, and he would go to his. This system was working beautifully... until.

I'll set the scene for you. It's the second week of December 2019. FBDG and I were at my house. I had made us dinner and we were enjoying a bottle of good bourbon while I washed dishes.

Him: That dinner was fantastic!

Me: Well, thank you!

Him: Better than any restaurant.

Me: *Goofy grin*

Him: I love it when you smile like that...

And then, he said ... IT...

Him: I love you so much!

We both stopped and froze like statues for the longest recorded awkward silence in the history of awkward silences.

Me: Um... you what???

Him: Uhhh... nothing?

Me: What did you say?

Him: *He's in full-on panic mode* I didn't say anything... you
didn't hear anything...

Me: No, no... I believe I DID hear you say something
there, mister.

Him: *He hangs his head* I'm sorry... I'm sorry that just flew
out. I couldn't help it.

Me: ....

We had about 2 more minutes of awkward silence then,
thankfully, my youngest walked in the kitchen. Nothing else was
mentioned about IT the rest of the evening. I just reasoned the
cause of those 5 giant words was a really good meal and really
good bourbon.

A couple of days later we were talking on the phone. Keep in
mind that this is the second week of December.

Him: I'm off work for the rest of the year as of the 19th, then
I'm driving to Florida to visit my sister and her family.

Me: That's cool.

Him: Yep, gonna make that looooong drive all by myself... there and back.

Me: Well, call me crazy, but I'm thinking if you drive there, you'd have to drive back.

Him: It's like an eleven-hour drive... and that's if you don't stop.

Me: That's a really long drive.

Him: Yep, allllll by my lonesome self.

Me: Well, I hope you have safe travels.

Him: It's such a long trip when you're alone.

Me: *I finally got the hint* Well I could probably go with you.

Him: Really? You'd want to spend that much time in a car with me?

Me: Sure! Why not?

Him: Ok, but only if you WANT to go with me. I was thinking about staying until the New Year.

Me: Oh, there's no way I could do that. I have all of my kids coming to my house for Christmas... on Christmas day. I would need to be back no later than Christmas morning.

Him: That's no problem at all.

Me: Well, my last day of school is the 20th. If you want, come over after work on the 20th, we can leave super early the next morning. There's just one favor I need to ask of you.

Him: Name it.

Me: I need to find, buy, and wrap all of my Christmas gifts the evening of the 20th. You game?

Him: No problem. I gotchu!

Me: Okay. I should probably remind you just how much I absolutely loathe shopping of any kind. We will be going to Wal-Mart; I already have the plan of attack mapped out to get us in and out of there in the fastest time possible.

Him: Sounds good to me.

Me: We'll go straight back to the house and have a wrap-fest in the living room.

Him: Perfect. Looking forward to it.

After FBDG let his true feelings for me slip, I started thinking about it. A LOT!

From the time I met him in October until that December, I asked if he would be willing to meet some really important people in my life. He agreed and so he did.

I had him accompany me to dinner with my dear friend and her husband asking them to tell me what red flags they see and what they thought of FBDG. They did not see any red flags.

I had him attend one of my band's gigs and asked my band brothers what red flags they see and what they thought of FBDG. They did not see any red flags.

I took him to a karaoke night out with my dad and asked him what red flags he sees and what he thought of FBDG. He did not see any red flags.

No red flags? How is that possible???

When I could sense FBDG was hinting at wanting me to accompany him on his road trip to Florida, knowing that so far there were no visible red flags, I decided to give him the ultimate test. It's much easier to get to know someone better when you're on a long road trip. Road trips can make or break a relationship. It was time for me to pull that trigger.

All went according to the plan we created. On the December 20th I got off work, met FBDG at a restaurant for dinner, we completed operation Christmas prep, packed his car, and at the butt-crack of dawn, we started our journey to Florida. The plan was to only stop for fuel, food, and answering nature. We got in the car, started talking and literally did not stop talking until we arrived at our destination. We had talked so much that we were both losing our voices. I bombarded him with so many questions. What he didn't realize was that it was his interview... his relationship interview. I broached topics I knew would be hot-button topics with him. I was ruthless.

Me: So, you were raised Catholic?

Him: Yes ma'am.

Me: I was very much NOT raised Catholic. Ever hear of the Assemblies of God protestant denomination?

Him: Yeah, I've heard of it.

Me: So, what's the deal with praying to Mary? Shouldn't we just pray to God because, yanno, he created Mary and she really doesn't have any extra pull there because, well, she was human as well?

I could see his wheels turning, and I anticipated him blowing up at me and calling me everything but a white woman. But you know what? He didn't. He didn't become angry, agitated, or flustered. AT ALL!!!

Him: Well, now that's your opinion... allow me to explain my side of this issue.

And then he proceeded to calmly explain his beliefs.

Calmly? Calmly explain? No yelling? No name calling? No irrational violence? Just... CALM??

Yep... calm.

Could it be possible to have a conversation with opposing ideals and opinions and remain calm? It was other-dimensional for me.

We spent the next 4 days with his sister, his brother-in-law, and his nephew. We did a few touristy things, we visited his aunt and uncle at their winter home there in Florida, and the longer we were together, the more I realized just how compatible we were. Never mind the relinquishing of the original agreement. Based on what I saw, based on what my important people told me about him, based on the lack of a red flag, I allowed myself to look at him as more than just a fun companion. There was one more test, one more little piece of information: the flutters test. You heard me correctly... the flutters test. What in the world is a flutters test? I'm so glad you asked me that. Up until this point, I hadn't allowed myself to even consider seeing him within the parameters of an intimate relationship. I knew he would willingly take care of me. I knew he would willingly take care of my children. I knew he would be only respectful, kind, and loving to me and my children. What I did not know for sure was, did I truly have the same feelings for him as he had for me: did this guy give me the love flutters?

We decided we would drive the first half of the trip home on Christmas Eve, then finish the trip Christmas morning. Our halfway point was Chattanooga, Tennessee. We stopped at a hotel, ordered dinner in and continued our non-stop conversation. That night as I tried to sleep, I thought about the previous days and weeks with this man. He had checked off every box on my "impossible" list, I was always so eager and excited to talk with him, I adored and respected his mind, I would much rather spend my time WITH him than without him. My life with FBDG was so much more fun, joyful, and my favorite aspect of our relationship... peaceful. This man was definitely NOT the big bad wolf disguised in a nightgown and nightcap. This man, I started to believe, was my prince charming.

Christmas morning, December 25, 2019, FBDG and I were only about 3 hours from my house when I decided to open up about my plot and my newfound realization.

Me: I need to tell you something.

Him: Ok? Shoot!

Me: ....

Him: Ok? *He had a panicked look wash over his face.*

Me: I'm trying to make sure I say this the right way.

Him: *He looked even more somber.* O...K?

Me: ....

Him: You're killin' me smalls!!! *Nervous chuckle*

Me: Ok… you know the reason I went on this trip with you, don't you?

Him: Because you wanted to???

Me: Yes, but no… I needed to see for myself.

Him: You needed to see for yourself? What, exactly, did you need to see for yourself?

Me: Well, did you notice how I was throwing sensitive-topic arrows at you?

Him: Yeah… what's THAT all about???

Me: Remember how you kept your cool in response to those "arrows"?

Him: Well, there's no reason to get all worked up over someone's opinion… it's just that. Opinions are like armpits everyone has two of them and they usually stink.

Me: Right… well I needed to see a few things for myself. I needed to see how you respond to conflict, and I needed to see if I had the flutters.

Him: The flutters?

Me: Yeah, you know… that fluttery feeling when you… have strong feelings for someone.

Him: You mean, like, twitterpated?

Me: Sure… po-TAY-to, po-TAH-to

Him: Ok?

Me: Well, I know you would willingly take care of me and my children and provide for our every need, but I needed to know that I'm with you not because of that, but because of the flutters.

Him: .... O...K??? What are you saying here???

Me: Well... yes.

Him: Yes what?

Me: Yes, I have the flutters.

Him: Sooooo... what—are—you—saying?

Me: I've decided to give you a shot... to give US a shot.

Him: REALLY??? *I watched the worry and panic leave his face and a giant grin appeared.*

Me: I do have one major request. I need to know you'd be willing to pursue a faith journey with me. I cannot be in a relationship with anyone who is not willing to have a relationship with Jesus. This is a deal-breaker.

Him: I believe I can do that. He took my hand and held it most of the way home.

We arrived back at my house in time to prep some food for the family festivities. When my kids arrived, I took them aside one-by-one and asked them to please tell me what red flags they have seen with FBDG. I asked them to please tell me SOME-THING that would give me reason to kick this guy to the curb. All four of them responded the same, "Mom, there are NO red flags. None at all. We like this guy!"

Over the years I've learned there are two sure-fire ways to de-termine if a person is a good person: a) when they're around children and 2) when they're around dogs. In both scenarios, watch how the kids and dogs respond. Kids and dogs just KNOW when they can trust someone. I didn't have a dog, so I could only go on what my kids told me; especially after everything they had endured in their lives. Because I trust my children's judgement more than any other, finally, at the age of 45, I believed I had found my soul mate. I found my FBDG that fit perfectly in the FBDG shaped hole in my heart.

I had finally found my prince charming!

CHAPTER 29

Lessons Learned:
THIS BETTER END RIGHT

As I mentioned before, I am profusely affected by movies, but it's not just physical violence that gives me literal pain. I have an identical response when I'm watching drama, suspense, action, thrillers, romantic comedy, and every other audiovisual genre imaginable. I become so engrossed in the story I'm watching, it's as if I'm involved in it along with the characters. I'm extremely particular when it comes to which movies I choose to invest my time in. Whenever I go to the theater to see a movie, as it begins, you will most likely hear me say the same thing every time: "This better end right!" If I'm talking to someone who has already watched something I'm interested in watching, I will inevitably ask them, "Does it end right?" Now, an ending being right or wrong is completely subjective; when it comes to a story, there is a myriad of possible opinions. What I consider a "wrong" ending isn't necessarily "wrong" to everyone. Nevertheless, my children are well aware of this phenomenon of mine, and I learned the hard way that when my children suggest a given movie, I need to investigate that movie and how I will feel after having watched it. The perfect example of this happened around the year 2018.

Child #3: Hey mom, are you familiar with the book The Boy in the Striped Pajamas?

Me: I don't think so. What's it about?

Child #3: It's about a boy in World War 2.

Me: Sounds interesting, why do you ask?

Child #3: They made it into a movie. Would you like to watch it with me and [child #4's name]?

Me: You know I love watching new-to-me stories with you two... I'd absolutely love to watch that with you.

Now, if I had asked my typical question, if it ends "right", maybe I would still have that entire box of tissues I went through as a result of the ending for which I was NOT adequately prepared. If you are not familiar with this story, The Boy in the Striped Pajamas, allow me to save you from the same grief and trauma inflicted on me. A little boy's family moved into a house on the property of a Polish concentration camp. The father was an officer in the Nazi SS and had been given the task to oversee this concentration camp. The little boy, Bruno, wandered away from the house, as little boys tend to do, and approached a fence where he saw people on the other side of the fence. They were all wearing striped "pajamas". There, Bruno met another little boy on the other side of the fence. They became friends. It seemed completely innocent. At the end of the story, we saw Bruno join his little friend on the other side of the fence. While Bruno was there, all of the people in striped "pajamas", including little Bruno, were gathered into a big room and as the scene panned out, we realize it was a gas chamber.

THE STORY DID NOT END RIGHT!!!

I was an absolute mess. The end of that story wrecked me on so many levels.

There may be some of you out there who can relate. Perhaps while reading this book, you might have thought, at times, that this story better end "right". I feel that to my core, my friend.

Well, how about I tell you the rest of the story and you can be the judge as to whether my story ends "right"?

Christmas day, December 25, 2019, I decided to give my FBDG a shot at an exclusive relationship. We spent most of our time together, barring work hours. I still had my little miracle house and would utilize it when I would start to feel overwhelmed or needed some time for myself. I kept it because it was my safety net for when, you know, when the red flags were finally out and blatantly obvious. And then, COVID hit. When the big shut-down happened, FBDG and I were together 24/7. I was teaching from his house via Zoom, and his I.T. job became exclusively remote.

Time out... I need to back up briefly in this story... remember when I mentioned that I had started smoking thanks to Voldemort? Well, when I met FBDG that first date, I was still a smoker. I did not know it at the time, but one of his "hard no's" was smoking. He said that when I asked if he minded me smoking and that I said I hate the stupid habit and want to quit but have not gathered enough strength to quit just yet, he gave me a free pass. I truly did hate smoking from the moment I started, but it became the one thing that could calm me. Letting go of that "security blankie" was a terrifying notion.

Ok... time in...

As I mentioned, FBDG was an I.T. specialist for the USDA. That meant sometimes he needed to travel to Washington, DC, or Kansas City to fix... whatever it is that an I.T. specialist for the USDA needs to fix. The end of June 2020, I was invited to accompany FBDG to Kansas City. We had the opportunity to go to a karaoke bar, enjoy some live music, and some good food. It was an amazing time getting to know each other better. I learned how genuine, considerate, empathetic, intelligent, giving, selfless, determined, and respectful this man truly was. I was so amazed at how wonderfully different he was from every other relationship I had ever experienced. I felt like this guy was absolutely too good to be true. I watched his every move looking for a red flag to pop up and waited for the other shoe to drop, because it's ME we're talking about. Me. You know, the woman with the figurative bulls eye on her chest who only had bad things happen to her.

Now, I still had no intention of ever marrying again. I made it a point to remind FBDG, often, that I don't NEED him in my life, I WANT him in my life. There is a huge difference between needing someone and wanting someone. I refused to be in a co-dependent relationship ever again... to this day, I adhere to this standard.

Everything was going so well. We spent a lovely work-vacay in Kansas City, our relationship was growing together through our shared faith journey. Would I finally have the life I'd always dreamed of? It was looking like that certainly could happen.

We had been home after our trip for about a week and FBDG mentioned he wasn't feeling well. He had a fever, congestion, cough, and said he felt like he'd been run over, multiple times, by a tractor-trailer. As a Navy veteran, he utilized the VA for his medical needs free of charge to him. The problem was, getting in to see his primary care physician was challenging at best. And, when he did see any physicians at the VA, the standard of care was abysmal. My FBDG felt bad enough that he went to the VA hospital emergency room. Because I have this knack for being a squeaky wheel and getting answers to all the questions, I wanted to go with him to make sure he was getting what he needed, however, we were in the middle of the pandemic shutdown, so I was not allowed to go with him. Even if we were married, I still wouldn't have been able to go.

So, he went to the Emergency room of John Cochran hospital in downtown St. Louis by himself. There, he tested positive for COVID-19. If you remember, at this time (the summer of the year 2020), there was a LOT of arguing as to the best means to treat COVID-19. To make matters worse, FBDG was already dealing with service-connected asthma and sleep apnea. The doctor at that ER told him he had COVID-19, and he should get rest, force fluids, and take Tylenol. Apparently, that was the best care the VA could offer. When FBDG arrived home, he immediately called his primary care physician. She said she would order more Albuterol and send a blood-oxygen meter to keep an eye on his blood oxygen level. FBDG did not improve, in fact, he was getting more and more sick as the day went on. The next day, when the blood-oxygen meter hadn't been delivered with the Albuterol, he decided to order one from Amazon same-day. He was in his house walking upstairs from the basement and was struggling to get to the top of the stairs. He had just gotten the blood-oxygen meter and put it on his finger. His blood oxygen level was 78. SEVENTY-EIGHT!!! He, again, called his primary care physician, to which he was told GO TO THE NEAREST ER! There was a hospital less than 5 miles from his house, so I drove him there. Again, they wouldn't let me go in with him. I sent him inside and begged him to let me know what was happening. I felt so helpless. All of those years of cancer treatment, my miscarriage, and my stillbirth came flooding back all at once. I was SO SCARED!

The hospital I took him to did not have a COVID wing, so it was decided that he'd be transported by ambulance to the VA hospital, John Cochran. I begged him to have them take him to Mercy hospital instead, but he was too weak to argue with them and they wouldn't listen to me because I was just a girlfriend. After he was triaged, he ended up in the ICU. I begged the VA people to please let me bring him his phone charger and anything else he needed. They let me drop off a bag with his belongings at the ER and had a nurse disinfect as best they could, then delivered it to FBDG.

We would video-chat via Facebook Messenger. A few days into his ICU stay, while we were chatting, the doctor approached FBDG.

Dr: Good afternoon [FBDG's name]. How are you feeling today?

FBDG: I'll be honest with you, doc. I am not feeling any better at all.

Dr: I figured as much. I was just looking over your chart and I see that you've been gradually declining in your condition. Your blood-oxygen level just doesn't want to increase. We have you on the highest O2 level that is allowable through your O2 mask.

FBDG: Yeah, the nurse told me about that.

Dr: [FBDG's name], I came here to let you know that if your numbers don't start to take a turn for the better, I'm going to have to intubate.

FBDG: Ok. Do what you have to do to get me better.

Dr: That's the other thing… as of yet, I have not been able to save any of our COVID-19 patients who have been intubated.

FBDG: ……………

Dr: [FBDG's name]? Do you understand what I've just told you?

FBDG: I think you just told me that if my numbers don't get better, you have no choice but to intubate me… and that I won't make it out of here alive.

Dr: Well, basically, yes… that's it in a nutshell. I'll be back to check on you in a bit.

FBDG: Ok, doc.

Me: Did that doctor say what I think he just said?

FBDG: His voice was soft and weak Yes, ma'am. He did.

Me: I'm sorry, but that's just not acceptable. *I was desperately trying to hold back my tears.*

Him: I'm sorry, baby. I'll try to get better.

Me: [FBDG's name] If you walk out of that hospital and come home to me, I will never touch another cigarette ever again.

Him: *He begins to take the deepest and fullest breaths he possibly could… trying to increase his blood oxygen level.*

You might be wondering why my promise to never touch another cigarette was such a motivator for FBDG. During one of our long talks at the beginning of our friendship, I asked him why he was so interested in me. He admitted that on his side of things in his dating choices, he had one hard NO and that was smoking. If the woman he was talking to was a smoker, he would say have a nice life and move on. His mother had died of stage 4 COPD because of smoking. But, on our first in-person meeting I had mentioned how badly I wanted to quit smoking but didn't feel strong enough just yet, so he wanted to see where our relationship would go before ending it. If anything was going to motivate FBDG, it would be my smoking cessation.

At that point, the nurse walked in, and I had to stop the video call. I had been on the front porch of my little miracle house smoking. I put that cigarette out, went to my bedroom, fell to my knees in a hysterical sobbing puddle of despair, and began crying out to my Abba-Father God. I wasn't angry, I wasn't cursing Him. I started praying with a terribly broken and contrite heart:

"Abba-Father, I know you have the perfect plan for me and my children. We've been through so much... and then You send [FBDG's name] to us. You bring us this beautiful beam of unconditional love and optimism, who is right now fighting for his life. I love him so much. Please, please don't take [FBDG's name]away from us. I just found him! The kids and I, we want more time with him. Please, God, heal him completely!"

No, I didn't need him in my life. I WANTED him in my life. He felt like he was that missing piece from my life. He didn't complete me at all... as I've said before, I was completely complete on my own. FBDG was the missing piece of decoration in my beautiful life's tapestry. He added so much vibrancy, so many new colors I hadn't imagined before, so much LIFE into my world. It felt so cruel for that to be taken away after merely 7 months as a couple.

Now, hold your horses here. My "Spidey-sense" is telling me you might be thinking "Please tell me this story ends right?!? DOES THIS STORY END RIGHT???"

Deep breath my friend...

Later that day, the day the doctor warned us of intubation, FBDG video called me.

Him: Hello beautiful!

Me: What's wrong?

Him: What do you mean what's wrong?

Me: Well, I'm so used to receiving bad news via a call, I just want to hurry up and hear it and get it over with.

Him: Oh, my sweet angel, no. This isn't bad news...

Me: It's not? Are you just trying to soften the blow?

Him: No, my love. They just did vitals.

Me: O...K????

Him: My O2 level

Me: YEAH???

Him: There's a slight increase... enough that they tried decreasing my O2 through the O2 mask and when they did, my blood-oxygen level stayed at the same level as the slightly increased level.

Me: *I start to cry*

Him: No... no, my love. This is not a cry-thing. This is a HAPPY thing.

Me: *Through blubbering sobs.* Not... sad... this... is... happy... tears... *I was starting to get the crying hiccups. Ever get those? It's pretty embarrassing when it happens as a 45-year-old.*

Him: Now, I'm not out of the woods by any means, but my blood-oxygen level improved enough that they've postponed my intubation to see if I continue improving.

Me: *Crying even harder.*

Him: Now, let's talk about that little promise you made... you know, how when I walk out of here on my own that you won't ever touch another cigarette???

Even through the O2 mask, I could see him smiling.

Me: That's right, my amazing man... you walk out of there on your own, I will never have another cigarette... EVER!

Little by little, my FBDG improved until the day I officially quit smoking: July 31, 2020. That's the day I drove to John Cochran VA hospital, picked up my soul mate, and took him home.

Five and a half months after living through that horrific life-threatening experience, January 17, 2021, my FBDG asked me to marry him. 9 months after that, October 23, 2021, I married my best friend, my soul mate, my biggest and most supportive cheerleader, my love, my FBDG. I would love to tell you all about that entire engagement, wedding, and honeymoon experience, but it will need to wait for another book. Wow! It looks like I'm planning an entire book series for you so keep an eye out for my next installment.

So, did we all live happily ever after?

If you ask my husband, I am positive he would tell you that absolutely yes, we are currently living our happily ever after. He believes that I was created in a lab for him so perfectly that I'm better than he ever could have imagined or designed. He would say that even though we've had our share of struggles in our marriage just like every marriage has their own brand of struggles, that does not negate our happily ever after. He would also tell you that neither one of us are perfect, that we've both made mistakes, but that doesn't mean we've forfeited our happily ever after. He would tell you that he's the luckiest and most blessed man to ever live. To that, I say, I LOVE YOU MY AMAZING MAN!!!

If you ask me, I am here to tell you that, much to my astonishment, my husband accepts me and all of my many "suitcases" full to capacity with my C-PTSD origins. And, despite all of the C-PTSD baggage I bring to our marriage, we are well on our way to our happily ever after. I am in awe of how this man loves me completely. He's showing me what genuine unconditional love is. It still feels so odd to me. As of the day I'm writing this, we've been married only 25 months; I still struggle with feeling that it's possible to be in a mutually respectful and loving marriage. He doesn't call me horrible names, he doesn't hurt me physically, emotionally, or mentally at all. He doesn't lie to me, doesn't cheat on me, doesn't gaslight me. He strives to lead us in our faith journey and is consistently trying to find ways to improve himself in his role as my husband.

Am I completely healed from all of my past trauma? Heavens no! To be honest, I don't know that I ever will be completely healed. Time will tell. I am doing my best to navigate my C-PTSD with the most amazing therapist who, I firmly believe, was sent to me by my Abba-Father God to try to help me find my way out of the C-PTSD jungle. No, I am FAR from being completely healed from all of my past trauma.

I've decided that I will not allow all of the trauma I've endured to be in vain. It's time I take my story, my multiple stories, and use them for good rather than evil. I need to take my stories of trauma, brokenness, pain, sorrow and grief, and I need to share my stories with those who are hurting. I need to share my stories with those whose experiences parallel mine. It's time I take a message of hope to a hurting world and bring love to those who desperately need encouragement in their time of despair, of hurt, of trauma. It's time I bring the wisdom I've gained from my 49 years on this earth to those who are where I once was in my misery and hopelessness. That's right my friend, it's time I turn the focus on YOU.

So, what are the lessons I can share with you? I have narrowed my plethora of choices down to 4 life lessons.

Life-Lesson #1: What happened to you when you were a child and unable to defend yourself is not your fault! Repeat after me: IT IS NOT MY FAULT! The fault lies with those people who, when they should have been protecting and nurturing you, they forced their pain and trauma onto you because they had been deeply wounded by someone else. It is NOT your fault!

Life-Lesson #2: Sometimes bad things happen to good people. I've heard it said that "it rains on the just and the unjust alike." That means no one is immune to pain, no one is immune to difficulties, NO ONE is immune to horrible experiences. It doesn't mean we're being "punished" for something. It doesn't mean we're bad people who deserve to go through trials and tribulations. What it does mean is that we're all human and we need to learn from those experiences. The death rate of humanity is 100%, so it's important to use the extremely short time we have on this earth not to wallow in our anger, hate, and depression but to instead spread peace, love, and positivity.

Life-Lesson #3: Forgiveness is key to healing. Forgiveness is giving up hope that the past could have been any different. Forgiveness frees up your energy to be used for something constructive rather than to drive you further into that deep dark pit of despair, despondency, and dejection. Forgiveness forces the eviction of those unforgiven people from your mind who have been living rent-free in there for way too long. If you want to experience healing, you MUST offer forgiveness.

Life-Lesson #4: You don't have to get to the end of your journey to experience wholeness. While wholeness is the ultimate goal, much like whitewater rafting, the journey to wholeness will have innumerable twists, turns, highs, and lows. It is so important to embrace the journey and to ride those waves of emotions along the way.

If you've stayed with me to the end of this book, first of all, from the bottom of my heart, THANK YOU! I hope you found something encouraging and maybe even uplifting in this book.

You might remember way back at the beginning in the forward I started with my own quote about my gratitude.

I'll wait while you go back to the forward to refresh your memory...

And now that I have shared these stories of my life with you in this book, these experiences that have molded me into the person I am today, I feel my quote more now than I ever have before:

"I wouldn't wish my life experiences on my worst enemy...

but I'm so very grateful for the journey."

ABOUT THE AUTHOR

What doesn't kill you makes you stronger. This is why Krista Hale Skapinski just might be able to bench press an 18-wheeler with her left pinky. Having survived one trauma, one tragedy, after another, it became common for her to hear it said to her "you should write a book" and so she did.

Her first book, "You Should Write a Book" is the result of a little bit of blood (literally), a whole lot of sweat, and too many 5-gallon buckets of tears to count.

Krista is a wife, mother, grandmother, and educator who earned her master's degree in education and retired after teaching music in the public school system for 25 years. She resides in St. Louis, Missouri and, in her spare time, you will find her playing piano and singing for her church praise band.

www.ingramcontent.com/pod-product-compliance
Lightning Source LLC
Chambersburg PA
CBHW021704120626
46545CB00004B/1402